W9-CAA-019

Personality
Assessment

Personality
Assessment

Richard I. Lanyon
Harvard Medical School

Leonard D. Goodstein
Arizona State University

John Wiley and Sons, Inc.
New York • London • Sydney • Toronto

Library of Congress Catalogue Card Number: 75-140552

ISBN   0-471-51740-2

Printed in the United States of America

10 9 8 7 6 5 4 3 2

PREFACE

Our aim in writing this book has been to present a relatively brief and general account of the area of psychological inquiry and practice usually identified as *personality assessment*. We have described the major methods and techniques used, including some discussion of their underlying rationale and manner of development, and have given a survey of the central contemporary issues and problems involved in this ever-expanding area.

In the preparation of this work, we have tried to keep in mind the needs of the wide range of psychologists and others for whom the field of personality assessment is relevant, including the clinician, the personality researcher, and the personality theorist. However, we have not oriented this volume toward any of these directions in particular, but have tried to balance the many conflicting demands for differential focus. The book is not intended as a manual for developing proficiency in the practice of personality assessment or in the use of any specific assessment device—these skills are the product of carefully directed study and extensive supervised practice. Instead, it is intended as a general introduction to the area of personality assessment and, as such, it might lay the groundwork for the later or the concurrent development of practical efficiency.

We begin (Chapter 1) with the historical development of personality assessment, in order to give a perspective for understanding contemporary practice. Chapter 2 contains a brief excursion into concepts and theory, placing the field in a broader context with respect to science in general and psychology in particular. Chapters 3 through 5 tell "how it is done," concentrating more on the principles underlying modern methods of assessment than on giving practical advice in using these methods. Chapters 6 through 9 discuss a number of important and basic issues in assessment, all related to the question of *whether* and *how* assessment should be carried out—from statistical, ethical, and professional viewpoints. The final chapter introduces some recent developments which could have important influences on the nature of personality assessment in the future.

In the handling of controversial issues, of which personality assessment has more than its fair share, our aim has been to steer a middle course between theory and practice on the one hand and research evidence on the other. Although we have relied upon empirical evidence as much as possible, we also have attempted to point out the often-ignored limitations of much of this evidence. Where there is no relevant evidence available, we have cited informed opinion and have indicated the need for additional research. We are aware of the frequent failure of contemporary clinical practice to accommodate to current research findings, and we hope to aid this accommodation.

The book is sufficiently broad to serve a number of purposes. For advanced undergraduate and graduate level courses in personality assessment, this book together with its companion volume of original source materials, *Readings in Personality Assessment*, should provide the comprehensive foundation which is necessary for the development of serious clinical, research, or consulting skills. For introductory courses in measurement or intermediate courses in personality, which may include the topic of personality assessment as one of several, the text is short enough to be assigned in whole. It also provides a readable introduction to the field for nonpsychologists, such as educators, ministers, social service and mental health workers, medical personnel, and informed laymen. To meet these needs we have presumed only minimal knowledge of academic psychology and have limited the use of statistical concepts.

The serious student of personality will notice that a number of topics have not been covered, such as physiological measures related to personality, the intensive study of individuals, the multitrait-multimethod approach to validity, and certain concepts that are currently central in personality research and theory such as repression-sensitization, cognitive complexity, body image, and ego development, to name a few. Also, some clinicians will feel that more space should have been devoted to clinical illustration of individual assessment instruments or to the integration of psychodiagnostic materials. It was felt that such additions would detract from the value of a book of this kind.

We are thankful for the comments and criticisms made by

students who used this text in graduate courses in personality assessment at the University of Cincinnati, the University of Pittsburgh, and Rutgers University, and for the careful and detailed suggestions of a number of reviewers. Many persons have shared the burden of the clerical work; in particular we thank Mrs. Elaine Lewis, Mrs. Barbara Aiduk, and Miss Sherry Traub. We especially thank our wives for their patience and support, and we hope that they will be able to share in the sense of accomplishment which they have helped us to feel.

RICHARD I. LANYON
LEONARD D. GOODSTEIN

August, 1970

CONTENTS

Personality
Assessment

1 HISTORY OF PERSONALITY ASSESSMENT

Man's interpersonal behavior is not only of immediate interest to his friends and neighbors but is also of general social relevance, and interest in personality assessment is long standing. If a prehistoric man attempted to decide upon the intentions of a strange visitor to his campsite by observing his stance, this might be regarded as a primitive effort at personality assessment. The later use of soothsayers and oracles to determine the veracity of peace offers from the enemy could be similarly viewed. There are many such early, informal procedures that antedate the development of modern psychology. Because of their historical value and because they illuminate some of the methodological issues involved in all personality assessment, we shall discuss several of these procedures that are still practiced to some degree in our society, despite their ascientific development and rather dubious contemporary status. They are astrology, palmistry, and phrenology, methods that are considerably older than any current professional assessment technique.

Astrology, Palmistry, and Phrenology

Astrology, the attempt to forecast events on earth through observation of the fixed stars and other heavenly bodies, is thought to have originated about twenty-five centuries ago in Mesopotamia. The belief that the stars were powerful gods led the ancients to conclude that human affairs could be foretold by study of the heavens. The personality of each individual, and the cause of events in his life, was determined by his horoscope (the configuration of the stars at the time of his birth). Personality assessment for an individual was accomplished by noting the moment of his birth and then getting the appropriate predictive information from one of a number of elaborate manuals or almanacs, not unlike the daily horoscopes that are still to be found in many newspapers. The extensive knowledge of the physical world gathered by man through the scientific revolution has done much to reduce serious interest in astrology, but it still remains popular with many people.

Although no evidence exists to show that the moment of birth determines personality, there has been some interest in and support for the proposition that the *season* of birth does have some modest consequences on later behavior. Some studies have shown that persons born during the summer months have slightly higher intelligence than those born in the winter (Pintner and Forlano, 1943; Orme, 1965), though there have also been inconclusive or opposite findings (Davies, 1964; Craddick, 1966). The most reasonable explanation for the positive findings seems to be that the extreme heat of the summer months may adversely affect the developing fetus, resulting in a lower level of cerebral functioning later in life for those infants carried through the summer months and born in the winter. However, definitive evidence is still lacking in the area. What is significant for the present discussion is the serious attention now paid to the problem by respectable scientific investigators. The question of a relationship between moment of birth and personality, a problem with its roots in astrology, has been restated in ways which make it amenable to investigation within the methodology of an empirical science.

Palmistry refers to the determination of an individual's characteristics by interpreting the various irregularities and folds of the skin of the hand. Palmistry is known to have existed as a standardized system in China as early as 3000 B.C., although its early beginnings and theoretical roots are lost in antiquity. In palmistry, importance is given to the lines of the hand, as well as to the swellings or *monticuli* between these lines. Each of these "signs" is interpreted in a specific manner. Thus a large Mound of Saturn, that portion of the palm directly below the third joint of the middle finger, indicates wisdom, good fortune, and prudence. Palmistry provides for a complete personality assessment of individuals by the reading of these signs. The complete absence of any reasonable explanation for the interpretative inferences, coupled with the clear knowledge that the monticuli and other characteristics of the hand can be changed by physical exercise, lead to a dismissal of palmistry as superstition and quackery.

Nevertheless, people claiming to be practitioners of this ancient art can still be found with little difficulty today and they have their ardent adherents. Much of the claimed success of palmists would seem to depend upon their ability to respond to cues such as voice, general demeanor, and dress, which are more relevant for assessing personality than are the "signs" of palmistry. Still another possibility is that the palmist offers such generalized trivial statements (for example, "Although you have considerable affection for your parents, there have been times of great discord") that they could apply to virtually anyone.

Meehl (1956) suggested the phrase "Barnum effect" to "stigmatize those pseudo-successful clinical procedures in which patient descriptions from tests are made to fit the patient largely or wholly by virtue of their triviality; and in which any nontrivial, but perhaps erroneous, inferences are hidden in a context of assertions or denials which carry high confidence simply because of the population base rates . . ." (p. 266). Tallent (1958) labeled this kind of personality assessment as involving the *Aunt Fanny* error because it contains mostly information that would be true of anybody's "Aunt Fanny." The degree to which any personality assessment procedure involves the Barnum or Aunt Fanny effect because it produces trivial, highly generalized personality description always needs to be carefully evaluated.

Phrenology, the art of personality assessment through the measurement of the external shape of the human skull, was given its major impetus by Franz Joseph Gall, a German physician and anatomist, late in the eighteenth century. This comparatively recent attempt to develop a complete system of personality measurement deserves a more careful scrutiny for several reasons: (1) there were reasonable theoretical assumptions underlying the system, (2) the system is completely empirical and thus open to scientific inquiry, and (3) the history of phrenology is recent enough to have provided fairly complete documentation.

Gall's basic assumption was that the human brain was the locus of control over human behavior, a view which is now uniformly accepted by psychologists. At the turn of the nineteenth century, however, the operation of the cerebral cortex was poorly understood and the current scientific view favored a strict localization of cortical action, with each function or faculty centered in a definite and specific region of the brain surface. The size of these regions created corresponding and observable alterations in the size of the skull, which could be used by the phrenologist to assess the many characteristics of the individual, including personality. For example, a protrusion of the skull in the area of honesty would indicate an honest individual. As was the case with astrology and palmistry, phrenology enabled its practitioners to give a complete personality assessment, based in this case upon the protrusions and contours of the skull. The basic assumptions concerning the specificity of cerebral functioning and the formation of the skull have now been clearly disproven, and thus the theory upon which phrenology rests is discredited.

It is critical to note that Gall was essentially empirical in his approach to the development of phrenology, attempting to relate behavior to brain functioning and skull shape through personal observation. To gather information about the brain, he examined the skulls of living persons and then attempted to study their brains through autopsy after death. He also examined the skulls of persons in mental hospitals, prisons, colleges, and other places where individuals of exceptional deficiencies or endowments could be found, hoping to be able to relate skull shape with the characteristics which had brought these persons together. Although this early attempt at the development of an empirical science of personality assessment is both noteworthy and laudable, it also points up the danger of unverified personal observations as the sole source of data in a scientific endeavor. The need for cross-validation of personal observations—that is, the objective demonstration of the same relationships in an independent setting—is as critical today as it was in Gall's time.

Paradoxically, it was not the lack of scientific validity of Gall's position that drew the most serious objections. Rather, the most strenuous indictments were based upon philosophical grounds (Davies, 1955). The critics of phrenology insisted that Gall's position was not unproved but unprovable; and even if provable, it was immoral. The confirmation of phrenology, according to these critics, would involve an acceptance of atheism, fatalism, and a denial of moral responsibility, the same issues which are raised in objection to contemporary deterministic views of human behavior. In the face of this violent and emotional criticism, however, the phrenologists themselves became defensive and dogmatic. What had originally been regarded as tentative and experimental now became dogma and gospel. Phrenology thus deteriorated from an experimental science, albeit one based upon inadequate assumptions, into a religion-like cult which was closed to any self-examination or modification based upon new data. The change doubtlessly served to hasten its fall from the respectability it once enjoyed.

The use of stable physical signs to assess personality characteristics is common to both palmistry and phrenology. The search for clear-cut relationships between the physical attributes of an individual and his psychological characteristics has been a continual one, reminiscent of Man's unending concern about the relationship between mind and body. This concern had an early expression in the humoural theory, an ancient physiology which remained current through the Middle

Ages. The theory proposed that the body contained four principal humours or fluids: blood, phlegm, yellow bile (choler), and black bile (melancholy). The particular proportion of these four ingredients in different people determined their "complexions" or personality characteristics, their physical and mental qualities, their unique dispositions. It was thus claimed possible, by reading the physical signs of the relative amounts of these humours in a given individual, to determine his distinctive personality.

Although our more complete understanding of the physiology of the human body has long put the humoural theory into disuse, the assumption that man's personality is a reflection of his physical body is also to be found in the modern work of Sheldon and his colleagues (Sheldon, Stevens, and Tucker, 1940). Sheldon's theory of *somatotypes* divides people into three major types, the ectomorph who is thin and fragile, the mesomorph who is powerful and muscular, and the endomorph who is round, soft and fat. According to the theory, each of these ideal types has a specific personality that is an innate consequence of that particular body build. The personality characteristics of most individuals, who are combinations of these three body types, are determined by the relative proportions of these body-type factors in their individual somatotype. Sheldon's theory has been the subject of considerable controversy, and the evidence for its validity is at best equivocal. Nevertheless, it is consistent with the age-old concern for discovering a simple link between mind and body.

It is not to be denied that there *are* significant relationships between certain physical signs (for example, trembling, sweating) and personality characteristics (for example, anxiety), nor that these relationships, though far from perfect, can be utilized in assessment. The unsuccessful attempts throughout history to rely on physical signs appear to have at least one of the following two characteristics: first, reliance on a theory which postulated that personality characteristics were *caused* by particular physical attributes; and second, lack of any logical connection between the physical sign and the personality attribute.

Astrology, palmistry, and phrenology, together with such methods as crystal-ball gazing, tea-leaf reading, and physiognomy (personality assessment from facial features) have not survived scientific investigations of their usefulness, and the practice of such dubious procedures is considered charlatanism today. Yet, as we have seen, certain aspects of these approaches continue to be identifiable in current psychological thinking, indicating that these notions do have some current influence. Also, it should not be assumed that their practitioners can never do better than chance in personality assessment. In many cases such persons are sensitive to the same subtle cues that trained clinical psychologists and psychiatrists use in their own intuitive personality assessments. The charge of charlatanism arises from the attempts of phrenologists and palmists to insist that their understanding of the person being studied results from the application of some technique or procedure that has now been demonstrated to be ineffective or useless for that purpose rather than from their superior intuitive assessment skills.

Influence of Psychological Measurement

Scientific personality assessment has its roots in the study of individual differences through psychological measurement. Most students of individual differences identify the opening of this area of inquiry as 1796, when a Greenwich astronomer's assistant, Kinnebrook, was dismissed because he had constantly observed the times of stellar transits almost one second later than his superior. It was later realized that this difference in *reaction time* was a stable one, and that people differed from each other in this and other measurable characteristics in a similarly stable fashion.

The study of individual differences was given considerable impetus by Darwin's work on evolution. In order to study the effects of human genetics, it would be necessary to identify clearly individual differences in those behaviors that had adaptability and survival value for mankind. Sir Francis Galton, a famous British scholar of the nineteenth century, became interested in the inheritance of these differences, and devoted the later portion of his life to their study. Although there had been previous attempts to categorize and measure what Galton called "intellectual faculties," Galton himself was the initiator of the measurement of the nonintellectual faculties, known more commonly at that time as "character and temperament."

Galton discussed the measurement of several such faculties in the *Fortnightly Review* of 1884. His statement ". . . that the character which shapes our conduct is a definite and durable 'something,' and therefore . . . it is reasonable to attempt to measure it," bears a strong resemblance to most contemporary views of personality, a topic to be explored further in the next chapter. Further, Galton proposed that the measurement of character should involve the same approach as ". . . that which lies at the root of examinations into the intellectual capacity," and he briefly discussed methods for the measurement of *emotion* and *temper*, using what we might term the behavior sample approach. For example, he suggested measuring emotion by means of instruments to record physiological changes in the individual during real-life stress situations. To investigate the practicality of this procedure, Galton himself actually wore a pneumocardiograph over his heart while delivering an important public lecture. He also suggested measuring pulse rate and changes in limb volume with the withdrawal of blood, all measures which are still used in psychophysiological research laboratories for studying emotional reactions. With regard to temper, Galton pointed out that small boys were expert in measuring the temper of a dog (that is, how much teasing a dog would tolerate before responding negatively), and he was convinced that similar techniques could be developed for the assessment of good and bad temper in humans.

The study of individual differences in the United States was pioneered by James McKeen Cattell, who took his doctorate in Leipzig with the pioneer of experimental psychology, Wilhelm Wundt. Cattell also worked briefly with Galton in England, then returned to the United States in 1888 and established the Psychological Laboratory at the University of Pennsylvania. Although his interests were mainly in the areas of psychophysics, perception, and reaction time, Cattell nevertheless had a strong influence upon the development of other psychological measurement devices, including personality tests, through his support for the practical utilization of psychological knowledge (Boring, 1929, pp. 532–540).

At about the same time in France, Alfred Binet, who had become enthusiastic about Galton's work on individual differences, began a series of studies of eminent persons in the arts and sciences. Binet used a standard series of experimental tasks, including observation on body types, head measurements, and handwriting. Some of these interests appeared to reflect the then-current influence of phrenology and other prescientific notions, and Binet, who was a careful and objective investigator, later discarded them as not leading to useful understanding of the persons being studied. Binet also began a series of investigations into mental functioning, which included personality, using a wide variety of tasks such as word knowledge, reasoning, and numerical ability. These investigations led to the development of the now-famous Binet tests of intelligence. Some of his tasks, which involved telling stories about pictures and identifying inkblots, were antecedents of what are now known as the projective tests of personality.

Thus, prior to 1915, research on the measurement of personality was preceded by work on the measurement of skills or abilities, and grew out of the early academic interest in the measurement of human individual differences. The faculties of character or temperament were considered to be "real," along with reaction times and perceptual abilities, in much the same sense as physical characteristics such as height and weight. Galton had introduced the use of direct behavior samples in real-life situations, and his work had stimulated considerable interest in both the United States and France. Two of Galton's followers, Karl Pearson and Charles Spearman, were playing a major part in the development of statistical procedures that provided powerful tools for later work in assessment.

At about this time, an English scientist named Webb (1915) published what seems to have been the first major attempt to summarize the important aspects of character through the intensive study of a large number of subjects. He obtained ratings of a large group of school- and college-age males on 40 or more qualities which had ". . . a general and fundamental bearing on the total personality." The ratings were obtained from persons who knew the subjects well, and the resulting data were treated by an early form of the statistical procedures which are now known as factor analysis. They were interpreted to indicate that the most basic aspect of personality was the ". . . consistency of action resulting from deliberate volition, or will." Webb's study is noteworthy both for its use of judges' ratings (that is, estimates by experts) and for its sophisticated statistical techniques. Webb also summarized two previous studies which had approached the scientific study of personality in a different way, through the use of what he called the "biographic method," an analysis of written personal life histories. These can be regarded as forerunners of the present-day "biographical data blank" approach to personality assessment.

Influence of Abnormal Psychology

At about the same time that academic psychologists were developing their interest in the measurement of normal human capacities and individual differences, other investigators were becoming involved in the formal assessment of *abnormal* human behavior. This interest stemmed from the practical need to classify and categorize the various kinds of psychopathology as well as the more theoretical need to gain a better understanding of the phenomena under scrutiny. Closely related to these efforts were the parallel attempts of Binet to develop clinical tests that would identify children who lacked the mental capacity to benefit from schooling and would provide theoretical information about their intellectual limitations.

It is generally considered that the earliest attempts at personality assessment with psychopathological cases involved word association procedures. Emil Kraepelin, the renowned German psychiatrist who was primarily responsible for our current psychiatric classification procedures, made some use of a "free association test" as early as 1892, and Sommer, one of his colleagues, suggested its use for differentiating various kinds of mental disorder in 1894 (Anastasi, 1961, p. 16). In the word association technique, the subject is presented with a stimulus word, frequently from a standardized list of such words, and is asked to respond as quickly as possible with the first word that comes to mind. The list is usually presented more than once, since the giving of different responses to the same word is believed to indicate a problem area. A record is made of the responses given and of the reaction time to each presentation. It is noteworthy that the technique had been also used by Galton and Cattell for assessing individual differences.

The use of word association as a method for the identification of unconscious personality conflicts was initially proposed by Carl Jung. Jung (1910) developed a standardized list of words that were regarded as especially useful in detecting areas of conflict or disturbance, indicated by excessively long reaction times, failures to respond, misunderstandings of the stimulus words, and other emotional reactions, such as stammering and blushing.

Another more formal approach to the use of word association was developed by Kent and Rosanoff (1910). Their standardized list deliberately omitted words which were especially likely to call up personal experiences, and they developed norms of common responses by administering the list to 1000 normal persons. By comparing the responses of normals with those of psychotics, they were able to demonstrate that psychotics gave strikingly fewer common responses than normals and that these differences were large enough to be of diagnostic significance in individual cases. Thus, the word association test can be regarded as the first practical psychometric device for identifying emotionally disturbed persons, although it is little used for this purpose today.

A similar concern with problems of adjustment led Heymans and Wiersma (1906) to develop a list of symptoms indicative of psychopathology. This list, revised by Hoch and Amsden (1913) and later by Wells (1914), was influential in generating the self-report personality inventory. The first such inventory was Woodworth's *Personal Data Sheet*, which was developed during World War I to diagnose the ability of soldiers to adjust satisfactorily to the strains and stresses of military life. Since it was obvious that there were not enough psychologists or psychiatrists available to interview each draftee personally about his emotional status, some more economical method was sought. A Committee on Emotional Fitness was appointed by the National Research Council to work on this problem under the chairmanship of Robert S. Woodworth. Their solution was a paper-and-pencil inventory, entitled the Personal Data Sheet to allay suspicion about its real purpose, which was a standardized psychiatric interview in printed form (see Symonds, 1931). The questions were based upon common neurotic symptoms and upon the reports of symptoms which were actually observed in men who had not been able to adjust to war and its stresses. The questions dealt with physical symptoms ("Do you ever feel an awful pressure in or about your head?"), fears and worries ("Are you troubled with the idea that people are watching you on the street?"), adjustment to the environment ("Do you make friends easily?"), unhappiness and unsociability ("Are you troubled by shyness?"), dreams, fantasies, and sleep disturbance ("Are you frightened in the middle of the night?"), plus some miscellaneous items. The score on this questionnaire was the number of items answered in the direction considered to be typical of maladjustment or psychoneurosis. Over 200 different questions were initially assembled, all capable of being answered yes or no. On the basis of preliminary testing with both college men and draftees, the list was reduced to 116. However, the armistice came before the final form could actually be used in practice. Later called the Woodworth Psychoneurotic Inventory, this self-report inventory was the forerunner of the many paper-and-pencil personality tests in use today.

During the same period, another noteworthy development occurred in personality assessment for clinical purposes. Hermann Rorschach, a Swiss psychiatrist, had been using the perception of inkblots as an approach to theoretical problems in psychology when he made the empirical discovery that the results could be used for making differential psychiatric diagnoses. His major work was published in German in 1921, but did not appear officially in English until 1942 (Rorschach, 1942). Although earlier investigators had used inkblots as free association material, they had limited themselves to an analysis of the thematic content. Rorschach's contribution was to attempt a systematic analysis of the subject's concern with the *formal* aspects of the blots, such as color, shading, apparent movement, and whether the subject preferred to consider the blot as a whole or in parts. He believed that these different perceptual approaches were related to different psychological processes or "structures" of the personality, and he advocated further research into this perceptual task, using an empirical, statistical orientation. Rorschach's work has been seminal both in stimulating research with his inkblots and in the development of other minimally structured stimulus situations, to which responses can be elicited and analyzed for the purpose of personality assessment. Rorschach's plans for greater validational research on his technique were interrupted by his untimely death at the age of 37.

The Past Fifty Years

It can be considered that the early days or beginnings of contemporary personality assessment lasted through 1920. By this date, the major influences which have been discussed in the two previous sections were in evidence, and two clear lines of development became apparent. Although these twin developments followed the directions pointed by the two divergent origins of personality assessment—the academic study of individual differences and the clinical assessment of psychopathology—they also reflected additional influences. In the development from clinical origins, emphasis was upon the global assessment of single individuals. Perhaps the most important additional influence was that of psychoanalytic theory, which assumed that the causes of behavior were "buried" far beneath the level of conscious awareness. In such a view, the most meaningful and useful understanding of an individual's personality should be based upon an analysis of these "deeper" aspects of his functioning, rather than the overt behavior which is readily available for superficial scrutiny. Also important was the influence of Gestalt psychology, with its implication that the personality of the whole individual was more than the simple sum of discrete behavioral responses or traits.

These concerns and influences directed the clinician interested in measuring personality toward a preoccupation with the hidden or covert aspects of personality, and led to the popularization of what Frank (1939) ultimately termed *projective techniques*. Projective methods were conceptualized as those which present the subject with a situation for which there are few clearly defined cultural patterns of response, so that he must "project" upon that ambiguous field "his way of seeing life, his meanings, significances, patterns, and especially his feelings" (Frank, 1939, p. 403). According to Frank, a projective test involves the presentation of a stimulus situation that elicits the private idiosyncratic meaning and organization of the individual's private world that he has brought to the testing situation and which is called into play in responding to the test demands. Frank regarded these methods as indirect ones which tap the pattern of internal organization and structure of personality without disintegrating or modifying the pattern as it exists, much in the manner of an X-ray of the body.

What are the projective methods? We have already discussed the word association method, which is seldom used nowadays in clinical practice. Rorschach's inkblot technique, however, found immediate favor among clinicians, especially those with a psychoanalytic orientation, as a means of assessing the state of the unconscious mind. Another group of projective methods, which Lindzey (1961) has called *constructive techniques,* was developed by Henry A. Murray and his colleagues at Harvard University in the 1930s (Morgan and Murray, 1935; Murray, 1938). Murray, with a strong interest in literary creation, developed the Thematic Apperception Test (TAT), in which subjects create stories about ambiguous pictures. According to Murray, the content of the stories reflects the subjects' past experiences and present needs. A similar constructive approach is to be found in Van Lennep's (1951) Four Picture Test, developed initially in the 1930s, and in such later instruments as the Blacky Pictures (Blum, 1950) and the Children's Apperception Test (Bellak, 1954). Another widely used group of projective procedures involves an analysis of the subject's own creative drawings and paintings. Although figure drawings of a man had been used for some time as a convenient method of estimating intelligence (Goodenough, 1926), it remained for Machover (1949) and Buck (1948) to popularize them as a projective method for personality assessment.

The second trend in personality measurement, that stemming from the interest of academic psychologists in individual differences, is exemplified by the work on paper-and-pencil personality inventories. Such devices could be readily administered to many individuals in a group, scoring was rapid and objective, and statistical procedures could be used in establishing norms, internal consistency, the relation between test scores and other behavioral measures, factor structure, and other aspects of the instruments. This approach emphasized the measurement of discrete traits or aspects rather than a global assessment of the whole personality. The test items involved in these instruments were often concerned with the more superficial and obvious aspects of overt behavior, and their susceptibility to deliberate faking posed many problems in interpreting the scores obtained.

Following Woodworth's original work, there were several rather immediate attempts to adapt his questionnaire to other groups (such as school children, juvenile delinquents, and college students), essentially by modifying the wording of the questions. A variation of the questionnaire procedure was developed by Pressey (1919), whose X-O Test presented the subject with lists of words rather than questions. The subject was asked to read the list and to cross out (hence the title of the test) the words that he regarded as wrong (such as spitting, smoking, recklessness), that made him nervous or anxious (such as loneliness, sin, pain), or that involved his likes or interests (such as camping, reading, kissing).

The item content of these early inventories was chosen for its *face validity:* that is, items were included if it was thought by the test developer that they would elicit different responses from well-adjusted and poorly adjusted subjects. The Bell Adjustment Inventory (Bell, 1939) is a somewhat more recent example of this approach to item selection and test construction. A different and more sophisticated technique for item selection is the *empirical approach,* where the actual responses of different subject groups are examined in order to determine which responses are characteristic of that group. Only those items that can be actually shown to differentiate the groups are included in the final form of the test. The empirical approach, used by Rorschach in the original development of his psychodiagnostic procedure, was employed by Edward K. Strong (1927) in the development of the Strong Vocational Interest Blank. Although a full discussion of interest measurement is beyond our scope here, Strong's work is noteworthy because it presents an important early model of the empirical approach to test construction. The empirical technique was also involved to some extent in the construction of the Bernreuter Personality Inventory (Bernreuter, 1938) and in the Humm-Wadsworth Temperament Scale (Humm and Wadsworth, 1935). The latter was the direct predecessor of the more carefully developed Minnesota Multiphasic Personality Inventory (Hathaway and McKinley, 1940; 1951).

One of the troublesome problems involved in the use of paper-and-pencil personality inventories was the tendency of some subjects to avoid giving socially undesirable answers to the items, such as admitting to being nervous, rather than making the more personally appropriate responses. The Minnesota Multiphasic Personality Inventory (MMPI) attempted to deal with this problem by including several *validity scales,* such as the lie scale, which give some measure of the tendency to respond in the socially acceptable manner. Concern with this problem also led to the development, in the 1940s, of the *forced-choice technique,* which was subsequently used by Edwards (1953) in his Personal Preference Schedule. Since the forced-choice procedure requires the subject to endorse one of two items of equal social desirability (or undesirability), it was presumed that his response would reflect something more than the obvious social acceptability of the single items.

Goldberg (1970), commenting upon the current proliferation of personality inventories, made a distinction between two kinds of inventories, based on the reasons for their development. The first group of inventories was developed in response to pressures from society to deal with specific applied problems. This category included the inventories dealing with the problem of personal adjustment as previously discussed, the ones measuring satisfaction and success in vocational choice, and the ones tapping aspects of academic achievement beyond what is predictable from measures of scholastic aptitude or intelligence. The second group of inventories was based more upon conceptions of the structure of individual differences than upon any societal or real-life considerations and was viewed as stemming from theoretical concepts about the nature of personality. This group included the inventory measures of introversion-extroversion and masculinity-femininity, and also the inventory measures based upon two influential theories of individual differences, Spranger's (1928) classification of "personal values" and Murray's (1938) scheme for ordering manifest needs. Although Goldberg's classification scheme was developed only for inventory measures of personality, it has clear relevance for other personality assessment methods. It also reflects the current usage of personality assessment devices and tends to cut across the two major historical influences on assessment methodology.

Most of the specific instruments and the methodological issues introduced above will be discussed in greater detail later. What, however, can be said about the present relationship of the two major historical influences, the self-report personality questionnaire and the projective technique? Over the years there has been a persistent tendency on the part of many followers of each of the two traditions— projective techniques and personality inventories—to have a strong negative emotional bias toward work in the other tradition. This tendency was probably heightened in 1939 by Frank's labeling of the former trend as "projective techniques" with the explicit statement that these instruments provided indirect measures of personality structure, and the implication that the then-more-traditional inventories were not coming to grips with the real stuff of personality. The most important consequence of this formation of two alienated points of view has been the loss of much clinical and scientific interchange between the two camps, and loss of the growth that might have occurred with greater cooperation and mutual respect. Thus, with the possible exception of Holtzman's Inkblot Technique (Holtzman, Thorpe, Swartz, and Herron, 1961), there have been negligible developments in the past decade that would represent a synthesis of the two traditions.

Some psychologists (for example, Levy, 1963) have argued that this distinction between projective and inventory devices is a spurious one. It is pointed out that self-report inventories can be, and most often are, responded to "projectively," and that the resultant personality "profiles" are used by skilled clinicians as the basis for a global interpretation of personality, in terms that involve far more than a simple description of overt behavior. On the other hand, the traditional projective techniques can be, and often are, objectively scored and then interpreted according to normative data and empirical evidence about the meaning of certain discrete response categories.

Although it can be logically argued that the traditional distinction between projective and inventory tests is really not an important one, the independence of their histories has been real enough to demand formal recognition. However, we see no reason to perpetuate a distinction which serves no useful purpose, and we shall attempt in the remaining chapters to transcend many of the usual differences between the two approaches.

The Nontest Instruments

Most of the preceding discussion has been concerned with what are usually termed personality tests. What about other formal approaches to personality assessment, such as biographical data sheets and behavior sample techniques?

The biographical data sheet, widely used for assessment purposes in industrial and business settings, has been little used on a routine basis for clinical purposes, with the exception of an interest in certain predictive or prognostic signs obtainable through such instruments as Phillips' (1953) scale for predicting outcome in schizophrenia. The Phillips scale is a method of estimating the premorbid adjustment of psychiatric patients by assigning differential weighing to various items in the patient's case history, mainly those behaviors involving heterosexual interests and relationships. Biographical data have also been used for many years in the development of "base expectancy tables" to predict whether or not a prisoner is likely to violate parole if it is granted to him. Such tables are discussed in detail in the July 1962 issue of the *Journal of Crime and Delinquency*. It is surprising, in light of the extremely high importance given to biographical information by professional mental health workers, that there is no widely used clinical instrument of this type. The work of Briggs (1959) clearly suggests that such instruments can be developed and are potentially very useful for clinical work.

In spite of illustrious beginnings in Galton's laboratories, the behavior sample technique has also seen only limited use in routine personality assessment. Notable exceptions have been the Hartshorne and May (1928) studies in personality and the U.S. Office of Strategic Services' clinical assessment project during the second World War (OSS Assessment Staff, 1948). More recently, behavior sampling has been used in behavior therapy research (for example, Lang and Lazovik, 1963) for the assessment of specific anxieties. In general, however, it must be concluded that neither the biographical data sheet nor behavioral sampling techniques have received the serious interest and concern that they would seem to deserve from researchers in personality assessment.

Multiple Methods of Personality Assessment

This historical overview would not be complete without some discussion of the development of procedures for comprehensive assessment by a group or panel of professionally trained assessors. In such a procedure the individuals to be evaluated are brought together in small groups for several days of study at an "assessment center," which is usually at a remote residential site. The purposes of this procedure may be to better understand individuals of this type, such as creative architects or clinical psychologists, or to select candidates for some difficult high-level position, such as astronauts or undercover agents. Of course, these procedures are also helpful in generally understanding the issues involved in personality and personality assessment. Taft (1959) has provided an illuminating summary of several attempts to develop multiple methods of personality assessment and has discussed the practical and theoretical problems involved.

Many different kinds of data may be made available to the panel of assessors. Typically included would be a variety of biographical data, intellectual evaluations, responses to self-report questionnaires and projective techniques, the proceedings of several interviews, and a variety of other behavior samples or situational tests which would be developed for their relevance to the particular group under scrutiny. Thus, one of the situational techniques developed for the OSS assessment program was a stress interview in which interrogators attempted to break down the "cover story" which the candidate had developed. Among the several problems inherent in this approach are how the many behavioral indices (test scores, ratings, and the like) should be weighted, how they are to be combined into a single predictor, and how criterion measures are to be developed.

The first multiple assessment program appears to have been developed by Henry Murray (1938) and his associates at Harvard, and consisted mainly of comprehensive and detailed evaluations of a series of persons in order to better understand the functioning of normal persons. Many of the techniques used by Murray were adopted for selection purposes during World War II, when both the United States OSS and the British War Office Selection Board employed the assessment center concept for selecting spies. Despite considerable difficulty, data were obtained to indicate the positive contribution of the selection programs. Between 1946 and 1951, an extensive multiple assessment program to improve the selection of promising trainees for the profession of clinical psychology was conducted by the Veterans Administration and the University of Michigan (Kelly and Goldberg, 1959). During a five-day stay at an assessment center, each trainee was comprehensively studied by a variety of procedures. Using ratings of later success as a clinical psychologist as the criterion for the usefulness of the procedure, the results were quite disappointing. The authors noted, however, that the group studied was already highly selected and rather homogeneous in a number of important respects, all of which would attenuate the obtained correlations. A similar study with more promising results was reported by Holt and Luborsky (1958), using psychiatric residents as the subjects.

With a somewhat different purpose but using essentially similar methodology, the group of psychologists at the University of California's Institute of Personality Assessment and Research (IPAR) have been investigating the personality characteristics of highly creative and successful persons in a number of disciplines, including architecture and mathematics. Their research reports (for example, MacKinnon, 1961) tend to offer strong support for the usefulness of this assessment center approach. More recently, this approach has also been applied by the Peace Corps to the selection of volunteers for overseas service and by one major American industrial company, the American Telephone and Telegraph Company, for evaluating middle-level managers (Bray and Grant, 1966). It would appear that the multiple assessment approach, particularly when it involves relevant behavior samples, is one of the more promising approaches to personality assessment.

Summary

A number of assessment methods such as phrenology, astrology, and palmistry are fascinating to many laymen but are not regarded

as having the documented utility required for their serious consideration by trained professional workers in personality assessment. Turning
to the professionally recognized assessment instruments, two historical
trends can be seen in their development. The first is traceable to the
original academic interest in measuring individual differences, and
has its most important consequences in contemporary paper-and-pencil
inventories, the self-report personality tests. The second originated in
the need for understanding clinically abnormal behavior, and is seen
as leading to the interest in and development of projective techniques.

There has been an unfortunate tendency for some professional
workers in personality assessment to develop strong positive feelings
about one of these trends at the expense of the other. Projective methods
are seen as subtle, rich, sophisticated, dynamic, and sensitive by those
who favor them, but as unscientific, vague, subjective, crude, and unreliable by those who do not. Inventory methods are scientific, efficient,
rigorous, reliable, and objective to their adherents, but superficial,
atomistic, artificial, and sterile to their detractors. While some differences may exist between the two approaches, especially in their historical development, the overemphasis placed upon these differences
has probably been detrimental to the development of the science of
personality assessment, so that the significant advances in recent years
have been few. A more integrated attack upon the yet unsolved problems of personality assessment would seem to be more useful than
the perpetuation of these disputes.

Although the predictive power of biographical data is known to
be satisfactory for many interpersonal behaviors, this source of information has not been widely used on a routine basis for clinical purposes. One context where biographical information has found regular
use is in multiple assessment procedures, where a group of individuals
are studied intensively over several days using a variety of methods.
The assessment center approach has been successfully used for purposes
of personality research and also for the selection of certain personnel
by the army, the Peace Corps, and industry.

2 CONCEPTS AND DEFINITIONS

In understanding any human enterprise, it is important not only to understand *what* is being undertaken, but also to understand *why* a particular course of action is being pursued. Why do psychologists undertake the task of personality assessment? What are the benefits that this enterprise can offer? In general, professional psychologists assess human personality for two major reasons: first and primary, to assist our understanding of the behavior of a particular person, that is, the *clinical* assessment of a single individual; and second, in the context of psychological research and theory building, to advance our *general knowledge* of human behavior.

The major use of personality assessment instruments in clinical and personnel psychology has been in the first context, the clinical assessment of the single person. Here, the aim is to come to some decision about the future course of action of a specified individual, or to make a prediction about his unique future behavior. It is this clinical or professional usage which has been the main reason for the development and continued existence of most of the better known assessment devices.

With regard to the second use of assessment, researchers in psychology employ personality assessment techniques for a number of reasons. Some wish to study a particular personality concept, such as rigidity, or ego strength, or need for achievement, either for its own sake or within the framework of some theoretical approach to personality. Another research reason for utilizing assessment techniques could be in the context of achieving a better understanding of a certain clinical syndrome or pattern of behavior. A third reason might be to reduce the range of individual differences within subject groups on a research task by sorting the subjects according to a distinctive personality characteristic. For example, a researcher evaluating the effects of a psychotherapy procedure such as relaxation training might decide to examine high-anxiety and low-anxiety subjects separately because it is suspected that these subjects will differ in their ability to relax. In research uses of assessment, the interest is typically in group differences rather than in a particular individual or in understanding the implications of the findings for the single person. The researcher is primarily interested in how the overall results shed light on some general fact or behavioral law which is reflected in the behavior of people in his experiment.

It would thus appear that the two major themes or influences which have defined and shaped our current knowledge in personality assessment are our involvement in solving applied, practical problems and our interest in a better theoretical understanding of human functioning. We have previously noted that Goldberg (1970) drew a similar conclusion after discussing the rise of interest in personality inventories. His conclusion might well be extended to include the entire field of personality assessment, as it seems clear that the interplay between these two themes, the applied or individual and the general or theoretical, has strongly influenced our present stage of development in personality assessment. Let us further examine these themes in order to enhance our understanding of basic concepts and issues. We shall focus our discussion on the clinical or practical role of assessment and introduce theoretical aspects as appropriate.

Clinical Assessment: The Empirical Approach

We shall begin with an analysis of clinical assessment procedures that utilize empirical knowledge. Taking a simple example, assume we have evidence that a particular response or set of responses (for instance, a score on a self-report personality inventory or a set of responses to a projective test) is highly correlated with some nontest behavior (the criterion). It might be that high scores on the ABC Test are known to be highly correlated with success in door-to-door selling, or that a large number of animal responses on the XYZ Test are highly correlated with unsuccessful rehabilitation following release from a mental hospital.

In the *empirical* approach to clinical assessment, the psychologist would need only to administer either of these tests, compare the obtained results with the empirical research findings, and make his prediction as to the probability of success or failure of the individual in either door-to-door selling or post-hospital rehabilitation. The psychologist usually neither knows, nor is he concerned about, the psychological or theoretical connection between the individual's test responses and the behavior to be predicted. In the empirical approach it is not necessary to understand *why* there is a connection between high scores on the ABC Test and selling behavior; it is sufficient to know that such a relationship reliably exists. Naturally, it is important to know the limiting conditions of this empirically derived relationship; that is, to know the particular groups of individuals and kinds of selling for which this relationship holds, and the circumstances under which it might break down. If we presume, however, that such information is available and that the individual is drawn from the segment of the population covered by a known empirical relationship, we can use this knowledge for prediction or decision making about that individual. The empirical approach might be schematically represented as follows:

Information from   Previous   Decision
assessment $\rightarrow$ empirical $\rightarrow$ about the
procedures   findings   individual

Depending upon such factors as the size of the relationship between the predictor and the criterion, the representativeness of the original empirical data, and the similarity of the current criterion to the original one, the professional psychologist will be more or less correct in his prediction or decision. Since there are a relatively small number of steps and inferences between the data and the decision, and it is not difficult to make periodic checks on the accuracy of the previously reported relationship, the probability of serious error is not great. However, it has been argued by Peak (1953), Loevinger (1957), and others that a purely empirical approach, with a total reliance upon observed relationships, is limited and superficial because the psychologist will not be able to develop any understanding, except on a primitive correlational level, of *why* his decision was a useful one.

The empirical approach to assessment involves a basic assumption. This is the assumption of interpersonal behavior consistency, that is, that there are enduring patterns of behavioral responses which transcend situations and which can be tapped and used for understanding particular individuals and people in general. The search for an understanding of these enduring characteristics of persons serves to identify the entire field of personality as an area of inquiry. Although a concern with the *nature* of these enduring characteristics is clearly the province of the more theoretically based approaches to personality assessment, the empirical approach must also assume their existence. It is particularly important to understand this assumption, because a number of psychologists have begun to question the existence of enduring interpersonal characteristics. This recent theoretical trend is one which conceptualizes personality in terms of complex learned social behavior, using the terminology of general behavioral learning theory. This approach, typified by the writings of Kanfer and Saslow (1965), Wallace (1966), Peterson (1968), and Mischel (1968, 1969), is discussed more fully in Chapter 10; here we simply note that it gives much less than the usual importance to a person's enduring characteristics as determinants of his interpersonal behavior. These writers deny that generalized dispositional tendencies have important effects on behavior, and regard the search for techniques to tap such tendencies as a waste of time. Rather, they place the greater emphasis on the current environmental determinants of personality-related behaviors, and on the relevant rewards and punishments which are operating on these behaviors. In this view, the understanding and prediction of an individual's interpersonal behavior would be made not so much from an assessment of his "underlying personality" as from an analysis of his overt responses and the environmental surroundings in which these responses were made. How much effect this trend will ultimately have upon the field of psychology in general and personal assessment in particular cannot be foretold at present.

Personality Description and Clinical Assessment

In the empirical approach to personality assessment the professional psychologist moves directly from the obtained psychometric data to the prediction or decision without considering any intervening processes. The empirical approach is data-based, and its use is limited to those situations in which the psychometric data have been shown to be of predictive value. In actual practice, this limitation turns out to be a serious one. While the data which we have may predict door-to-door salesmanship, we are also interested in sales potential in a whole variety of situations. Similarly, while our empirical data may refer to success in post-hospital rehabilitation, we are also interested in post-prison rehabilitation and other related situations.

We could argue that all that is required under these circumstances is to extend the empirical approach to these new situations; that is, to collect additional new empirical data in each specific situation of interest. Unfortunately, however, this is typically not what happens in practice. Rather, the existing data are interpreted in more general terms, using the nonspecific language of personality description, and then they are used for prediction or decision making. Thus, persons scoring high on the ABC Test become characterized in general terms such as high in "salesmanship" and persons giving many animal responses to the XYZ Test as low in "rehabilitation potential." The personality description approach to assessment might be schematically represented as follows:

Information from assessment procedures	→	Personality description	→	Decision about the individual

It is possible to regard this approach to clinical or individual assessment as a theoretical one, but we prefer not to do so. Our reasons are that there is very little "theory" involved other than common sense, and the choice of the concepts involved in this kind of procedure is primarily determined by pragmatic rather than theoretical considerations. Thus, our decision to use the ABC Test of "salesmanship" or the XYZ Test of "rehabilitation potential" would be made because we are interested in the behaviors that presumably can be predicted by these instruments, and there is minimal "theory" involved either in developing the tests for this use or in employing them in this practical manner.

It seems advisable at this time to state more precisely what we mean by a *theory*. Marx (1963) identified three general meanings of "theory" in contemporary psychological writings. The most general use is in reference to any conceptual process in science in contrast with the empirical, or observational, aspects. A second use is in reference to any generalized explanatory principle, one which ordinarily involves a statement of functional relationships among variables. The third usage, which both Marx and the present writers endorse as the preferred one, refers to a group of logically organized or deductively related laws, typically based upon empirical observations. This usage is more closely aligned with those of the more developed sciences, and also has a closer relationship to the concept of a *system*, in that this latter term broadly refers within psychology to a cluster of theoretical propositions and methodological biases. Taking the third usage as the criterion, it is readily apparent that there are few viable personality theories. In the remainder of our text, the term *theory* is restricted to this third usage, and much of what is often termed theory will be regarded by us as rational, a priori, or common-sensical.

The reader should note that there is nothing intrinsically incorrect, either theoretically or methodologically, with the procedure of assessment through description. Indeed, if there were data available to suggest that the ABC Test did identify those who would become successful salesmen in a variety of settings or that the XYZ Test could predict who would respond unfavorably to rehabilitation efforts under a number of different circumstances, no serious objections to this kind of procedure would be raised. Unfortunately, the literature in personality assessment is replete with examples demonstrating that this is not the case. Rather, it would appear that indices developed for predictive or decision-making purposes are relatively specific to that situation, and they become much less effective when the situation to be predicted differs in any substantial way. It is always necessary to make an empirical check on the generality of the predictive data. The ABC Test must be checked to see whether it works with new samples of men who may be older or younger or better educated than the original sample, or to see whether it will predict life-insurance sales as well as door-to-door sales of encyclopedias. If we do not empirically verify the generality of our conclusions, we run the risk of making incorrect predictions and bad decisions, and sometimes we will perform worse than if we had used pure chance to make our choices. The major problem involved in using such descriptive constructs as "salesmanship" or "rehabilitation potential" is that their looseness represents a clear invitation to many potential users for abuse.

The procedure of using the empirical relationships between test scores and nontest behaviors to support the utility of an abstract, generalized construct introduces the important concept of *construct validity* (Cronbach and Meehl, 1955) which is further discussed in Chapter 6. What should be understood at this point is the existence of a frequent problem in the applied use of personality assessment procedures—the assumption that a test score or index is indicative of some generalized internal characteristic of the respondent in cases where there is precious little data available to support such an assumption.

The Language of Personality Description

Before becoming involved with matters of theory in personality assessment, let us discuss the language that we tend to use to describe personality characteristics. Phrases like "sleeps more than usual," "works energetically on a problem," or "has never been observed to cry," would represent rather clear and specific descriptions of directly observable behavior. In describing personality, however, either in our ordinary conversation or as professional psychologists, we usually wish to go further than this. We are usually interested in descriptive concepts that tap the more basic characteristics of the individual.

Cultural anthropologists have suggested that a study of the words used in ordinary language by a culture will provide some clues as to what is regarded in that culture as basic and important. The observation that the Eskimo language has many single words denoting different kinds of snow and that the Polynesian dialects contain single words indicative of complex kinship relationships which can only be explained in English by phrases is seen as evidence that snow and kinship are areas of importance in these cultures. Therefore we can assume that personality characteristics which are regarded as basic in our culture will ordinarily be denoted by single-word personality adjectives. Thus, rather than the behaviorally descriptive phrases used in the preceding paragraph, both ordinary personality descriptions and formal assessment reports would tend to characterize such an individual as lethargic, energetic, or stolid.

In this view, the more basic or important a particular personality characteristic is felt to be, the more likely is it to find its way into our natural language as a single word. The position has been clearly articulated by Gordon Allport (Allport, 1937; Allport and Odbert, 1936) and more recently reviewed by Norman (1963c) and Goldberg (1970). A related assumption is that important characteristics will have many synonyms associated with them which will provide the culture with nuances of meaning for these important characteristics.

The language that is used for characterizing personality is usually regarded as having some generalized explanatory value; that is, it is considered as providing something more than a mere description of an observable event. At the very least, personality descriptions are seen as suggesting the operation of some enduring response dispositions or characteristics of the individual. Generalized response dispositions are typically termed *traits* and, when they refer to those dispositions that have implications for intra- or interpersonal adjustment, they are regarded as personality traits. This term is used in contrast to *states*, which are more transitory and ephemeral. For example, anxiety as a trait would suggest a continuing, generalized condition of the individual, while anxiety as a state would suggest a more transitory or momentary condition. One of the problems in personality description is that traits are often assumed from behaviors which are only indicative of states.

The Structure of Personality

Allport and Odbert (1936) were able to cull almost 18,000 different trait names from *Webster's Second Unabridged Dictionary*, while Norman (1963c), using the Third Edition, developed a list of over 40,000 characteristics. Although both were able to reduce their lists rather substantially (to 4500 and 2800, respectively), the enormity of the problem of organizing and systematizing such a mass of material raises the question of the structure of personality. The question here is how to arrange these many traits or characteristics in some systematic, understandable, and logical fashion, such as the chemists have done for the elements in the periodic table.

If one considers science to be essentially a matter of the discovery of truth, then the problem is to determine how these personality characteristics are arranged in nature, that is, to discover nature's "building blocks." If, on the other hand, one's view of science is that scientists impose explanatory constructs upon their observations of the natural world in order to assist them in understanding certain phenomena and that there is no "real order" to the universe, then the task is to develop useful explanatory constructs. In this latter view, the primary problem in the study of personality is to develop useful ways of organizing or conceptualizing personality structure and functioning. The work of Raymond B. Cattell (1957, 1965) is a carefully reasoned presentation of the former or "discovery of the truth" viewpoint as applied to the organization of personality traits, while George Kelly (1955) has been a vigorous proponent of the latter or "creative" point of view. It should be emphasized that in the discovery point of view it is presumed that there is only a single correct view of personality structure, while the creative view accepts the proposition that there may be several different, and even equally useful, ways of viewing the structure of personality. Since most psychologists would appear to be implicitly, if not explicitly, committed to the creative view, the reader may begin to understand why there are so many different concepts and ideas about personality, personality structure, and personality assessment.

Definitions of Personality

The problem of defining personality is a difficult one, and a very wide variety of definitions have been suggested over the years. Thus, Allport (1937) was able to delineate no fewer than 50 meanings for this term. Allport's analysis exhaustively traces the history of the concept of personality, beginning with the early antecedent *persona*, which referred to the theatrical mask first used in Greek drama, and documents its diverse meanings in such fields as theology, philosophy, sociology, linguistics, and psychology.

Even when the matter of defining personality is approached from a purely psychological viewpoint, the diversity is great. In their text on personality theory, Hall and Lindzey (1957, p. 9) have stated that "no substantive definition of personality can be applied with any generality." The historical and theoretical reasons for this diversity of thought and lack of agreement among psychologists are complex and lengthy, and the reader is referred to the chapter by Sanford (1963) entitled "Personality: Its Place in Psychology" for a careful discussion of the issues.

Hall and Lindzey (1957, p. 9) have argued that personality is best defined by "the particular empirical concepts which are part of the theory of personality employed by the observer." The typical *measures* of personality in use today, however, tend to be atheoretical. As stated by Angyal (1941), most personality tests involve the measurement of elements of personality that are random or arbitrary, although they may be of practical significance, such as leadership, dominance, or anxiety. American psychologists, particularly those interested in personality assessment, have tended to adopt an implicit definition of this sort for personality, reflecting their concern for usefulness ahead of theory. The definition employed in this book also will reflect such a position. Thus, we shall define personality as those *enduring characteristics of the person which are significant for his interpersonal behavior*.

All definitions of personality suggest many questions, and ours is no exception. What are the antecedents of these "enduring characteristics?" To what extent are they inherited, learned in early childhood, or developed in later life? Under what conditions and to what degree can they be expected to change? These and related questions bring us deeper into the subject of personality theory; indeed, it is around such questions that the major differences in personality theory are found. These problems are actively dealt with by most of the major contemporary personality theorists (see Hall and Lindzey, 1957, for lucid and readable accounts), each of whom takes a somewhat different stand. From the viewpoint of personality *assessment*, however, they need not directly concern us, since we can pursue our subject with only minimal involvement in personality theory per se.

Personality Theory and Personality Assessment

Although it would be useful to have a universal, internally consistent conceptual language for personality description, none exists. As indicated in our brief discussion of the structure of personality, there is much disagreement about how best to even approach this task. Instead, each of the major personality theorists has attempted to develop his own conceptual system, which has little or no integration with any other system. Most approaches to assessing personality have been theoretically neutral, but the personality descriptions produced by each have tended to involve the language of one or another personality theory. For example, in psychoanalytic or Freudian theory, it is considered that differences in personality stem from individual differences in the amount of available psychic energy (libido) or in the methods of handling this energy. Concepts such as ego, superego, and Oedipal conflict refer to mechanisms and processes in the flow of energy. Thus, if we were to explain an individual's behavior as due to a strong ego, or to unresolved Oedipal strivings, we would be using the language of Freudian personality theory. In another language system, that of "trait and type" personality theory, personality is described as a simple additive combination of many separate characteristics. Using this language, we might say that the individual was very hostile, or had strong dominance characteristics, or was extroverted. As yet another alternative, if we were to employ the language system of stimulus-response learning theory as applied to personality, we might describe the individual as having failed to learn an appropriate discrimination, or as behaving according to a certain reinforcement schedule.

To repeat, personality descriptions resulting from assessment procedures are often couched in the language of a particular personality theory. We must not be misled, however, into believing that the assessment procedures are therefore based on careful theoretical considerations. A few of the major methods of personality assessment do have some theoretical identification, but most are theoretically neutral, and the language of the assessment procedure is chosen according to the theoretical sympathies of the test constructor rather than because the assessment procedure is derived directly from the theory or satisfies its assumptions. It is too often a simple matter to rename the concepts used in a procedure with those of another theoretical language system, without any significant difference either in the procedures involved or in the level of understanding achieved.

Which theory offers the best language to use in the description of personality? There are no simple rules for assessing the relative merits of the existing sets of personality concepts, and certainly none upon which the major theorists would agree. Hall and Lindzey (1957, Ch. 1) have suggested that the critical test of the utility of a theory is the amount of significant research it generates. Using this criterion of utility, the generally atheoretical nature of personality assessment procedures is perhaps an indictment of the current state of personality theory.

Theoretical Approaches to Personality Assessment

Let us try to see what is involved in the theoretical approach to clinical assessment. For the purposes of this discussion we shall ignore the issue of which assessment procedures the psychologist chooses and how he collects, analyzes, and integrates the information produced by these procedures. We shall simply note that the information is processed and a description of the individual's personality is offered by the psychologist, phrased in the language of his favorite theory of personality. For example, let us suppose that an individual being considered for psychotherapy is referred to a psychologist of Freudian persuasion for a personality evaluation. After completing the steps involved in a clinical personality assessment, the psychologist forwards his report, including his finding that the patient has an unresolved Oedipal conflict. The psychologist further recommends that the patient be seen in therapy by a dominant male therapist as the optimal arrangement for the resolution of the conflict. It should be clearly apparent that the conclusion that the patient requires a male therapist does *not* stem directly from the assessment data, but rather from some theoretical considerations on the part of the psychologist. This process might be schematically expressed as follows:

Information from assessment procedures	$\rightarrow$	Personality description	$\rightarrow$	Personality theory	$\rightarrow$	Decision about the patient

In order for this decision to be a useful one for the patient, three conditions must hold true: (a) the psychologist's interpretation of the assessment data must be correct within the framework of the particular personality theory he is using; (b) his understanding of the theory must be adequate enough to enable him to make a decision which is consistent with the demands of the theory; and (c) the theory itself must be a useful one. If the patient subsequently *deteriorates* in therapy with a dominant male therapist, the psychologist will be somewhat at a loss to know why, because of the lengthy chain of inferences leading to the original decision. Any one or any combination of the three conditions might not have held true. Or the failure may have been a function of therapist incompetence, unfavorable changes in the real-life circumstances of the patient, or a multitude of other considerations.

On the other hand, suppose the patient did improve in therapy. What could be concluded from this event? Success with the one single individual does not validate this rather long chain of inference; for one thing, the same extraneous factors listed above (favorable real-life circumstances of the patient, or extreme competence of the therapist) may have been operating. Success by several dominant male therapists with several similar patients takes us further toward the desired validation but not the whole distance, since the chain of inferences might well contain redundancies or compensating errors. The validity of this approach to individual assessment cannot be adequately determined by observing the outcomes of decisions based upon it, but must be investigated through careful step-by-step study of the inferential chain. In other words, validating the assessment technique is closely tied to validating the personality theory utilized in the chain.

Comparison of Theortical and Empirical Approaches

Let us contrast the steps involved in this theoretical or inferential approach with those which would be involved in the empirical approach to the same problem. We would assume that the psychologist knows, from previously reported empirical research, that patients with certain kinds of responses on a particular assessment instrument improve more quickly with male than with female therapists. When faced with the decision of recommending the sex of a therapist for a prospective patient, he would administer this assessment instrument, compare the patient's responses with the empirical research findings, and make his decision as to a male or female therapist solely upon that basis. Given the current state of personality theory, the clinician has a greater probability of correctness in his decision making if he uses the empirical rather than the theoretical approach. There are fewer steps and inferences between the data and the decision, which reduces the probability of error, and it is comparatively easy to recheck the correctness of the previously reported relationships.

It is possible to argue that the empirical approach is not personality assessment at all, at least not in any strict sense. The inferential step of attributing some underlying enduring characteristic to the respondent, that is, of making inferences about his personality, has in a sense been bypassed. However, empirical processes have traditionally been so closely tied with personality assessment, particularly in the context of establishing the "validity" of personality tests (see Chapter 6), that they must be regarded an integral part of the field.

One might reasonably ask which of the two approaches—theoretical or empirical—generally should be the better one to use. There is no simple answer to this question. On one hand, the existing theories of personality are not sufficiently explicit to offer any superiority to prediction through the theoretical approach. On the other hand, this approach offers more for the ultimate advancement of the field, so that its development will be slowed if empirical procedures are always favored for applied work.

It is possible, in principle, to develop an assessment instrument directly from a theory of personality. In such a case, the individual's responses would be immediately meaningful within the context of the theory, and no additional inferential activity by the clinician would be necessary. Thus, the step labeled "personality description" in the last diagram would be eliminated. One of the few instruments which are clearly and explicitly based upon theory is the Blacky Pictures Test (Blum, 1949), which is discussed in Chapter 4. Although such approaches are scientifically rather sophisticated and offer much hope for the development of basic knowledge about personality, once again it must be stated that personality theorizing is not sufficiently advanced for them to be generally useful at the present time.

Methods of Personality Assessment

The term *personality assessment* refers to the process of gathering and organizing information about another person in the expectation that this information will lead to a better understanding of the person. Understanding another individual and his personality typically involves making some prediction about the future behavior of that person in rather specific terms. Among the kinds of predictions to be made could be his probability of vocational success in a variety of areas, his response to different kinds of psychological treatments, or his probablity of demonstrating certain socially undesirable behaviors. The task of the professional psychologist often involves participating in a variety of decisions concerning other people, based upon his assessment of their personality.

All of us, however, are continually involved in gathering a variety of unsystematic information about the behavior of people around us, and we are continually, if not with complete awareness, making inferences about their personality characteristics from our observations. Statements such as "I know him pretty well," or "I've known him for a long time but I don't understand him at all," reflect our everyday ways of talking about our knowledge of another's personality. The study of these informal processes of data collection and of the ways we organize and analyze the information is a fascinating one. How well can one get to know another's personality in this manner? Are some people more effective in this respect than others? On what basis? What psychological processes are involved? Extended analyses of the present-day answers to these and related questions can be found in Bieri, Atkins, Briar, Leamen, Miller and Tripodi (1966); Sarbin, Taft and Bailey (1960); Taft (1955); and Vernon (1964), especially Ch. 2.

The informal or intuitive processes by which we get to know and understand people with whom we are closely involved are similar to those employed by the psychotherapist in understanding his patient. The informal approach is characterized by the large amount of time which it requires, and also by the lack of specificity about the manner of both data collection and data analysis. Each observer is expected to proceed with the task of understanding the other person at his own pace and in his own, nonspecified fashion.

Although the informal, intuitive approach is fascinating, it will not be considered beyond this chapter. We shall be primarily concerned with the formal, systematic ways of going about the assessment task— the methods used by the professional psychologist in his formal role as an expert assessor of personality. We shall emphasize the situations in which the psychologist or other professional person uses standardized assessment instruments in a systematic manner in the assessment situation. The interview, an unstandardized personality assessment technique but a major assessment method in use today, will also be considered briefly.

How might standardized assessment tools be classified? Here we shall identify three groups of instruments; the first consist of those generally regarded as *personality tests*. The discussion of personality tests, both inventories and the so-called projective techniques, and of the many problems surrounding their use and interpretation, will fill the major portion of this book. A second group of instruments makes use of specific factual information about the individual's present status and his past history, the kind of information which might be obtained from a biographical data blank or a carefully structured interview. This method, the *biographical data method,* is widely used in personnel selection in industry and will be discussed in Chapter 5. A third group of instruments provides miniature models of real-life situations, in which the behavior of interest can be observed directly. For example, an instrument for assessing the subject's stress tolerance would consist of a structured and standardized situation in which the individual would be required to perform under some artificially produced stress. The situation normally would be arranged so that the behavior could be directly observed without the person being aware of what was happening. This method of assessment, through the use of *behavior samples*, will also be discussed in Chapter 5.

Some psychologists have felt that certain personality tests, notably the projective techniques, are more appropriately regarded as standardized situations for eliciting a behavior sample. They consider that the projective testing situation represents a standardized model of an interpersonal interaction with ambiguous demands, and that the entire situation—the projective test materials (such as ink blots or pictures), plus the examiner, plus his instructions, plus the immediate environment—constitutes the assessment "instrument." This is a fruitful approach to the analysis and understanding of projective tests and their contribution to personality assessment; we, however, have taken the more straightforward and traditional direction of grouping the projective techniques together with the other personality tests.

The Choice of Assessment Procedures

How does the psychologist decide upon which instruments to use in a particular assessment situation? The psychologist traditionally uses an interview, tests, biographical and other case data such as supervisory ratings or school records, and whatever additional assessment tools he may choose, in order to provide information about the individual under study. Although the steps involved in normal clinical assessment may be more organized than those in the informal intuitive method of assessment, there is still much variability among psychologists in their manner both of data collection and of data analysis. There are no standard procedures for gathering data that are followed universally by psychologists, and the assessment instruments chosen by a particular psychologist will be a function of his training and experience, his idiosyncratic preferences, and his familiarity with the current literature.

One recurring problem in choosing assessment methods involves deciding between formal personality tests and the informal intuitive methods. Although it is usually not the case, let us assume for the purposes of this discussion that the end results of the two methods would be comparably useful, that is, both methods would yield equally correct predictions.

In choosing between the methods, the *time factor* is one important consideration. It may well be that a decision must be reached about a patient by noon tomorrow because he is going on court trial, or because he is being considered for discharge. To initiate a lengthy informal intuitive procedure at this stage would not be expedient. However, if the patient had previously been seen in psychotherapy for several months, his therapist could give us his intuitive assessment very quickly.

Economic factors must also be considered in making a decision about which method to use. To assign an individual to an informal assessor for an extended period of time is obviously an expensive business, and would rarely be done for the sake of assessment alone. However, if the person were a hospital patient in a well-staffed ward, a routine duty of the ward staff might well be to gather the informal data needed for such an assessment. Another situation where intuitive assessment would be prohibitively expensive is in the routine screening of large numbers of persons, such as for draft into the armed forces. Standardized assessment techniques, which can be administered to large numbers of persons simultaneously in a short time, have an obvious economic advantage.

Thus, the choice between these or any other assessment procedures will be influenced by considerations of practical efficiency. In this regard, a crucial factor will often be the availability of a person or persons who have been able to make the kind of observations necessary for an informal intuitive assessment over an extended period of time. If a competent assessor of this type is available, he should generally be utilized. To state the conclusion another way, the decision as to which assessment method to use should ultimately be determined by the *relative gain* or payoff of the alternative courses of action.

There may be occasions when it is not justifiable to apply any assessment procedure at all. Taking all factors into consideration, if the losses (in time, expense, increased hostility of the patient, loss of staff morale) more than offset the gains (additional pertinent information about the individual, increased probability of making the optimal prediction or decision), then it would be better not to use any assessment procedure. Unfortunately, there has been little systematic research on the relative payoffs of assessment techniques. Further, many hospitals, clinics, industries, and schools have been using the same assessment procedures routinely over many years with little information about, or even interest in, the efficiency of these procedures. Hathaway (1959) considered the time actually spent by clinical psychologists in routine clinical assessment and estimated that if an empirical evaluation of their efficiency were made, more than 40 percent of these activities would be abandoned.

Personality Tests and Ability Tests

We have previously indicated that the major focus of this book will be upon personality assessment through the medium of standardized assessment instruments, typically referred to as *personality tests*. The more general term *psychological tests* includes, in addition to personality assessment instruments, an extensive array of devices for measuring *abilities*.

How might we differentiate between ability tests and personality tests? Some of the attributes of an individual which are typically regarded as personality traits could also at times be considered as abilities, especially for tasks involving interpersonal interactions. For example, are leadership and persuasiveness more appropriately considered as personality or ability factors? As pointed out by Anastasi (1961, p. 33), any distinction between these two kinds of domains is to some degree arbitrary. Traditionally, the term "ability tests" has been used to identify instruments which assess skills or achievement in cognitive, intellectual, and motor areas. As an alternative to the term "ability tests," Cronbach (1960) has suggested "*maximum* performance test," a term which conveys the following concepts: (1) the individual is expected to perform as skillfully as he can, and (2) there are specific right and wrong answers to the test items. Cronbach further suggested that personality tests might be better regarded as tests of *habitual* performance, or instruments which are expected to identify the individual's typical modes of responding, when he is specifically informed that there are no right or wrong answers. While the arbitrariness of distinction is not eliminated by Cronbach's suggestions, the types of individual differences involved in these two categories are made more specific.

One reason for discussing ability tests in the present context is that the methods and techniques employed in ability testing have provided important models for the development of personality tests. However, the degree of success enjoyed by ability tests has not yet been realized in the field of personality assessment. Although the predictions about real-life situations made from carefully constructed ability tests can be considered fairly satisfactory, the same cannot be said for personality tests. Some of the reasons for this difference lie in the lack of widely accepted personality concepts; others involve fundamental questions as to what is meant by "measurement." Nevertheless, personality tests modeled on the traditional ability-testing procedures have probably now reached their maximum degree of refinement. Thus, further improvements in personality assessment will probably have to come from new approaches to the problem, rather than from further refinements of the traditional methods.

Summary

Psychologists undertake personality assessment for two reasons, corresponding to two general themes underlying the development of the field: for the clinical assessment of single individuals, and to advance knowledge of human behavior through research and theory. In clinical assessment, the simplest approach is prediction based on known empirical relationships between the assessment results and the behavior to be predicted. A disadvantage of this procedure is that it adds little to a broader understanding of the processes involved. One assumption basic to all traditional personality assessment procedures is that one's interpersonal behavior has some consistency over time and across different situations. This assumption is questioned in recent theoretical approaches to personality through behavioral learning theory, in which much greater emphasis is placed on environmental conditions in determining behavior at any time.

A common approach to personality prediction is first to construct a personality description by generalizing from known empirical relationships, and then to make predictions on the basis of the description. This approach is sometimes regarded as "theoretical," but the term "theory" in this text is reserved for more rigorous procedures involving sets of related laws. A serious problem with prediction from a general personality description is that the known empirical relationships are frequently generalized beyond their applicability.

Researchers have attempted to ascertain the structure of personality in our culture by identifying and analyzing the many thousands of trait words in the English language. There are two points of view about personality structure: (1) that a "true" structure exists, and will be eventually discovered, and (2) that any number of structures may be imposed upon natural human behavior in an attempt to understand it better. There is no agreed-upon definition for the term personality, and in this text we adopt an atheoretical, practical definition, which regards personality as *those enduring characteristics of the person which are significant for his interpersonal behavior.* Personality descriptions resulting from assessment procedures are usually couched in the specific language of one or another theory of personality, but this does not mean that the assessment is based on the theory. In fact, the science of personality is not yet sufficiently developed to permit a truly theoretical approach to personality assessment.

There are a variety of methods of personality assessment—informal and intuitive methods, interviewing, formal standardized procedures, biographical data, and behavioral samples. Most of this book will be devoted to a consideration of standardized assessment procedures. The choice of which assessment procedure to employ in any given situation depends on economic factors, the available time, and other aspects of practical efficiency.

In the development of personality assessment procedures, the well-established methods for assessing skills and abilities have generally been used as models. However, it appears that personality assessment procedures based on these models have now reached their maximum degree of refinement, and further developments will have to come from new approaches.

3 RATIONAL-THEORETICAL APPROACHES TO ASSESSMENT

We have touched upon a number of basic issues involved in developing and using personality assessment instruments. They include the problems of how the test situation can be standardized, what stimuli can be used to evoke meaningful and useful responses from test-takers, and what type of responses should be observed in order to understand and predict those human behaviors usually subsumed under the rubric *personality*. Chapters 3 and 4 will be specifically concerned with these issues. Following a discussion of the characteristics of assessment techniques, we shall examine the most widely used assessment devices. This procedure will serve to present and illustrate the problems mentioned above, and to give the reader some familiarity with current assessment devices and practices.

CHARACTERISTICS OF STANDARDIZED ASSESSMENT PROCEDURES

An examination of the standardized assessment procedures in common use shows that they tend to meet the following conditions: (1) the stimuli to be used in the assessment process are identical for all respondents and are always presented in the same fashion; (2) there are available *norms*, or frequency distributions of responses, either formal or informal (intuitive), so that responses can be assigned to a specific place within an anticipated range; and (3) there are useful personality and behavioral correlates of the to-be-observed responses. We say that assessment procedures *tend* to meet these criteria because the strictness with which the criteria are employed, particularly the latter two, varies. Nevertheless, each of these elements is present to some extent in all techniques which are considered formal assessment procedures.

The above conditions suggest three dimensions that could be useful in characterizing personality assessment procedures. The first dimension concerns the variety of relevant responses made by the test-taker and observed by the examiner and might be termed the *degree of response structure*. It should be clearly noted that here we are *not* referring to differences in the degree of structure which is imposed upon the testing situation by the examiner. A high degree of structure or standardization of procedure is an important condition for any formal assessment device. Thus, the procedures for administering the Rorschach are, or should be, just as inflexible as those for giving the Minnesota Multiphasic Personality Inventory (MMPI). Most paper-and-pencil personality inventories, such as the MMPI, also can be regarded as rather highly structured with respect to respondent behaviors, since the only responses to be made and observed are indications of "true" or "false" to a series of personal statements. Whatever other responses the test-taker might otherwise make are discouraged by the preliminary instructions and tend to be ignored if they are made despite the instructions. Since the MMPI is taken either by sorting cards into "true" and "false" piles or by marking an IBM answer sheet, variations in such behaviors as vigor or response time are not recorded, and neither the MMPI scoring procedure nor its interpretive system permit the use of such data. Rorschach's inkblot test, on the other hand, would be regarded as relatively unstructured in the present sense because the examiner generally observes and records a wide range of respondent behaviors, and considers all of them to be relevant response material. Included are the portion of the blot to which the person has responded, the stimulus characteristics of that portion of the blot—for example, the form, color, or shading—that determined each given response, the actual content of each response, the respondent's body position and movement, his changes in pitch, volume, loudness, and rate of speech, any spontaneous comments about the situation, and other features of the respondent's style of expression.

A second dimension on which assessment procedures differ is the degree to which published formal norms are available. Structured inventories, such as the MMPI, with a smaller range of relevant responses, more readily lend themselves to the development of formal norms. These norms are usually developed by the test authors and are presented in tabular form, frequently with conversion tables for easy translation into some standard score form. For example, the

MMPI scales employ "T-scores," with a mean of 50 and a standard deviation of 10. Later research often provides specific norms for working with homogeneous groups of various sorts (for example, Lanyon, 1968). Projective techniques, on the other hand, with a larger range of responses to be considered, generally do not have formal norms available. Instead, the clinician who uses these procedures must build informal norms based upon his own experience, so that the development of skills in the use of projective techniques becomes complex and time consuming. While there have been some attempts to develop formal norms for these assessment procedures, especially for the Rorschach (for example, Beck et al., 1961; Hertz, 1951), the results have by no means been generally accepted or integrated into clinical practice.

A third dimension which might be useful for characterizing personality assessment devices is the usefulness of the instrument. By usefulness, we mean the extent to which the test-taker's responses will permit understanding and prediction of some of his nontest behaviors. A very useful instrument would enable relatively precise predictions to be made about socially important behaviors, such as success in a particular occupation or prognosis in psychotherapy. Less useful instruments are either less precise in their predictions or deal with socially less significant behavior, such as performance on an experimental laboratory task. The term *validity* is similar to usefulness but is more precise, and refers to the existence of a demonstrated relationship between certain test responses and a particular nontest characteristic of the person. Thus the number of validities, or valid relationships, that a test possesses, and the importance or significance of these relationships, determine the test's usefulness. This topic is discussed more fully in Chapter 6.

The position of an assessment instrument on each of these three dimensions—degree of response structure, availability of norms, and usefulness—to some degree is established by a more basic aspect of the instrument. We are referring to the method of construction of the instrument, and more particularly, to the method employed in selecting the stimuli. In general, there are three major approaches to or strategies in the construction of formal assessment devices: (1) rational-theoretical; (2) empirical; and (3) internal consistency.

1. A test may be based upon purely rational, face-value, or common-sense considerations. For example, we might include the item "I frequently find myself worrying about something" in a test of manifest anxiety, since it would be reasonable to assume that on an a priori

basis, manifestly anxious subjects would be more likely to respond affirmatively than nonanxious subjects. Rationally derived tests are developed by selecting or constructing stimulus materials that *seem* to tap the behavior in which the test author is interested. A test might conceivably also be devised to be congruent with a particular theoretical view of personality, and it would assess concepts within that theory. The Blacky Pictures Test (Blum, 1950), which involves drawings portraying the adventures of a pup, Blacky, and his family, best approximates a theoretically derived personality test, in this case based on traditional psychoanalytic theory. The test-taker's responses to the drawings are scored and interpreted as indices of the amount of conflict in the various psychoanalytic stages of psychosexual development. Since there are no theories of personality which, strictly speaking, meet our preferred definition of a theory (see Chapter 2), and since most rationally based tests do involve some theoretical considerations, the discussion to follow considers rational and theoretically based tests together. Thus, a continuum of *rational-theoretical* derivation is conceptualized, with a priori inventories nearer to the rational end, and tests such as the Blacky Pictures nearer to the theoretical end.

2. The basis for a test can be *empirical;* that is, there is an empirical basis for believing that the test should work in the manner described by the test author. Each test item might be selected according to its power to discriminate between two groups of interest, such as people with sales potential from people in general, or it might be that a global score of some kind is shown to discriminate between two groups.

3. A test might be developed on the basis of the *internal consistency* of the items. For example, a fairly large number of test stimuli might be administered to a group of respondents, and those items whose responses are closely related or intercorrelated are assumed to tap the same psychological variable. Such statistically defined variables are then used as indices of aspects of personality functioning.

It should be emphasized that these three approaches to test development are not mutually exclusive. For example, the development of the so-called empirically derived instruments has almost always involved an initial rational or theoretical selection of items to be put to an empirical test. Similarly, the internal consistency approach typically follows some rational or theoretical assembling of the items. What we have done, however, is to classify instruments as predominantly based upon one approach or another. As stated previously, psychologists interested in personality and assessment have often tended to employ the word "theory" in a loose or colloquial sense. Thus they might consider certain tests to have a stronger theoretical base than we shall give them credit for here.

RATIONAL-THEORETICAL APPROACHES

Perhaps the most obvious approach to test development is the strictly rational one, where we expect the test items to act as stimuli for directly eliciting the information in which we are interested. *Woodworth's Personal Data Sheet*, described in some detail in Chapter 1, is an early example of purely rational derivation. It asks the same questions that a psychiatrist or a clinical psychologist would ask when directly examining a patient to determine his level of adjustment. As noted above, the assumption is made that the responses to such test items as "Do you sleep well?" or "Do you get rattled easily?" are valid indices of the level of adjustment of the respondent, in the same way as the responses to an oral examination are assumed to be. We shall have more to say about these assumptions later in the chapter; first we shall describe some of the more widely used instruments in the rational-theoretical category. Tests which fall toward the rational end of the continuum will be considered first.

Sentence Completion

Sentence completion is a technique or a method rather than a single specific instrument, although commercially marketed instruments representative of the method are readily available (Forer, 1950; Rohde, 1967; Rotter and Rafferty, 1950). The respondent is presented with a series of items consisting of the first few words of a sentence, and his task is to provide an ending for each of these beginnings or stems. The stems are developed to elicit responses that illuminate various aspects of the individual's feelings and behaviors. Thus, his attitudes and feelings toward his mother are assumed to be tapped by the stem "My mother and I . . . ," and his techniques for handling strong emotions are presumably seen in his response to the item "When I am angry or upset, I . . . ." Sentence stems in the third person are also employed, such as "His greatest wish was . . . ," and the projective hypothesis is used as a basis for reasoning that the responses to these third person stems are informative about the subject's own desires.

Of the several commercially available instruments, the Rotter Incomplete Sentences Blank (Rotter and Rafferty, 1950) has perhaps enjoyed the widest use. In addition to qualitative, clinical inferences that might be drawn from the content of the individual's responses, the Rotter Incomplete Sentences Blank also contains a rationally derived quantitative scoring scheme that yields a single index of adjustment-maladjustment. There are 40 sentence stems, all of which are rather brief and nonspecific, such as "I feel . . . ," and "Marriage . . . ." Each response is scored, with the aid of the examples provided in the manual, on a seven-point rating scale for degree of maladjustment. The reasonably high levels of reliability and validity reported in the manual for this maladjustment index have tended to be substantiated in later studies (Goldberg, 1965).

In general, the available evidence about the usefulness of the sentence completion method can be summarized as follows (Goldberg, 1965):

1. There is little research evidence to indicate that any of the formal aspects of responses to sentence completion items, such as reaction time, response length, or grammatical or spelling errors are systematically related to any personality-relevant behaviors. There is also little evidence to support the use of impressionistic or clinical analyses of the content of the responses, although adequate studies of such an approach are difficult to conduct.

2. The more structured approaches to content analysis, such as Rotter's scoring procedure, have been demonstrated to be useful. This finding is intuitively reasonable, since an instrument developed to assess a single, clearly defined variable or dimension like adjustment-maladjustment can be expected to be valid or useful for that particular purpose. Further, the focus upon a single dimension tends to result in relative homogeneity of items, enhancing the consistency or reliability of the instrument, which in turn enhances usefulness. However, it should be pointed out that the clinician interested in describing and understanding a broad range of personality and behavior will probably be dissatisfied with an instrument yielding only a single score.

3. Employing first person stems seems to provide somewhat more useful responses than third person stems, although the evidence is not unequivocal.

4. The specificity of the content of a response can be controlled by the specificity of the sentence stem. That is, the stems can be worded so that the responses are more or less delimited. For example, the stem "Marriage . . . " elicits a wider range of responses than the stem "My marriage has been . . . ." It is yet unclear which of these two types of stems elicits the more significant responses.

In order to illustrate the usage of the sentence completion method, the first five sentence stems of the Rotter Incomplete Sentences Blank are given below, together with the completions which were provided by an 18-year-old college male freshman seeking help for personal problems.

1. I like . . . music, leisure time, and sports.
2. The happiest time . . . is when I'm performing.
3. I want to know . . . what I don't know.
4. Back home . . . it's very nice.
5. I regret . . . many things, but only slightly.

The nature of the objective scoring system for degree of maladjustment is as follows. The scoring manual (Rotter and Rafferty, 1950, p. 55) would give a score of 6, representing the extreme of maladjustment, to a response such as ". . . to know if I am going crazy," given to the first stem, "I like . . . ." The response ". . . most everything" to this stem would receive a score of 0, representing the extreme of adjustment. The response ". . . to observe people" would receive a score of 3, the neutral category with respect to adjustment-maladjustment. The particular response which was given by the above client would be scored 2, or slightly on the "adjusted" side of the neutral point. With the aid of similar scoring examples, the response given by the client to the second sentence stem would be scored 3. The complete set of 40 responses given by this client yielded a total score of 134, placing him at about the 70th percentile with respect to maladjustment according to the norms provided in the ISB Manual.

Qualitative or subjective inferences typically also are drawn from sentence completion responses. For example, the client's response to the second stem might be taken to suggest exhibitionistic needs, and further evidence to support or contradict this tentative hypothesis would be sought from the remainder of the test. Likewise, strong dependency needs might be inferred from the fourth response. The fifth response, which contains a mild contradiction, might be interpreted as reflecting a personality conflict, perhaps involving guilt.

Edwards Personal Preference Schedule

A commonly used paper-and-pencil inventory is the Edwards Personal Preference Schedule (EPPS), which is also one of the more psychometrically sophisticated of the rational-theoretical instruments. Edwards' avowed purpose in developing the test was "to provide quick and convenient measures of a number of relatively independent normal personality variables" (Edwards, 1959, p. 5). The 15 variables were selected from the list of "manifest needs" listed in the theoretical writings of Murray (1938), and include such needs as achievement, affiliation, deference, nurturance, and order. To assess each need, the EPPS uses nine brief statements that bear a rational, common-sense relationship to that need. Thus, the need for achievement is tapped by such statements as "I like to do my very best in whatever I undertake," and "I would like to accomplish something of great significance." Although the EPPS has sometimes been considered to be derived directly from Murray's theoretical writings on personality, its basic reliance upon common-sense considerations, particularly in item development, should be emphasized.

The sophistication of the EPPS is found in its *forced-choice* format. Pairs of self-reference statements are presented simultaneously to the respondent, who in each case is to choose the statement which is the more self-descriptive. There are 210 such choices for the respondent to make, and he can endorse the set of statements related to each need from zero to 28 times. Every need is paired twice with every other need, requiring each statement to be repeated three or four times. The strength of a particular need is determined by the number of times, out of the 28 options, that the respondent chooses or endorses the statements representing that need. Fifteen additional pairs are included in order to evaluate the consistency or reliability of an individual's responses.

Why was the forced-choice technique employed? Edwards (1953, 1957) was concerned by his finding that the frequency of endorsement of any self-descriptive statement was highly related to the judged *social desirability* of that statement. The general issue of the complex effects of social desirability upon personality test responses will be dealt with in some detail in Chapter 7; we shall simply indicate here its role in the construction of the EPPS. Edwards decided, upon the basis of his findings, that people ordinarily respond to test items according to the social desirability of that item rather than according to its specific personality content. Thus, the failure to control for social desirability led to a failure to fairly evaluate the respondents' personality characteristics. Edwards attempted to circumvent this difficulty in his construction of the EPPS by arranging the statements in pairs within which the alternatives were approximately matched on social desirability, and requiring respondents to endorse one statement from each pair. He reasoned that the choice could not now be made on the basis of social desirability, so that persons must choose according to their own personality characteristics.

The development of the EPPS represents an innovative attempt to deal with the problem of social desirability, although later research (for example, Heilbrun and Goodstein, 1961a; 1961b; Rorer, 1965) has shown that the problem is far from resolved. Briefly, the research tends to suggest that the forced-choice format reduced but failed to remove the influence of social desirability; more important, however, is the finding that the predictive usefulness or validity of such questionnaires appears to be determined in part by the extent to which the factor of social desirability is still present. As mentioned above, this problem will be explored in detail in Chapter 7 under the heading *response sets*.

The use of a forced-choice format also raises other problems. In the case of the EPPS, the respondent is in effect asked to distribute 210 endorsements over 420 items. Put another way, he must indicate 210 points' worth of personality needs, regardless of whether or not this degree of "need" exists. The result is an EPPS profile which reflects a rank order of needs as they apply to the respondent. Such procedures, which allow comparisons of an individual's characteristics within himself but are limited in the degree to which they permit inter-individual comparisons, are termed *ipsative*, and they raise special problems in the interpretation of test scores. Still another problem posed by the forced-choice format is that the scale scores thus obtained are not statistically independent of each other since, by the nature of the forced choice, an elevated score on one dimension will force a lower score on another dimension. Since most statistical operations assume the independence of scores, many studies involving the interrelationship of EPPS scores are difficult to interpret. Thus, it can be concluded that Edwards' attempts to deal with the problem of social desirability have not been completely successful and have created, in turn, several new and difficult problems.

Despite these problems, the rational derivation of the EPPS might lead us to expect it to be a reasonably useful or valid instrument. Edwards (1959, p. 19) has shown that the scores are reasonably stable or reliable. Yet recent reviews of the EPPS (Radcliffe, 1965; Stricker, 1965) have concluded that the evidence for its usefulness is poor, despite the more than 300 reported studies which have examined it (Buros, 1965, p. 195). One important exception is the achievement scale, which has been shown rather consistently to be correlated with academic achievement in both high school and college.

Study of Values

Another personality assessment instrument that utilizes a paper-and-pencil questionnaire format and which takes some account of a theoretical viewpoint is the Study of Values (Vernon and Allport, 1931; Allport, Vernon, and Lindzey, 1960). Utilizing the theoretical views of personality advanced by Eduard Spranger (1928), the Study of Values aims to measure the relative prominence of six basic interests or motives in personality: theoretical, economic, aesthetic, social, political, and religious. The theoretical man is dominated by the discovery of truth and his chief purpose in life is to bring order and systematization to his understanding of his world. The economic man is concerned with that which is useful, and is very much in keeping with the typical stereotype of the successful American business man. The aesthetic man is interested in form and harmony, and his primary concern is with beauty rather than truth or utility. The social man is concerned with love for other people in an altruistic or philanthropic sense, a selfless love for mankind. The political man is primarily dominated by power, by control over people and events, and by needs for personal influence and renown. The religious man is concerned with a sense of unity, a need for establishing a kind of transcendental understanding of the universe in some personal way.

The format of the test, like the EPPS, is ipsative. Part I consists of 30 forced-choice item pairs in which each value is paired twice with every other value, and Part II consists of 15 forced-choice item tetrads in which each value is compared with all other combinations of three other values. The test is self-administering and self-scorable.

The Study of Values was originally published in 1931 (Vernon and Allport, 1931) and was revised in its present form in 1951. Although there is good evidence for the stability or reliability of the separate scores, there is a serious question about their unidimensionality and degree of independence. Hundleby (1965) felt that even factor-analytic studies were not conclusive about the nature of the interrelationships among the scores, a problem complicated by the ipsative format of the test. It should be noted that the fairly wide use of the Study of Values for demonstration and research purposes has been connected only minimally with Spranger's theoretical views, which have had little impact upon contemporary personality theory.

Much of the research into the usefulness of the Study of Values has involved comparisons among scores of different occupational groups and students in different colleges and different curricula, demonstrating the different values of such groups. These differences are interesting and lend some support to the use of the instrument for research purposes, but are not sufficiently large to justify its clinical usage for individual assessment.

Rorschach Psychodiagnostic Technique

The Rorschach Psychodiagnostic Technique, or Rorschach, is usually classified simply as a projective technique. However, if we classify it according to the strategy employed in its development as a clinical instrument, the Rorschach is best regarded as rational-theoretical. The presumed relationships between Rorschach responses and the personality characteristics of respondents are based largely upon assumptions and hypotheses developed by Hermann Rorschach, the Swiss psychiatrist who invented the test, and several generations of his followers; and also upon common-sense considerations. In addition, there is a strong theoretical aspect to its development, since many of the interpretative dimensions stem from Jungian personality theory. There have also been a variety of attempts to conceptualize the Rorschach within other theoretical frameworks, and these efforts have been evaluated by Zubin, Eron, and Schumer (1965). As a further point of interest, the original derivation of the Rorschach was to some extent empirical, since Rorschach himself compared the responses of certain patient groups in developing his concepts about the instrument. However, the contemporary clinical usage of the instrument, based upon the writings of Rorschach (1942), Klopfer et al. (1954), Beck et al. (1961), and many, many others, is based primarily upon rational considerations.

In administering the Rorschach, the examiner shows the respondent a series of ten symmetrical inkblots, five achromatic and five chromatic, and asks him to describe what he can see in these blots, or "what they remind you of." The order of presentation is invariant and the examiner records the individual's responses verbatim, including any spontaneous comments as well as nonverbal behavior such as card turning. The respondent is permitted to give as many or as few responses as he wishes. Following this initial free association period, there is an inquiry or post-test interview in which the examiner, bearing in mind his interest in the specific formal Rorschach scoring categories, repeats the individual's responses back to him and asks him to specify the particular characteristics of the blot that determined each response.

Perhaps one way of understanding the development of the Rorschach is to examine Rorschach's initial work and how it has led to contemporary Rorschach interpretation with its emphasis on the formal characteristics of the responses. Hermann Rorschach's original interest was in fantasy (Zubin, Eron, and Schumer, 1965, p. 172), which he studied through perception of small, colored geometric forms. Finding that these geometric forms were too limited as stimulus material, he started to experiment with inkblots. When he began to use his patients as subjects for these perceptual experiments he was surprised to note that there were stable relationships between certain inkblot perceptions and psychiatric symptoms. Encouraged by these findings, he began a more systematic investigation of the responses of a number of diverse patients groups and started to speculate about the reasons for these relationships.

Since Rorschach was primarily interested in perception, he paid particular attention to the formal aspects of the individual's responses rather than to the content. He noted the number of responses, the reaction time, whether the response was determined solely by the form of the response or whether color or perceived movement were also involved, and so forth (Rorschach, 1942, p. 19). As part of his speculation, he developed fairly complex hypotheses about the relation of color and movement responses to the dimension of extroversion-introversion, based in part upon Jung's theoretical interest in this dimension.

The current clinical usage of the Rorschach has varied little since the test's inception. As Zubin, Eron, and Schumer have noted (1965, p. 178), most of the current rationale, procedures, and even interpretative phrases ascribed to various test response characteristics can be found in Rorschach's original monograph, which was initially published in German in 1921. Since Rorschach himself considered many of these relationships as highly tentative and requiring additional research, this is indeed a surprising state of affairs, the more so since the subsequent half century has seen the publication of over 2000 articles and books dealing with this instrument. Rorschach's own empirical commitment and his feelings of tentativeness about his findings appear not to have strongly influenced the subsequent course of events.

Zubin, Eron, and Schumer (1965, pp. 238–239) made a careful analysis of the many validity studies of the Rorschach. They concluded that the generally contradictory research forces a rather unfavorable view of the usefulness of the instrument and that clinical or impressionistic use of the Rorschach is likewise unsatisfactory, despite the many claims to the contrary. They further concluded that a global approach, in which the Rorschach is seen simply as one element in a clinical interaction between subject and examiner, is probably more fruitful than the traditional one with its emphasis upon formal response analysis. In such a clinical interaction (Sarason, 1954), emphasis is upon how the subject responds to the test stimuli in the presence of another person, and the examiner is concerned with the many subtle interpersonal cues which are present during the interaction. Here, the Rorschach is regarded as a standardized stimulus in an interpersonal interaction and as facilitating the examiner's task of building subjective, informal norms for interpreting the entire interaction.

The manner in which the Rorschach is traditionally used clini-

FIGURE 3-1. A reproduction of Card IV from the ten Rorschach inkblots.

cally can best be illustrated by discussing responses that were actually given to one of the stimulus cards. Figure 3-1 shows a reproduction of Card IV from the ten Rorschach inkblots. Klopfer and Davidson (1962, p. 10) have described the stimulus characteristics of this card as follows.

The blot material of Card IV appears massive, compact, yet indistinct in shape. This card is black-gray all over and highly shaded. Because of its massive structure and dense shading, it appears ominous to some people. Thus monsters, giants, gorillas, or peculiar-looking people are seen sitting or approaching, or the blot looks like a dense forest with mountains and lakes. The frequency of the giant, ape, or monster type of response has prompted some clinicians to refer to this card as the "father card." They believe that attitudes toward paternal authority are revealed because of the combination of masculine aggression and dependent needs related to shading.

Subjects who are prone to select details for their responses may perceive the large side areas as "boots," or the top side areas as "snakes" or a "female figure diving." Two other areas that are easily delineated are the lower center portion and the small top center area, frequently associated with sexual responses.

The shading of the card, if not disturbing to a subject, may suggest furriness; in that case the blot is frequently seen as a fur rug.

A 23-year-old female psychotherapy outpatient gave the following responses to this card. The question marks in the inquiry phase indicate places where the examiner asked clarifying questions about the *location* of the percept (What parts of the blot are you referring to?) and its *determinants* (for example, What about the blot suggested a monster?).

Free Association Phase	*Inquiry Phase*
IV 1. Sort of looks like a monster with big feet.	A cute little thing. Really a dashing little monster. Such a friendly little guy. Got a big tail, though. (?) The whole blot. (?) Really looks like a monster, but a friendly one.
2. When I turn it round, it just looks like—when you mount an insect it has wings and legs—looks like a mounted insect. Sort of cute insect. Maybe a little moth.	You lay him out flat. Only partially mounted. Person hasn't finished yet. You can tell by the lighter color that its wings are turned over. (?) The lighter gray. (?) Again, the whole blot.

The first response would be scored W F+ (H), indicating that the location of the percept was the whole blot (W), that the determinant was form, or shape (F), that the form perceived was appropriate or realistic (indicated by the + sign), and that the content of the percept was human-like, but not distinctly human ((H)). The second response would be scored W FC'+ A, indicating a whole response (W), a realistic form integrated with the perception of achromatic color (FC'+), and animal content (A).

In traditional Rorschach interpretation, at least three kinds of material are considered to be significant: the formal scoring categories, namely, the distribution of percepts over the various location and determinant categories, the nature of the perceived content, and the general language with which percepts are described. Only the most tentative hypotheses would be made from each individual percept, and heavy reliance is placed upon the response pattern as a whole.

Predominance of W or "whole" locations, when combined with a high level of form appropriateness, is traditionally interpreted as reflecting "the ability to organize material, to relate details, to be concerned with the abstract and the theoretical" (Klopfer and Davidson, 1962, p. 131). A high degree of form appropriateness is also considered to indicate a concern with the reality situation. The presence of achromatic color responses in any quantity is interpreted as indicating either hesitation in responsiveness to external stimuli or an unhappy mood. With regard to content and language, the client's recognition of a "monster" and the manner in which she divests it of its threatening nature ("cute," "little," "friendly") might be seen as illustrating one method of adjustment to perceived threat, by denying and even "reversing" the threatening elements. The fact that a satisfactory compromise is reached at the end of the inquiry ("a monster, but a friendly one") might be taken as a tentative indication that this particular defense mechanism operates satisfactorily for the client. This hypothesis might be tempered slightly after examining the next response, in which the percept has been reduced not only to an insect but a dead one, and the client again calls it "cute," perhaps suggesting that she is still finding it necessary to reassure herself that no threat exists. Pinning it out on a board might be seen as yet a further attempt to remove the threat. The use of "him" rather that "it" in the inquiry might be taken as a tentative cue that the threat has its basis in human interactions, particularly involving males. Obviously, such statements as these would only be regarded as tentative hypotheses, to be confirmed or negated by the client's responses to the other nine cards.

Holtzman Inkblot Technique (HIT)

Generally speaking, workers interested in unstructured or "projective" personality tests have tended to ignore problems of formal measurement, such as norms and unreliability. In 1954, however, a project was begun to develop " . . . a completely new approach to inkblot testing, one which is designed from its inception to meet adequate standards of measurement while preserving the uniquely valuable projective quality of the Rorschach" (Holtzman et al., 1961, p. 10). The materials were specifically designed to tap the same variables as the Rorschach, yet the method was designed to obviate a number of serious psychometric problems inherent in any quantitative use of the Rorschach, problems which center about unreliability due to the great variation in responses from subject to subject. Out of a very large number of inkblots produced by a variety of methods, Holtzman and his coworkers developed two parallel forms of 45 cards each. In these preliminary investigations the ˙ stimulus cards were administered to samples of normal persons (college students) and mental hospital patients. The two major criteria for selecting the final stimulus blots were that they should provide maximum discriminatory power between the two groups, and that the blots should enable maximum reliability of the scoring categories being studied. These categories included many traditional Rorschach variables such as location, form appropriateness, color, shading, and movement, categories whose personality interpretation is based on rational grounds. Thus, we shall consider the HIT as a rationally derived instrument despite the empirical basis of the selection of the actual HIT stimuli.

The HIT cards are shown one at a time to the individual, who is to give a single response to each card. The responses are then scored for 22 different variables, selected for their relative independence, reliability of scoring, and judged relevance for understanding personality. In addition to the five scoring variables listed above, they include form definiteness, space, anxiety, pathognomic verbalization, and five different content categories. The advantages claimed for the HIT include: (1) simplified psychometric treatment, since all subjects would give the same number of responses; (2) independence of responses, since each would be given to a different stimulus; (3) utilization of recent Rorschach research to improve upon the response elicitation properties of the cards; and (4) the establishment of reliabilities through the correlation between parallel forms.

A great deal of reliability information has been developed by Holtzman et al. (1961), all of which indicates that the stability or reliability of most scores is quite satisfactory, a considerable improvement over the Rorschach. An exception is found in the relatively low test-retest reliabilities, some of which are lower than 0.5, even with intervals of as little as one week between test and retest. Extensive normative data are presented on both normal persons and psychiatric patients. The manual reports substantial correlations of HIT scores with those obtained from the Rorschach, suggesting that the same variables are indeed being tapped by these two instruments. On the other hand, there are very few significant relationships reported between HIT scores and either scores from paper-and-pencil inventories or ratings of overt behavior. These findings are explained by Holtzman et al. as a consequence of the fact that the significant variables in personality and psychopathology are neither directly observable nor measurable by inventories.

The HIT has been favorably received in recent reviews (Forer, 1965; Thetford, 1965) as a carefully reasoned and thorough solution to the problem of adequately measuring the significant variables of the Rorschach. However, as Eysenck (1965) pointed out, there is little or no generally acceptable evidence to support the usefulness of these variables in personality assessment.

Thematic Apperception Test

The Thematic Apperception Test, more commonly known as the TAT (Murray, 1943), is another traditional projective device which is here classified as rational-theoretical. The stimulus materials consist of 31 cards, 30 depicting various scenes and people, and one blank card. In the standard presentation, the respondent is shown 20 cards chosen according to sex and age, although in the typical clinical presentation fewer than 20 cards are generally used. The TAT is introduced as a "test of imagination," and the respondent is asked to tell as dramatic a story as possible to each card. He is instructed that each story should include what has led up to the event depicted in the card, what is happening at that moment, what the people in the story are feeling and thinking, and finally the outcome of the story. The examiner records the stories verbatim as they are given. Murray (1943) also recommended that the examiner attempt, in a post-test interview, to determine the source of the story—whether personal experience, from friends, or from books or movies.

Although Murray was not the first person to use the picture-story method, he did the most to popularize it as both a clinical and research tool. Apart from one or two isolated studies in the early 1900s, the earliest clinical application of the procedure was that of Schwartz (1932), who used his Social Situation Picture Test as a diagnostic aid to psychiatric interviews with juvenile delinquents. The TAT was developed as a method for eliciting unconscious fantasy material from patients in psychoanalysis (Morgan and Murray, 1935). Indeed, the final selection of the TAT cards was based upon how much relevant information the TAT responses contributed to understanding the personality characteristics of individuals who had already been studied in detail by other methods.

The popularity of the TAT has given rise to a number of other story construction tests. The Children's Apperception Test (Bellak, 1954) and the Michigan Pictures Test (Hartwell et al., 1951) are rather similar in procedure to the TAT. In the Four Picture Test (Van Lennep, 1951), the subject is presented simultaneously with four colored pictures and is instructed to incorporate them in a story. In

Shneidman's (1951) Make-a-Picture-Story Test, respondents are given various background scenes and cardboard cutouts of a large variety of people from which to construct their own pictures, to be used as a basis for stories. In general, these techniques are based upon the same assumptions and utilize the same interpretative framework as the TAT, although there is much less evaluative research available on them.

Two rational assumptions that guided Murray's initial work with TAT were: (1) that the attributes of the hero, or main character, in the story represent tendencies in the respondent's own personality; and (2) that characteristics of the hero's environment represent significant aspects of the respondent's own environment. Thus, the traditional use of the picture story technique involves an interpretative analysis by the examiner, first, of the intrapsychic state of the individual, as reflected in his description of the story heroes, and second, of the environmental pressures he experiences, as reflected in his descriptions of the heroes' environments. For example in the first TAT card, which shows a boy peering at a violin, the story might reflect the boy's resentment (an inner state) at his parents who insist upon his practicing (an environmental pressure) when he wishes to do something else. Murray's (1938) own theoretical system would discuss these inner states as *needs* and the environmental or external pressures as *press*. However, the use of the TAT does not require the adoption of Murray's system, so that this instrument cannot be regarded as having a strong theoretical base.

As with the Rorschach, there have been a number of attempts both to develop quantitative scoring schemes and to construct formal norms for the data derived from an analysis of TAT responses. Perhaps the most widely used scoring system is that of McClelland (McClelland et al., 1953). McClelland was concerned primarily with the *need achievement* dimension, and with assessing motivation in various research endeavors rather than clinical diagnosis. Another system is Eron's (Zubin, Eron and Schumer, 1965), which has been shown to be useful in research but appears to have found little clinical application. Murstein (1963) has provided an excellent summary of a variety of scoring and interpretative schemes for picture stories. However, the typical clinical usage of the TAT and the other picture-story methods remains rather informal and idiosyncratic.

How useful or valid is the TAT as a personality assessment procedure? Although the volume of literature on the TAT is large (it is third in this respect, preceded only by the Rorschach and the MMPI), its status as a proven, clinically useful instrument is still in doubt.

Many of the problems associated with the clinical use of the TAT—lack of standardized procedures and formal normative data, low reliabilities, overenthusiastic and undercritical acceptance of intuitive hunches about the supposed meaning of certain responses—are also present in the Rorschach and other unstructured techniques.

One particularly troublesome problem with the TAT is the difficulty of determining whether an indicated need or personality characteristic will be present in the subject's overt behavior in real-life situations as opposed to existing only on the fantasy or unconscious level. This is especially important since the TAT is commonly regarded as helpful in understanding the content or "dynamics" of behavior; yet, for example, the person with strong needs for attention and recognition that are expressed overtly is very different behaviorally from the "Walter Mitty" character with equally strong needs that do not find behavioral expression because of some suppressive or inhibitory mechanism. Murstein (1963) has summarized the research pertaining to one specific aspect of this problem: the relationship between the judged aggressiveness of the heroes in TAT stories and the overt aggressive behavior of the subject. He concluded that the relationship was generally positive but was complicated by the operation of a number of other variables, such as guilt over aggression, the objective amount of hostility depicted in the TAT pictures, and the specificity of the aggressive acts.

An additional consideration worth noting concerns the "hero assumption" described above. Lindzey and Kalnins (1958) were able to demonstrate the validity of this assumption in two rather important ways. First they were able to show that the figures identified by the respondent in a clinical interview as most like himself were, indeed, the same as those judged to be the heroes in his TAT protocol. Second, the aggression ascribed by the subject to the TAT heroes increased following experimentally induced frustration, while the aggression ascribed to other figures did not. These findings tend to support the assumption that the picture-story hero often does possess characteristics of the story teller.

Figure 3-2 shows one of the stimulus cards of the Thematic Apperception Test. According to Henry (1956, pp. 254–256), the stimulus properties of this TAT card are as follows.

Murray's description. The portrait of a young woman. A weird old woman with a shawl over her head is grimacing in the background.

Manifest stimulus demand. An adequate accounting will include only the two figures plus some explanation of their being together in this position. Generally, the interpretation of subjects is about as Murray gives it.

FIGURE 3-2. A reproduction of one of the TAT stimulus cards.

However, recently we have seen in female subjects over seventy interpretations in which the "weird old woman" becomes a gently smiling and helpful person. Close examination of the face of the older figure suggests that "weird" and "grimacing" are not necessary connotations.

Form demand. The two figures are the only major details, though the facial features of the older woman can be differentially perceived.

Latent stimulus demand. In subjects in the middle-age range, this appears to be a stimulus relating older to younger. Thus, for the mature woman, threats of old age appear prominent. In the younger adult, apprehension over control by an older woman appears more prominent. A basic stimulus selected by many subjects, especially women, is one which portrays the old woman as some symbolic representation of a part of the younger; her evil self, her self when aged, etc.

Frequent plots. Most generally, the younger woman bears a family relationship to the older woman who is influencing or advising in some way. In about one-third of the stories, the older woman is seen as adversely influencing. In about one-third of the stories, a second plot will appear in which the older woman is a symbolic representation of the younger woman.

Significant variations. Of importance here is the issue of whether the subject sees the two figures in the same reality plane (mother-daughter) or whether one is a symbolic representation (my bad self, me when old, etc.). In addition, if treated in this fashion, the particular ideas toward the good and evil or other parts of the self should be specially viewed. In the light of the possibility of some, especially older, subjects seeing the background woman as kindly, responses to her should probably be watched more carefully and attention paid to the extent to which projection rather than reality observation is involved in attributing adverse influences.

The following story was given by the same 23-year-old female who contributed the Rorschach material discussed earlier in this chapter.

Well, there's a young woman in the foreground and an older woman in the background, and the older woman looks as though she has planned something that will be harmful to the younger woman, who looks very naive. And in fact the older woman has planned to keep the younger woman captive, and to make her serve her, for the rest of the older woman's life. But although the girl is naive, she's also rebellious; and by asserting herself with other people and getting a group of friends she's able to move out of the—not exactly spell, but she's able to break the bond that the older woman has around her. Right now she's just beginning to realize that she is being put in a position like this, but she's still very much under the control of the older woman, because these two have lived together for a long time. In fact, the younger woman was raised by the older woman. She's still very much under her control as I said, and she has strong feelings of guilt and fear of facing the world on her own. But fortunately she is able to make friends. At this point, though, she hasn't broken the bonds and she feels very confused, like she's being drawn between two poles. Ultimately, she's able to go out and make friends, and getting to know people and the different ways they have from the ways the old woman had taught her, she's able successfully to face the older woman, and defy her control, and go out and live a life of her own.

This story follows the stimulus demands of the card to a considerable extent; that is, the client reacted to the card much like most people her age. Thus, we would not be justified in coming to an immediate conclusion that she has any special problem in her relationships with older women. Also, a typical TAT interpretation would draw material from ten or more cards, and would regard whatever hypotheses are gleaned from an individual story as quite tentative, to be strengthened or disconfirmed by the remainder of the stories. From the present story, the following details might be considered of interest.

The older woman's control over the younger is perceived as long-standing and as having caused some rather central personality problems. However, the younger woman is seen as taking the initiative in developing other friendships in order to provide emotional support for the break which she plans with the older woman. Her ambivalence over these plans is seen in the use of the words "rebellion," "guilt," and "confused." The younger woman is perceived as displaying perhaps a somewhat lesser degree of anger and resentment toward the older than one would expect after having been trained as a life-long captive and servant; and the severity of the confinement, together with the younger woman's expression of guilt rather than anger, suggest a situation where anger is perhaps repressed. There is also the younger woman's determination and ultimate success, though this comes about through defiance of the older woman rather than a resolution of conflict, again suggesting more anger than is overtly acknowledged.

Although themes of apprehension over control by an older woman are relatively common in stories given by younger persons to this picture, the strength of the conflict as represented by the guilt, the severity of the control exercised, and the absence of appropriate expressions of anger by the younger woman suggest the tentative hypothesis that such a conflict does exist for this client. The client's inability to resolve the fantasy conflict successfully lends further support to this hypothesis. A TAT analyst might also suggest that the client's ability to put forward a rational plan for younger woman while still acknowledging her confusion and naivete suggests good potential for improvement in psychotherapy. Naturally the experienced clinician would search for additional support for these tentative hypotheses elsewhere in the client's TAT responses.

Picture Drawing Techniques

It is widely believed that creative works (especially in the fine arts, and drawing and painting in particular) reflect the personality of the artist. It should be noted that a demonstration of the validity of this assumption for trained artists would not necessarily establish its validity for people with little or no formal artistic training. It is, however, this latter assumption that underlies the use of picture drawing techniques in the assessment of personality characteristics.

The use of drawings in psychological evaluation was first popularized by Goodenough (1926), who developed a standardized procedure for evaluating the intelligence of children from their drawings of a man. As a result of a growing interest in interpreting the qualitative aspects of such drawings, two techniques have become widely used. One of these is Buck's (1948a; 1948b; 1949) House-Tree-Person or H–T–P technique, in which the respondent is required to draw first a house, then a tree, and finally a person, each on a separate sheet of paper. In the second, Machover's (1949) Draw-a-Person (DAP) test, the respondent first draws a person of either sex, and then is asked to draw a person of the opposite sex. In the interests of brevity, we shall confine our discussion to the Machover DAP, recognizing that most of our evaluative remarks are equally cogent for the H-T-P and other drawing procedures.

In administering the DAP, the respondent is given a pencil and an $8\frac{1}{2}$ by 11 inch sheet of blank paper, on which he is instructed to "draw a person." The examiner inconspicuously observes the individual, noting such behavior as the total time involved, the sequence in which the drawing is completed, any spontaneous comments, and so on. When this drawing is completed the individual is given a fresh sheet of paper and told to "Now draw a man (woman)." Machover recommends reassuring him, if necessary, that the test has nothing to do with his drawing skills, and also persuading him to draw any parts he appears to have omitted. It is also recommended that the individual be asked a series of questions to encourage his free associations to the drawings, such as "How old is the person drawn?" and "Is he married?"

The major portion of Machover's (1949) book is devoted to rules of interpretation involving the qualitative aspects of the drawings. These rules were apparently derived from the author's clinical experience as well as a variety of rational considerations, most of which reflect a psychoanalytic orientation. The rules provide for a description of the personality characteristics of the respondent with a strong emphasis on his psychopathology. They include the following sets of categories: head, parts of the face, facial expression, neck, contact features (arms and hands, legs and feet, fingers, toes), other body features, clothing, structural and formal aspects, conflict indicators (erasures and shading), and differential treatment of the male and female figures. One of the rules that can be regarded as representative of rational considerations involves the interpretation of the manner in which the shoulders are drawn: "The width and massiveness of the shoulders are considered the most common graphic expression of physical power and perfection of physique" (p. 71). The rationale underlying some interpretations is more difficult to comprehend; for example, "The Adam's apple . . . has been seen mostly in the drawing of young males as an expression of strong virility or masculine drive. Special interest in the Adam's apple has been restricted to the sexually weak individual who shows little differentiation between male and female characteristics and is uncertain about his own role" (p. 58).

Swensen (1957, 1968) and Roback (1968), in their reviews of the research literature on the DAP, concluded that there was little support for Machover's interpretations or hypotheses, and indeed that more of the data directly contradicted her contentions rather than supported them. Swensen further noted that the available evidence indicated the test-retest reliabilities of the various content and structural aspects of the drawings to be quite low, although the overall quality of the drawings (rated according to their realism or correspondence to life) was fairly constant. The research also suggested that the judged overall quality of the drawing is related to the gross level of adjustment of the subject. The evidence on this relationship was more recently reviewed by Lewinsohn (1965) who reached the same conclusion. Also on the positive side, Swensen (1968) suggested the possibility that future research that controlled for overall quality of the drawings might lead to more satisfactory findings with respect to specific personality variables. Despite the generally negative findings, the clinical usage of picture drawing techniques has been very high, with the DAP second only to the Rorschach in frequency of use (Sundberg, 1961).

Figure 3-3 shows two drawings which were reported and interpreted by Hammer (1968), another leading authority in this area. Hammer's interpretation is given below.

The nuanced language of drawing projection is particularly suited for stating the complexities and human contradictions as they balance and interrelate within a single personality. At such times, the apparent contradictions can be seen to possess an inner harmony, as in the musical

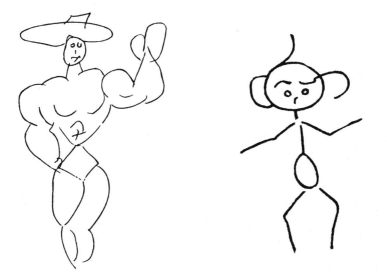

FIGURE 3-3. Human figure drawings done by an 18-year-old male.

statement and counterstatement of a fugue. Figure 3-3, drawn by an eighteen-year-old male caught stealing a TV set, constitutes such a pictorial statement. Beneath the obvious attempts at an impressive figure of masculine prowess, there are more subtle trends of the opposite: of inadequacy and inconsequentiality. The muscle of the drawn figure have been inflated beyond the hard and sinewy, into a puffy softness as if it is a figure made of balloons; the legs taper down to insubstantiality and, finally, absent feet, and an incongruous hat is placed on the boxer making comical his lifting of one gloved hand in victory. . . . On the one hand, emblematic of his defenses, his drawn achromatic person is the "twenty-year-old" boxer with muscles flexed and a weight-lifter's build. Beneath this inflated image, however, on the crayon drawing of a person—which, due to the impact of color, tends to tap the relatively deeper levels of personality (Hammer, 1958)—he offers now only a "six-year-old boy" who then looks even more like an infant than a child: with one curlicue hair sticking up and the suggestion of diapers on (. . . shown here in black and white). The ears are rather ludicrous in their standing away from the head and, all in all, the total projection in this drawing is that of an infantile, laughable entity, rather than the impressive he-man he overstated on the achromatic version of a person. Beneath his attempts to demonstrate rugged masculinity (which may have culminated into the offense with which he is charged), the patient experiences himself as actually a little child, dependent and needing care, protection, and affection (p. 375–376).

Blacky Pictures Test

In Chapter 2 we suggested that most attempts to develop personality assessment procedures have been theoretically neutral, although the personality descriptions which stem from them are often couched in the language of some particular personality theory. For an assessment procedure to be regarded as theoretically derived, the actual stimuli employed to elicit the relevant responses would have to be selected on the basis of a viable personality theory and the entire assessment procedure would be closely interwoven with that theory. As stated previously, since there are no rigorous theories of personality, we have utilized a general classification of *rational-theoretical* tests; and within this framework, the best established test toward the theoretical end of the continuum is the *Blacky Pictures Test* developed by Blum (1949, 1950). This test is based upon the traditional psychoanalytic theory of psychosexual development, which holds that children typically pass through three distinct and critically important stages in their personality development. In the first or oral stage, the child's primary preoccupation is with oral satisfactions—eating, sucking, chewing, and other stimulation involving the mouth. The anal stage is the period in which the child is made aware of the need for controlling his eliminative functions and learns to achieve the required control. In the phallic stage, there is an awareness of the sexual organs as a source of satisfaction and a preoccupation with this satisfaction. Psychoanalytic theory involves a vast number of additional complexities, but what is important for us is the notion that excessive deprivation, or excessive gratification, at any one of these stages may lead to the child becoming "fixated" at that stage. That is to say, his later personality characteristics, especially his ways of handling conflict may reflect his experiences at the fixated stage of development. Thus, a child who received excessive gratification at the oral stage might develop an "oral dependent" personality, where he would handle his psychological conflicts by expecting to have his needs met by others with little effort on his part, in an adult restructuring of the helpless role of the suckling infant. A child who was deprived of gratification at the anal stage may develop "anal retentive" personality characteristics, such as strong feelings of possessiveness about material things, stubbornness, and hoarding behavior. These examples suggest how psychoanalytic theory regards the roots for adult behavior to be established in the early psychosexual development of the child.

It follows from the Freudian theory of psychosexual development that if we can discover an individual's reactions and attitudes connected with the oral, anal, and phallic aspects of his psychosexual development, we will have obtained significant information about his personality and about the sources of any overt or latent personality conflicts which he may have. The Blacky pictures are specifically designed to yield such information. The test materials consist of twelve cartoons portraying the life of Blacky, a puppy of indeterminate sex, and his family, consisting of Papa, Mama, and another sibling. Each scene was developed in order to tap what should be a potential conflict area for Blacky according to the psychoanalytic theory of psychosexual development. For example, the second picture, designed to assess "oral sadism," shows Blacky snarling as he vigorously shakes his mother's collar in his teeth. The other pictures are similarly designed to measure such psychosexual concepts as anal sadism, penis envy, sibling rivalry, and guilt feelings. The respondent is presented with each picture, asked to make up a story telling what is happening and why, and is then asked a series of multiple-choice questions about the pictures. He is also asked which cards he likes and which he dislikes. It is assumed that these evaluations, together with the respondent's report of Blacky's mood as unhappy, angry, frightened, and so forth, are indicative of his own response to these potential conflict areas. Since the connections between the stimulus materials and the inferences to be drawn from responses to them are quite subtle, and since there is little general understanding of psychoanalytic concepts, the Blacky test does not require self-awareness on the part of the respondent and is typically regarded as a projective technique.

The scoring and interpretation of responses to the Blacky pictures are relatively complex procedures. Blum (1950, 1951) initially provided scoring directions for assessing the strength of 13 different psychosexual areas, and more recently (Blum, 1962) he proposed a 30 variable scoring system, based upon factor analytic research on the previous scoring schemata. According to Sappenfield's (1965) review, the scoring of the Blacky test is sufficiently reliable for research purposes but is not adequate for individual clinical assessment.

How useful or valid is the Blacky test? There is little published evidence concerning the utility of impressionistic clinical analyses of Blacky test responses, although it is likely that the instrument is widely used in this fashion in psychoanalytically oriented clinical settings (Sappenfield, 1965). On the other hand, there are a considerable number of positive research findings in which the Blacky test has been successfully used to demonstrate the validity of certain aspects of psychoanalytic theory, one of the primary uses for which it was developed. Sappenfield, in reviewing some of these studies, considered that their success was facilitated by the availability of the careful and explicit scoring instructions contained in the manual. Thus, one study showed a connection between the development of peptic ulcers and oral erotic conflicts (Blum and Kaufman, 1952), while another confirmed the predictions made from psychoanalytic theory about paranoia, using the Blacky test responses of paranoids and other psychotic patients (Aronson, 1953).

To summarize, the Blacky Pictures show some evidence of being a useful instrument for testing certain aspects of psychoanalytic theory in a research setting, though there is little published evidence to support its use as a clinical assessment device.

Bender Visual Motor Gestalt Test

The Bender Visual Motor Gestalt Test (Bender, 1938, 1946), which was initially developed within the Gestalt school of psychology, also has an easily identified theoretical base. Originally an orientation for the study of perceptual phenomena, the Gestalt approach soon spread into virtually all aspects of psychological theorizing. Briefly, it was based in the notion that events could only be understood by studying them in their entirety, as opposed to studying their individual elements, because the *configuration* of the elements, a critical component of the "whole," would otherwise be lost.

Bender (1938) studied the visual-motor perceptual skill of young children from a Gestalt point of view, noting the gradual development of their ability to perceive "wholes" and relationships when shown drawings of incomplete figures and other simple patterns. Reasoning that the individual's entire psychological development was reflected in this particular aspect of his functioning, Bender proposed that overall level of mental skill could be assessed from visual-motor perceptual performance, and she based her development of test materials on that assumption.

The test stimuli for the Bender Gestalt consist of nine 4 by 6 inch cards, each of which contains one of the original patterns used in early Gestalt perceptual research studies. The respondent is shown the cards one by one and is asked to copy the patterns on a single sheet of blank 8½ by 11 inch white paper. Bender originally interpreted the drawings according to the principle that "any deviation in the total organism will be reflected in the final sensory motor patterns in response to the given stimulus pattern" (Bender, 1946, p. 4). For guidance in interpretation, Bender presented illustrations of the responses of normal children at various age levels. She also presented illustrations of the response patterns of various psychologically disturbed groups which she considered to be identifiable with the instrument, based on the assumption that psychopathology is caused by early childhood trauma, which subsequently interferes with the maturation of the ability to perceive Gestalts or "wholes."

Although it can be argued that any *quantitative* scoring of Bender Gestalt responses would be inconsistent with the theoretical insistence of the Gestalt viewpoint that the "whole" is more than the sum of its parts, Bender (1938) did offer a tentative scoring scheme for measuring the maturational level of children using their responses to the test stimuli. A number of other scoring systems have been developed, probably the best known being that of Pascal and Suttell (1951). In this system the individual's drawings are assessed for their deviation from the standard on 105 different details. Numerical values are given and totaled to give a single score. The reliability of such scoring schemes is generally rather satisfactory, and they have served to point up the test's correlation with factors like intelligence and education.

The theoretical basis of the test indicates that its validity should be assessed, at least initially, from its degree of success in discriminating among subjects who differ in their development of the visual-motor Gestalt function, or the capacity to organize perceptual "wholes." A number of studies have shown that a fairly adequate mental age score can be derived from the test responses of children between the ages of 4 and 12 (Billingslea, 1963), a conclusion not inconsistent with Bender's initial assumption. It is also possible to make a gross differentiation of normal persons from various groups, especially those with cerebral brain damage, although these findings are much less clear-cut (Billingslea, 1963; Blakemore, 1965).

Many clinicians argue that a variety of qualitative aspects of a subject's Bender Gestalt responses, such as the relative size of the drawing, the strength of the impression, and the relative placement of the figures on the page, are useful indices to the personality of the individual. Although much use is made of the responses in this manner, empirical efforts to demonstrate relationships with molar personality characteristcs have been rather unsuccessful (Billingslea, 1963; Blakemore, 1965). These negative findings should not be surprising in view of the fact that Bender's original theory and her selection of the test stimuli have only the most tenuous connection with personality functioning, at least on the level of the assessment of observable behavioral characteristics.

In summary, the theoretical basis of the Bender Visual Motor Gestalt Test as a measure of personality functioning is not a sound one; neither the theory nor the test stimuli seem to be firmly grounded in personality functioning. It is thus not surprising to find that the test lacks validity for personality assessment.

RATIONAL–THEORETICAL ASSESSMENT DEVICES: SOME COMMENTS

In Chapter 2 we indicated that clinical assessment of personality initially involved collecting data about the individual, data that hopefully enable us to understand and predict other aspects of his behavior. The critical issue is how the psychologist decides which data are worth collecting, that is, which data will have predictive or informative value. It is clear that there are many different kinds of data that *may* be useful, and often it is difficult, if not impossible, to decide in advance which of them will yield worthwhile clues about an individual's personality characteristics. Indeed, the history of personality assessment is replete with techniques, such as phrenology and astrology, which have proven to be "blind alleys" because the data involved were not related to personality attributes.

Since the range of information that could have usefulness in personality assessment must be regarded as practically infinite, the selection of the data to be considered must involve some choice on the part of the assessor, unless it is to be completely random. In personality tests based on purely rational considerations, the initial selection of the test stimuli is based upon the assumption that there will be meaning or significance in the test responses because of the very nature of these stimuli. The more importance that is given to considerations of a particular theory of personality, the closer the test would be classified to the theoretical end of the rational-theoretical continuum. Let us first consider problems which arise from the purely rational aspects of this strategy.

In the case of the rationally derived *questionnaire*, the basis for item selection is obvious in the content of the item. Thus, the assumption is that anxious persons will admit their anxiety when directly questioned about how they feel. The rationale for the so-called projective techniques is not quite so obvious, especially to the layman. The assumption, for example, that emotional persons will respond more to the colored portions of a series of inkblots than nonemotional persons stems from several sources: from some crude theoretical notions about responsivity to color in general, from a logical analysis of the nature of man and how he behaves, and from informal empirical observations of man and his behavior. For simplicity, we have lumped this all together and called it a rational basis. Some more strictly theoretical and empirical elements are perhaps also involved, but these elements tend to be of limited significance in the current literature and folklore surrounding projective techniques.

Rationally derived questionnaires seem to depend for their usefulness upon at least three specific assumptions. (1) It must be assumed that the respondent is competent to judge himself with regard to the questions asked. (2) We must rely upon him to share the truth about which he is assumed to be aware. (3) The test stimuli must be assumed to be clear and unambiguous in their meaning.

Most psychodynamic views of personality would tend to deny the validity of the first two assumptions. Such views hold that most people tend to hide unpleasant truths from self-awareness, as a way of avoiding the anxiety that the admission of these truths would arouse. Thus, individuals would be least likely to provide useful responses in the very aspects of personality where assessment is most important. In addition, most persons are well aware of the possibility of dissimulation, of deliberately not revealing unpleasant truths about themselves because of the social consequences of admitting them. Both of these considerations are among the most frequently mentioned objections to rationally derived instruments.

Concerning the third assumption, the psychological meaning of the stimulus can be thought of as varying among persons in two ways: (1) as a consequence of the defensiveness just discussed, and (2) because of individual differences in meaning stemming from differences in individual experience or personal learning history. Thus, the questionnaire stimulus "I often have headaches" may elicit an affirmative response from one subject for whom "often" is once a month and a negative response from another subject for whom "often" is once a week. In other words, selecting unambiguous stimuli is by no means a simple task.

It is just these idiosyncratic differences in the psychological meaning of the stimulus materials that originally gave rise to the concept of using test stimuli "projectively." The major assumption underlying projection in this sense is that individual differences in responses to ambiguous stimuli are functionally related to some underlying, habitual characteristics of individuals, their personality. An allied assumption is that the relationships between the stimuli and responses are known or knowable to the test developer on some rational basis. However, because of the subtle nature of these relationships, they are not readily known to the subject, thus reducing the effects of defensiveness or deliberate simulation upon his responses. As it turns out, it is this very subtle or tenuous nature of the relationship between test response and assumed personality characteristic that provides the most serious objection to the traditional projective instruments.

Although the rational selection of the content of test stimuli often may not be a *sufficient* basis for test usefulness or validity, it seems to be a *necessary* basis. That is to say, without some rational connection between test response and the characteristic to be assessed or criterion to be predicted, the likelihood of establishing a satisfactory level of validity is much reduced. Thus, an important consideration in selecting test stimuli would appear to be that the meaning of responses to the test stimuli should be inherent in the stimuli themselves or in the fashion they were selected.

A clear illustration of this point is found in the research reported by Norman (1963a, 1963b) using questionnaire items. Faced with the problem of assessing the personality suitability of candidates for desirable jobs (where the defensiveness of the respondents could be assumed to be high), Norman attempted to develop "subtle" items whose meaning would not be clear to the respondents. For several groups of college students, friends' ratings were obtained on five personality dimensions. These ratings were then used as personality criteria to be predicted from the students' responses to three sets of test stimuli. The first test employed personality-descriptive adjectives (obviously related to the criterion), the second required preference ratings for various occupational titles (intermediate in their relationship to the criterion), and the third required preference ratings for geometrical designs (very subtle in their relationship to the criterion). Using the criterion group approach, to be described in Chapter 4, Norman constructed a series of personality scales from the results of each test. His results clearly indicated that only the scales based upon the first test (the self-descriptive adjectives), which were the most obvious in their meaning, were at all consistently related to the criterion.

The importance of rationality in test stimuli was also illustrated by Duff (1965) using the MMPI. Following the lead of Seeman (1952, 1953), who had demonstrated that the MMPI contained both obvious and subtle items, and that subtle items were difficult for the test taker to simulate or "fake," Duff listed the MMPI items which originally had discriminated normal persons from three particular psychiatric groups: conversion hysteria, psychopathic personality, and schizophrenia. Expert judges were then asked to indicate which items, on the basis of their content, appeared to be appropriate for one of these discriminations or another. That is, the judges were asked to pick out the items which one would rationally expect to be relevant for these discriminations. After identifying the rational or obvious (content relevant) and the nonobvious or subtle (content irrelevant) items in this manner, Duff compared the validity of the two kinds of items by examining the responses of patients in the appropriate diagnostic groups. His findings clearly indicated that the content relevant items, that is, those with rational or face meaning, discriminated to a greater degree than did the so-called subtle items. Substantially the same point was made by Goldberg and Slovic (1967), whose findings are examined more carefully in Chapter 4.

The findings of Norman and Duff, among others, tend to support the viewpoint that although rational derivation is in itself not a sufficient demonstration of a test's utility, stimulus materials with no observable relevance to the criteria are unlikely to be consistently useful.

Influence of Theoretical Bases. The present status of personality assessment instruments with a substantial theoretical base is not salutory. There are relatively few such instruments available, their contribution to our knowledge of personality function in either an applied or a theoretical sense has been minimal, and they tend to offer little to the practicing clinician who is concerned with describing and understanding an individual patient. Thus, their promise as the most sophisticated approach to the problem of understanding personality has not as yet been realized.

There are at least two reasons for this state of affairs. First, there are few approaches to personality which qualify to be called theories, as has already been noted. Further, contemporary psychological theorists have shown relatively little interest in developing new molar personality theories. Instead, far more attention is being given to constructing microtheories that attempt to deal with more limited behavior sequences than those typically subsumed under the rubric of personality. The personality theory which has been most viable in instigating the development of personality tests has been Freudian psychoanalytic theory, which can claim the Blacky Pictures Test, the IES (Id-Ego-Superego) Test (Dombrose and Slobin, 1958), and others.

The second reason for the atheoretical basis of current assessment devices is the preoccupation of psychologists who are interested in test development with psychometric technical refinements rather than with clinical usefulness. The increasing demand for a high level of technical specialization among psychometricians may have tended to isolate them from both the theorizing and research in other areas, work which may have important implications for test development (Anastasi, 1967). There is clearly a need for both technical sophistication and theoretical understanding in the area of personality test development.

Summary

This and the following chapter introduce basic issues in the development of standardized personality assessment procedures. Such procedures tend to meet several conditions: (1) the stimuli and their manner of presentation are invariant, (2) norms exist for the responses of interest, and (3) the personality or behavior correlates of these responses are known. These conditions suggest several criteria for the classification of assessment devices: degree of response structure, completeness of norms, and degree of usefulness or validity. We have chosen a more basic classification—the manner in which the assessment stimuli were originally selected. Three categories are employed: (1) *rational-theoretical*, where the stimuli have common-sense appeal and are based to a lesser or greater extent in a particular theory of personality; (2) *empirical*, where the stimuli are chosen solely on the basis of their demonstrated utility; and (3) *internal consistency*, where the dimensions to be assessed are defined statistically. The most common rational-theoretical instruments are as follows:

In the *sentence completion* method, subjects write endings to a variety of sentence beginnings designed to elicit personality relevant material. This method has been most widely used in a "clinical" or impressionistic manner, though several scorable forms are available, and research findings suggest that standardized content scales have the best validity.

The *Edwards Personal Preference Schedule* (EPPS) is a paper and pencil inventory yielding scores on 15 "need" scales. In order to counter the tendency to answer all questionnaire items in a socially desirable direction, Edwards employed the forced-choice technique of presenting the statements in pairs matched for social desirability. However, later research has indicated that the validity of the test was not enhanced by this procedure. The *Study of Values* is another forced-choice paper and pencil inventory, developed to assess Spranger's six basic interests or motives in personality. There is evidence for its utility in research applications but not as an individual assessment device.

In the *Rorschach* test, the subject is shown a series of ten inkblots, and his responses are categorized according to a number of formal characteristics. The original discovery of stable differences in response among groups of psychiatric patients was made accidentally, and Rorschach's tentative speculations about the reasons for these differences are still regarded by many clinicians as authoritative, despite massive research evidence to the contrary. A global approach, in which the test is regarded as a standardized stimulus within the total context of a clinical interaction, might prove to be more fruitful. The *Holtzman Inkblot Technique (HIT)* was designed to measure the basic variables assessed by the Rorschach, while avoiding a number of serious psychometric problems inherent in the Rorschach. Although the HIT does measure these variables satisfactorily, there is little evidence that it is useful in personality assessment.

Picture story techniques, of which the Thematic Apperception Test (TAT) is the most popular, require the subject to make up stories about pictures depicting personality relevant scenes. It is generally assumed that the behaviors and feelings of the main characters (heroes) of the stories reflect the subject himself. A number of standardized schemes exist for scoring the content and other aspects of the stories, but the clinical use of picture story techniques is generally impressionistic. In *picture drawing* methods, the subject is given blank paper on which to draw something, often a human figure. Apart from a gross relationship between the degree of realism of the drawing (if a human figure) and the subject's general level of adjustment, such drawings have as yet been demonstrated to have little value.

Perhaps the most theoretically oriented of the established assessment devices is the *Blacky Pictures Test,* based in the traditional psychoanalytic theory of psychosexual development. A standardized scoring system is available, and there is evidence to indicate that the system provides valid information for research purposes. The *Bender Visual Motor Gestalt Test,* designed within the theoretical framework of Gestalt psychology, assumes that all phases of human development, including personality, are reflected in perceptual functioning. It appears to yield a fairly satisfactory "mental age" score for children, but seems to have no demonstrated validity for assessing personality.

In general, how valid are assessment procedures which are based entirely on rational considerations? The assumptions which would need to be met in order for a rational basis to be *sufficient* for validity appear to have little support. However, there is evidence that a rational basis for stimulus materials is *necessary* if an assessment procedure is to have potential validity. There seem to be two main reasons for the lack of assessment instruments with a good theoretical base. (1) There is more interest in building "microtheories" to explain elemental aspects of personality than in developing the broader theoretical structures that would be needed as a basis for a general assessment device. (2) Test constructors have often tended to become absorbed in the technical refinements of their procedures at the expense of practical utility.

4 EMPIRICAL AND INTERNAL CONSISTENCY APPROACHES

In Chapter 3 we introduced three different strategies or approaches to the construction of formal assessment devices: (1) rational-theoretical, (2) empirical, and (3) internal consistency. We discussed in some detail the first of these approaches and the problems involved with it. We shall continue with an exposition of the remaining two strategies together with some general comments about the issues involved in their use.

EMPIRICALLY-BASED APPROACHES

In Chapter 2 we introduced the use of test responses for the *prediction* of behavior in real-life situations without the intervening step of involving any personality characteristics. In order to review this approach and to indicate that such a strategy is applicable to any kind of stimulus material, we shall draw some hypothetical examples involving the Rorschach inkblots. If, for example, every patient who gave responses of "decaying flesh" or "rotting flesh" on two or more cards of the Rorschach was later confirmed to be schizophrenic, the diagnosis of schizophrenia could be made directly from this sign without any intervening assessment of assumed personality characteristics.

Essentially the same approach can be used for the assessment of the underlying personality characteristics themselves. To illustrate again from the Rorschach, if all subjects who gave a response of "several people asleep" were later found to be unusually passive in their dealings with the environment, then we would have an *empirical predictor* for the personality characteristic of passivity.

In these examples from the Rorschach, it might be possible to infer a rational or even a theoretical connection between the individual's test response and the personality characteristic which was predicted. The recognition of such connections is irrelevant to empirical prediction. Although there will often be recognizable connections in addition to the empirical one, their nature is simply not of concern in purely empirical prediction. In a strictly empirical approach, the responses having predictive value would be determined by trial and error, and not by utilizing rational or theoretical hunches about possible relationships. However, such an approach is rarely followed and most of the instruments discussed below include rational or theoretical considerations in their derivation, especially the former. For convenience, however, we shall refer to them as empirically based.

We shall now illustrate how the empirical approach can be used with paper-and-pencil questionnaires, using *dominance* as the personality characteristic to be predicted. The initial step is to identify a clear-cut and readily obtainable behavioral index of the attribute; that is, to formulate an *operational definition* of dominance. For our present purpose, we shall define dominance as "the characteristic involved in seeking elective public office." We then obtain a group of dominant persons (that is, people who sought or are seeking elective office) and a group of nondominant persons (those who have not sought office). It is assumed that both groups are equally willing to cooperate in our undertaking and that they are matched on relevant characteristics such as age, education, and socioeconomic status.

Both groups are asked to respond to a large number of questionnaire items, let us say 200. We could use items inquiring about the subject's likes and dislikes, his interpersonal relationships, his political orientation, or anything at all. In truly empirically based instruments, the items would be randomly selected from a universe of all such questionnaire items, if such a pool were available. In our hypothetical example, let us suppose that one of the items is "I like people with blue eyes," to be answered "true" or "false" insofar as the respondent is concerned.

Let us further suppose that we learn, by comparing the responses of our office-seeking, or dominant, or criterion group with those of the non-office-seeking, or nondominant, or control group, that 90 percent of the criterion group have responded "true" to this item while only 15 percent of the control subjects have answered "true." We have discovered a diagnostic "sign" for identifying dominant people; and each of our 200 statements would be similarly examined, typically using rigorous statistical criteria, in order to determine whether or not it too is a sign of dominance. By identifying all the items that reliably differentiate our criterion and control groups, we would have constructed an empirical dominance scale, and a dominance score would be generated for each person by totalling the number of discriminating items which were answered in the criterion direction.

It should be obvious that, depending on the level of significance established for the selection of items, at least some proportion of the items would have been identified as valid on the basis of chance alone. For example, if a five percent probability level is used to identify discriminating items, then five percent of the items in the total item pool will be "selected" by chance alone. Inclusion of such chance items is what is typically referred to by statisticians as committing a Type One error. In order to guard against errors of this nature, it is imperative that the items selected be *cross-validated*. That is to say, the item pool should be administered to further criterion groups which are demographically and otherwise rather similar to, but independent of, the original groups. In terms of the above example, either the complete item pool, or a portion of it, should be administered to another group of persons identified as dominant and to another control group. Those items selected by chance alone would not be the same in both administrations (except for a negligibly small percentage), and therefore those which are selected in both procedures can be assumed to be "true" discriminating items. A less elegant, but more typical, procedure for cross-validation is simply to test on a new group the discriminating power of a scale which is composed of those items selected from the initial administration.

The method of empirical derivation, illustrated above with questionnaire items, can in principle be applied to any set of test responses, such as preference for geometric designs, responses to inkblots, or endorsement of self-descriptive adjectives. It is only necessary to establish that a reliable difference exists between the criterion and control groups in the proportions of responses to the stimuli.

There are certain disadvantages to assessment devices that are empirically derived. Although these instruments may be useful practically, they provide us with little basic or theoretical information about operation of personality variables in behavior. Further, there is no assurance that the procedure will yield *any* discriminating items, since the items in the initial pool may not be sensitive to whatever differences exist between the two groups. Last, it should be pointed out that extreme care is necessary in interpreting the personality attribute that an empirical scale is presumed to be measuring, since there may be other differences between the criterion and control groups which will distort the meaning of the scale. Thus, later research might demonstrate that our hypothetical dominance scale measures strength of political feelings rather than what is generally agreed to be meant by dominance, and it would therefore have little utility in identifying persons who are interpersonally dominant.

Duff (1965) and Norman (1963b), whose work was discussed in Chapter 3, took the position that it is most useful to have the content of the test stimuli related in some rational manner to the particular aspect of personality in which one is interested. However, Berg (1959) has argued strongly that the rational content of the test stimuli is unimportant. He has crusaded for the use of a greater variety of test stimuli, such as abstract geometric designs, requiring only that they should elicit enough variability of response to permit the discovery of empirical relationships. Berg's "Deviation Hypothesis" was tested by Goldberg and Slovic (1967), who investigated the relationship between content validity and empirical validity for a variety of kinds of possible personality inventory items, including nonverbal items. They found that "items of low face validity generally had low validity coefficients, while items of high face validity had validities that were distributed over the entire range of the distribution (e.g., some presumably relevant items actually were valid discriminators, while others were not)" (p. 467), These findings directly contradict Berg's point of view, and give experimental support to the notion that content validity is a necessary but not sufficient basis for empirical validity. As indicated above, most test constructors using empirical derivation techniques have tended to follow the method endorsed by Goldberg and Slovic—they employ rational considerations in selecting the original item pool and then focus on empirical comparisons of the responses of the criterion and control groups.

The general issue raised by Goldberg and Slovic seems to us to be a clear one. Their results raised a serious question about the usefulness of the Deviation Hypothesis as an explanatory concept in personality assessment. Although this hypothesis may be of limited use in explaining responses in procedures where the stimuli are highly ambiguous, it does not seem to apply in situations of low stimulus ambiguity; that is, it does not apply to most self-report questionnaires. The implications of this argument for the empirical approach to personality assessment also seem to be clear, and are consistent with the conclusions reached in Chapter 3 that (1) the content of the items to be empirically evaluated is critical, and (2) investigators need to spend considerable time and effort in selecting the items to be used. The Deviation Hypothesis is further analyzed in Chapter 7.

Minnesota Multiphasic Personality Inventory (MMPI)

Construction of the MMPI was begun in the late 1930s by Hathaway and McKinley (1940, 1951), who were motivated by their recognition of a need in both clinical psychiatric research and practice for an objective multidimensional instrument to assist in the identification of psychopathology. They were interested in developing an instrument that would provide for a comprehensive sampling of behavior of significance to psychiatrists, yet would involve a simple presentation so that it could be used with individuals of limited intelligence and education.

They compiled more than one thousand items from psychiatric examination forms, psychiatry text books, previously published attitude and personality scales, and from the authors' own clinical experience, and prepared them in a self-report (true or false) format. The number of items was reduced to 550 through the course of revisions. The items are presented to the respondent either in a printed booklet or singly in a deck of small item cards. The test is scored for ten or more basic psychiatric and personality scales, as well as three "validity" scales.

Generally speaking, each scale was empirically developed by contrasting the responses of nonpsychiatric control subjects with those of patients in a particular psychiatric diagnostic category, using the traditional system of diagnosis which stemmed from the work of Kraepelin in the late nineteenth century. More than 800 carefully studied psychiatric patients constituted the pool of clinical subjects, while approximately 1500 control subjects were drawn from hospital visitors, normal clients at the University of Minnesota Testing Bureau, local WPA workers, and general medical patients. The individual diagnostic criterion groups generally numbered 50 or fewer, although in some cases additional groups were utilized in efforts to improve the discriminating power of the scale. For example, more than a dozen scales were developed in an unsuccessful effort to obtain satisfactory discrimination among the subcategories of schizophrenia (Hathaway, 1956, p. 108). The schizophrenia scale finally chosen for inclusion in the inventory was the fourth such scale attempted, and proved to be the most satisfactory of previous and subsequent efforts.

The usual method of item selection was to consider a basic pool of those items which showed a statistically significant percentage frequency difference between the responses of the criterion group and the control subjects. Items were excluded if the frequency of response for both groups was very high or very low, if they failed to differentiate among additional relevant groups, or if the group difference appeared to have an irrelevant basis, such as marital status. Further items were often eliminated from a scale if they showed an overlap in validity with some other diagnostic category. No item, however, was ever eliminated from a scale because its manifest content appeared unrelated to the category in question. The articles documenting the original construction and validation of the MMPI have been reprinted by Welsh and Dahlstrom (1956).

In the construction of the basic MMPI scales, every effort was made to utilize responses only of psychiatric patients whose symptoms were clear-cut and who were relatively free from psychiatric signs other than those qualifying them for their particular diagnostic category. The categories and the resultant scales are as follows:

Scale 1. Hypochondriasis (Hs). These patients showed an exaggerated concern about their physical health, often with complaints about physical problems which in fact had a psychological basis.

Scale 2. Depression (D). Characterized by intense unhappiness, poor morale, and lack of hope about the future, these patients were relatively pure cases of depression.

Scale 3. Hysteria (Hy). These patients, who had been diagnosed "psychoneurosis-hysteria," had psychologically based physical symptoms coupled with *la belle indifference* or bland unconcern about their condition.

Scale 4. Psychopathic Deviate (Pd). All the criterion subjects used in developing this scale had shown notable difficulties in social adjustment, with histories of delinquency and other antisocial behavior.

Scale 5. Masculinity-Femininity (Mf). This scale was derived from the responses of a rather small group of homosexual males, all of whom were relatively free of other psychopathology.

Scale 6. Paranoia (Pa). Although rarely diagnosed as paranoia, these patients showed paranoid symptoms such as ideas of reference, suspiciousness, interpersonal sensitivity, feelings of persecution, and delusions of grandeur.

Scale 7. Psychasthenia (Pt). The subjects in this criterion group, mainly patients, showed unreasonable fears, high general anxiety, feelings of guilt, and excessive doubts.

Scale 8. Schizophrenia (Sc). These patients were all diagnosed as schizophrenic without regard to the various subtypes of the disorder.

Scale 9. Hypomania (Ma). These patients showed the milder degrees of manic excitement typically occurring in manic-depressive psychosis, characterized by excessive activity, easy distractibility, elevated mood, and a rapid but disjointed flow of speech.

One additional scale, social introversion-extroversion (Si), was later added to the nine basic clinical scales.

The three validity scales developed in order to enhance the clinical usefulness of the MMPI were constructed as follows. (1) The *L* or lie scale, designed to provide a basis for evaluating the subject's general frankness, contains 15 rationally selected items reflecting socially desirable but rather improbable behaviors. (2) The F or infrequency scale, intended as an aid to recognizing random or other invalid respondents, contains items that are answered in the same direction by at least 90 percent of the normal subjects, and is thus a measure of how similar the subject's responses are to those of people in general. (3) The K or defensiveness scale was developed as a correction or "suppressor" scale to improve the discriminating power of several of the clinical scales, by correcting for varying degrees of subtle test-taking defensiveness. It was constructed by comparing the responses of normals with those of patients whose clinical scale scores were in the normal range and who could thus be assumed to have responded to the items defensively.

It soon became apparent that the MMPI could not be used successfully in the manner originally intended, since high scorers on a scale often did not fit into that particular diagnostic category. Further, it was recognized that large numbers of apparently normal people achieved high scores on the clinical scales. However, it was found that useful clinical and personality discriminations could be made by examining combinations or *patterns* of scores, and it is in this manner that the MMPI is currently used. The large volume of research literature involving the MMPI, second in quantity only to that on the Rorschach, has been summarized through 1960 by Dahlstrom and Welsh (1960). Several empirically based interpretative manuals are also available (Drake and Oetting, 1959; Gilberstadt and Duker, 1965; Lanyon, 1968; Marks and Seeman, 1963).

The MMPI is open to a number of criticisms. Perhaps the most frequently voiced concern is that some of the scales are highly correlated, indicating a considerable degree of redundancy. Similarly, Block (1965) has shown that many of the "pathological" items are highly similar in nature, creating a redundancy in items as well as scales. Other common criticisms are that the test is too long, that it contains items about sex and religion which are offensive to many people, and, as previously noted, that many normal persons achieve high scores on the clinical scales.

Although the MMPI has not been completely successful in its original purpose, the classification of psychiatric patients, there is much empirical support for its usefulness in identifying other aspects of personality functioning in the psychopathological domain. It is clear also that the current use of the MMPI requires a skilled clinician with considerable experience in its interpretation. Many of the problems

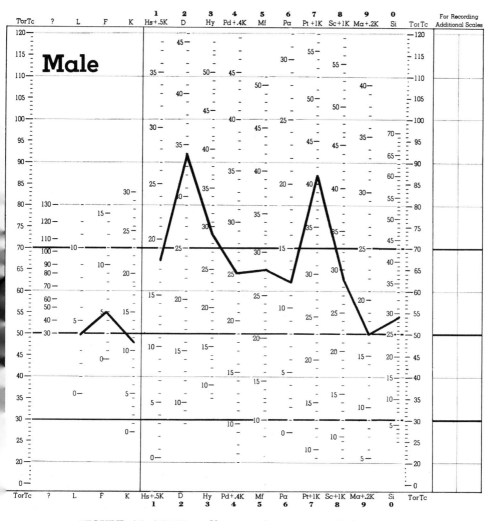

FIGURE 4-1. MMPI profile suggesting anxiety and depression.

surrounding its current widespread use stem from the fact that it was not designed for the assessment of normal personality, so that neither the items nor the scales are optimal for this purpose.

The contemporary clinical use of the MMPI is illustrated as follows. Figure 4-1 shows the MMPI profile of an adult male client seeking help in a community mental health center. The numbers on the sides of the chart represent a standard score system with a mean of

50 and standard deviation of 10. The K-correction (see text) has been added to the raw scores on the Hs, Pd, Pt, Sc, and Ma scales.

In order to give a satisfactory interpretation of these responses we should have some idea of the *base rates*, or relative frequencies in the population of interest, of the various personal characteristics which are suggested by the test responses. This concept will be discussed in detail in Chapters 6 and 8. The most noteworthy psychological features of persons giving MMPI profiles of the general pattern shown in Figure 4-1 are anxiety and depression; thus, in a community mental health center where the base rate of these characteristics is fairly high, we could suggest with considerable confidence that anxiety and depression are psychological problems of major concern to this client. If a psychiatric label is given, it would almost certainly involve some category of neurosis. Detailed information about such profiles, based upon both empirical and clinical findings, has been reported by Marks and Seeman (1963) and by Gilberstadt and Duker (1965). For example, according to the latter source, which is based upon the characteristics of male patients seen in the psychiatry service of a VA hospital, the most common (and discriminating) complaints of such clients include insomnia, obsessions, anxiety, depression, nervousness, tension, worry, tiredness, and gastrointestinal problems. Typically they have high standards of performance, are capable of developing good emotional ties, and tend to become overwhelmed and dependent under accumulated stress. However, reality orientation remains good, and in a hospital setting, improvement is usually fairly rapid.

California Psychological Inventory (CPI)

The California Psychological Inventory or CPI (Gough, 1957) was specifically designed for the multidimensional or multiphasic description of normal personality—the task to which the MMPI had been put. Gough, who had a strong interest in devising measures with broad psychological and sociological relevance, used the empirical approach with a variety of criterion groups. The CPI consists of 468 self-reference items, of which 200 appear in the MMPI, to be answered "true" or "false" in the same manner as the MMPI.

The CPI yields scores on fifteen personality and three validity or response bias scales, most of which were constructed empirically. The empirical personality scales are: dominance, capacity for status, sociability, responsibility, socialization, tolerance, achievement via conformity, achievement via independence, intellectual efficiency, psychological mindedness, and femininity. For some of these scales, the criterion groups were identified by a directly obtainable behavioral index. Thus, the socialization scale was derived by comparing the responses of juvenile offenders and high school disciplinary cases with those of normal high school students (Gough and Peterson, 1952); and similarly, the achievement via independence scale employed criterion groups defined according to course grades (Gough, 1953). For other scales, where behaviorally based groups were more difficult to obtain, criterion groups were defined by judges' ratings. For example, the dominance scale was developed by asking fraternity and sorority members to nominate the five most dominant and five least dominant members of their group (Gough, McClosky, and Meehl, 1951).

Four additional scales were constructed through internal consistency analyses, utilizing a combination of the rational selection of items and statistical refinement of the initial item pool. These four scales are social presence, self-acceptance, self-control, and flexibility. The usefulness of all 15 scales was further demonstrated by comparing the scores of a number of additional behavioral and personality groups.

The three validity scales are similar in nature to the validity scales of the MMPI. The wellbeing scale, designed to identify persons who exaggerate their misfortunes, was empirically constructed by comparing the responses of normal subjects who simulated severe conflict with those of actual psychiatric patients. The good impression scale, also empirically developed, was designed to identify exaggeration of one's personality characteristics in the positive direction. The communality scale, similar to the MMPI F scale, indicates the degree to which one's responses are like those of most normal subjects.

To facilitate the clinical interpretation of individual CPI profiles, the 18 scales are organized into four groups or clusters: (1) measures of poise, ascendency, and self-assurance; (2) measures of socialization, maturity, and responsibility; (3) measures of achievement potential and intellectual efficiency; and (4) measures of intellectual and interest modes. This grouping of scales generally has been supported by independent factor analytic studies of the CPI (Crites, Bechtoldt, Goodstein and Heilbrun, 1961; Mitchell and Pierce-Jones, 1960). In interpreting a test profile, the test manual suggests initially observing the overall elevation of the profile as an index of the respondent's social and intellectual functioning, and then comparing the relative levels of the four scale clusters. Further information is gained by observing the highest and lowest scale scores and by studying combinations of scales. The manual also provides lists of adjectives that were chosen by judges in an assessment program as descriptive of high and low scorers on each scale. This list contains some awkward contradictions, which might be a function of the scales, the rating procedure, or some other inconsistency. The manual gives a considerable amount of normative and correlational information about the scales, as a basis for further interpretative hypotheses and research.

Although the redundancy of the scales makes for some problems in interpretation, the evidence presented in the manual demonstrates some validity for each of the scales when judged against behavioral criteria. An example of this type of validity evidence is seen in a study by Goodstein, Crites, Heilbrun, and Rempel (1961), who compared the mean CPI profiles of college undergraduates seeking counseling for personal adjustment problems with a comparable group reporting vocational-educational problems and a control group who had not sought counseling. The three groups differed in the anticipated manner on overall elevation of their CPI profiles, and also showed psychologically meaningful differences in profile patterns. In general, reviewers have tended to regard the CPI as a reasonably useful instrument for the multidimensional description of the normal personality (Crites, 1964; Kelly, 1965).

The contemporary clinical use of the CPI is illustrated by Figure 4-2, which presents the CPI profile of a 41-year-old male research scientist who was tested as part of an industrial management development program. As was the case with the MMPI, the numbers on the sides of the chart represent a standard score system with a mean of 50 and a standard deviation of 10. The 18 CPI scales are presented along the horizontal axis in the same order in which they were described in the text.

Applying the interpretative rules suggested above would lead us to view this man as a self-assured, poised, rather forceful person with little self-doubt or uncertainty about himself. At the same time his sense of responsibility, his willingness to accept rules and proper authority, and his self-control seem less well developed; and his achievements, both those gained through conformance and those gained through independence, are probably modest. Quite aware of and sensitive to others, he is quite open to change and may even be impulsive at times. However, he appears rather satisfied with himself, and can be rather closed-minded and intolerant of others, especially when he feels that his principles are being violated. One might conclude that this man is an ambitious and socially skillful individual who lacks the impulse control and conscientiousness necessary to realize his ambition. His sensitivity to others coupled with his unwillingness or inability to respond completely to this awareness might lead others to view him as manipulative and controlling.

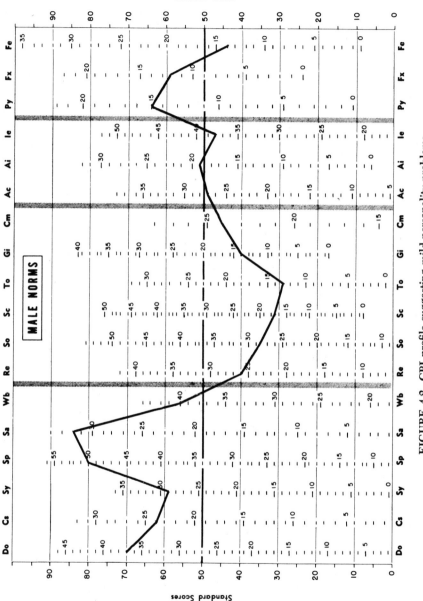

FIGURE 4.2. CPI profile suggesting mild personality problems.

This characterization was very much in keeping with the man's supervisory evaluations, which noted that he "has never realized his potential as a scientist." These evaluations further noted his very high needs for autonomy, making it very difficult for him to hear or accept supervisory feedback. His impulsiveness and his impaired interpersonal relationships led to a variety of morale problems in his laboratory and he was generally regarded as having limited potential for higher managerial positions or promotions.

Empirical Personality Assessment Devices: Some Comments

Although the empirical development of the tests discussed above and others of this type offer built-in evidence of their ability to discriminate between groups, they can often be criticized on the grounds that the test authors have failed to cross-validate the scales on independent samples of the criterion and normal groups. The absolute necessity for cross-validation has already been strongly emphasized; as a concrete example, let us imagine a pool of 1000 self-reference questionnaire items which can be answered positively or negatively. If we take two arbitrary groups—for example people with blue eyes and people with brown eyes—the two groups will differ in their responses to some of the items by sheer chance. Specifically, if we noted the differences that would be expected to occur by chance less often than five percent of the time, we would identify about five percent, or 50 or the 1000 items, that could be advanced as an empirically derived test for eye color differentation. Yet these items would have been selected on the basis of a statistical artifact and would probably have no stable relationship to eye color. Thus, if we repeated the item analysis on two different groups of blue- and brown-eyed subjects, the second resultant scale would contain 50 *different* items—another chance selection from the 1000 items. Needless to say, these two scales would be of no value in discriminating between further criterion groups. Since the extent to which empirically derived scales capitalize on chance variability is not always clear, independent demonstration of their discriminative ability is essential.

Other problems are raised by the use of the empirical method. The criterion groups are ordinarily selected to be pure and often extreme instances of the behavior domain to be tapped. Thus we would use rather "obvious" schizophrenics in developing a schizophrenia scale, and highly dominant versus perhaps passive individuals in developing a dominance scale, although we are typically interested in employing the scales to identify, not extreme individuals, but persons more in the middle of the continuum. It is frequently a moot point as to whether the items are either logically or empirically relevant for identifying less extreme instances of the phenomena.

We have already noted that empirically derived tests add little to our theoretical understanding of the characteristic under study, and that in practice it would seem best to combine the empirical approach to test construction with rational considerations, especially in the initial choice of the item pool. It is believed by many (particularly among psychometricians) that empirically based personality tests, because of their built-in evidence of practical usefulness, are the most promising instruments available at the present time.

THE INTERNAL CONSISTENCY APPROACH

The third approach to the construction of personality tests is the one based upon the internal consistency of the test items. It can perhaps best be described by way of example. Suppose we have collected the responses of a large number of subjects to a number of test stimuli. The nature of the test stimuli is not important for the moment, except that they are usually selected to provide a balanced coverage of the particular behavior domain in which the test constructor is interested. Thus, most of the tests which have been developed on the basis of this strategy involve self-reference questionnaire items, though in principle they could equally well involve inkblots or geometrical forms. Let us further suppose that we have as stimuli 50 self-reference questionnaire items, all of which can be answered "true" or "false."

Since we are unsure, at this stage of our test development, about what characteristics our items are tapping, we might be seen as having responses to 50 different "scales," each of which had a possible "score" of 0 or 1. It would obviously be desirable to have a method for examining such a large mass of responses on other than an individual basis. We note that the responses to some items tend to be correlated, so that persons who answer "true" to item 13 may also be very likely to answer "true" to items 15, 25, and 36, and "false" to items 8 and 39. We would also expect other item clusters to exist. In other words, a subject's "score" on any item can to some extent be predicted by his "score" on other items; the items in each cluster are intercorrelated because they have a common basis for variability. The statistical procedure for identifying such clusters of items, or *factors*, is known as factor analysis. As might be expected, the first step in a factor analysis is to correlate every item with every other item. The resulting matrix of intercorrelations is then treated by a series of complex statistical procedures in order to identify the factors or grouping of items. Incidentally, the same steps could be followed using scales rather than items in order to determine the factorial structure of a multiphasic instrument such as the MMPI or CPI.

When a factor, or cluster of items, is identified in this manner, it is assumed generally that these items are tapping the same psychological variable, because they tend to elicit consistent responses. In our example involving 50 items, let us suppose that we have been able to identify four clusters each involving ten items, and that the remaining ten items did not correlate significantly with each other nor with any of the four identifiable clusters. Factor analysis has reduced our original 50 variables to four, and we can describe an individual as he represents himself by his scores on four scales derived to represent these factorial variables. If these four factors are reproducible by the same steps in other, similar groups of normal persons, then we might assume that we have isolated four central traits of normal personality structure.

What do factor-analytically derived scales really measure, and how do we know what these factors mean? Certainly they have a specific statistical meaning, since they are defined in part by statistical procedures. We can also look for rational meaning, both in the original selection of the items and in what items contribute to the particular factor. For example, the composition of Welsh's (1956) MMPI factor *A* was such that he described it as a measure of anxiety or emotional upset. The procedure for naming factors is always rational or clinical, and empirical validity evidence must be accumulated before it can be concluded that the behavior domain involved in the factor is the same as that typically described by that name. Thus, the decision about the usefulness of terming Welsh's MMPI factor *A* an anxiety factor must depend partly upon whether persons with high scores on that scale are judged to be clinically anxious. Although the meaning of a factor is built into it in a statistical sense, the full nature of its meaning is not made clear by the statistical procedures.

An additional question is whether or not factors are *real* traits, the psychological essence of personality. This question is a highly complex one and has given rise to a variety of views among researchers in this area. On the one hand, Cattell (1965) views the particular factors that he has proposed as natural unitary structures in the domain of normal personality, natural elements that are logically equivalent to the atomic elements in the physical world. Eysenck (1953) has taken a similar, although less extreme view. On the other hand, Jackson and Messick (1958) have suggested that the major factors that are identified through the factor analysis of self-report inventories are mainly "response distortions" which should be regarded as distinct from the content of the scales. At the very least, however, it can be said that factor analysis is a useful technique for studying both the internal composition of individual scales and of the several scales in a battery or in a multiphasic instrument.

The Guilford Tests

Guilford (1959), who favors a trait approach to personality description, has employed factor analysis to arrive at the most parsimonious set of traits for describing normal personality functioning. After several factor analyses of many sets of self-report questionnaire items, he developed three separate inventories: Inventory of Factors STDGR (Guilford, 1940), Inventory of Factors GAMIN (Guilford and Martin, 1943b), and the Personnel Inventory (Guilford and Martin, 1943a). The Guilford-Zimmerman Temperament Survey (Guilford and Zimmerman, 1949) was developed later to cover, in a single inventory, ten of the 13 traits of the original three inventories. These were: general activity, restraint vs. rhathmia, ascendance, sociability, emotional stability, objectivity, friendliness, thoughtfulness, personal relations, and masculinity. Two empirically derived falsification scales, similar to the validity scales of the MMPI and CPI, were added later, together with a "carelessness-deviancy" scale, similar to the MMPI F scale (Jacobs and Schlaff, 1955). Although there is some evidence that some of these factorially derived scales do measure the traits for what they were named (Guilford, 1959, pp. 185–187), their relationships to other indices of the same traits have generally been shown to be fairly minimal.

Thurstone Temperament Schedule

Thurstone (1949, 1951) performed his own factor analysis on Guilford's original data and concluded that seven rather than 13 factors were sufficient to describe the main dimensions of personality. He developed the Thurstone Temperament Schedule to measure these factors, which he named active, vigorous, impulsive, dominant, stable, sociable, and reflective. As might be assumed, the same evaluative comments directed towards the Guilford instruments can be applied to Thurstone's test.

Sixteen Personality Factor Questionnaire (16PF)

Based upon extensive factor analyses of self-report inventories, biographical data, and behavior observation, Cattell (1965) has defined 16 factors which he regards as the "source traits" of normal personality structure, suitable for measurement on an inventory. Since some of Cattell's factors do not readily correspond to any readily named personality trait, he has developed his own nomenclature, such as *parmia* (implying parasympathetic nervous system domination) versus *threctia* (implying susceptibility to threat). (Cattell, 1965. p. 95.)

The 16PF test, a self-descriptive questionnaire, is available in three forms. Forms A and B, each containing 187 items, and a shorter form C, with 105 items, all yield scores on the 16 source factors. To insure adequate reliability, it is probably advisable to use more than one form, especially in individual descriptive work. Considerable normative information on the factor scores is available (Cattell and Stice, 1957), although the evidence for their predictive utility is limited (Lorr, 1965).

Factor-Analytic Personality Assessment Devices: Some Comments

The more one studies the literature on factor analytic approaches to personality measurement, the more bewildering becomes the array of factors that must be comprehended. The sheer number of different factors, coupled with the inability of factor analysts to agree about the factorial composition of the same set of data, would seem to render untenable Cattell's belief that there is anything "real" about factors. Fortunately, however, such a belief is not a necessary prerequisite for the use of the factor analytic approach.

The typical factor analysis does not involve a completely predetermined procedure; rather, certain decisions are based upon the "clinical" judgment of the factor analyst, which in turn partly determines the resultant factorial structure. This reliance upon judgment may help clarify why the factorial structure of a set of data suggested by one analyst does not resemble that proposed by another. Further, the degree of similarity between two different factor analyses is difficult to determine without a careful study of the statistical aspects of the data. For example, without such a careful study it would be impossible to determine that Norman's (1963c) emotional stability factor is not the same as the emotional stability factor described by Gordon (1963), but seems to be a combination of this and the ascendancy factor.

In recent years, one important area of agreement has emerged among factor analyses, at least the ones involving self-report inventories. There has been a fair degree of consistency in reporting the existence of two major independent or orthogonal factors (for example, Block, 1965; Jackson and Messick, 1958; Welsh, 1956; Wiggins, 1968), and there has also been broad agreement on how these two factors should be named. They are appropriately described by the labels *extroversion* and *neuroticism*, which are the names chosen by Eysenck (1960) for the two factors which he articulated and described as centrally important to the theoretical understanding of personality.

An alternative to a two-factor theory of personality was demonstrated by Norman (1963c), who proposed a system of five relatively orthogonal (independent) and easily interpreted personality factors. The factor names and the polar anchoring adjectives for each of these scales are presented in Figure 4-3. The work leading to the delineation of these particular factors was previously reviewed by Mischel (1968), and began with the identification by Allport and Odbert (1936) of 18,000 trait names. This list was reduced by Allport (1937), using personal judgment, to the 4504 clearest and most stable traits, then

Factor Name	Number	Abbreviated Scale Labels	
		Pole A	Pole B
I. Extroversion or Surgency	1	Talkative-Silent	
	2	Frank, Open-Secretive	
	3	Adventurous-Cautious	
	4	Sociable-Reclusive	
II. Agreeableness	5	Goodnatured-Irritable	
	6	Not Jealous-Jealous	
	7	Mild, Gentle-Headstrong	
	8	Cooperative-Negativistic	
III. Conscientiousness	9	Fussy, Tidy-Careless	
	10	Responsible-Undependable	
	11	Scrupulous-Unscrupulous	
	12	Persevering-Quitting, Fickle	
IV. Emotional Stability	13	Poised-Nervous, Tense	
	14	Calm-Anxious	
	15	Composed-Excitable	
	16	Not Hypochondriacal-Hypochondriacal	
V. Culture	17	Artistically Sensitive-Artistically Insensitive	
	18	Intellectual-Unreflective, Narrow	
	19	Polished, Refined-Crude, Boorish	
	20	Imaginative-Simple, Direct	

FIGURE 4-3. Personality factor structure suggested by Norman (1963c).

to 171 by Cattell (1957), using empirical judgments of semantic meaning. Rating scales developed from future refinements of the list formed the basis for comparing a number of diverse subject groups by means of peer rating procedures (see Chapter 5), and the resulting personality factor structure appeared to be highly consistent across the different groups. The data were collected by having each person in a rating group nominate one third of the other members in the group for Pole A of each rating scale, and one third for Pole B. Each member's score on a scale was then determined by averaging the ratings which he received.

Whether these five factors "truly" represent personality structure must be considered in light of the two positions on the structure of personality which were discussed in Chapter 2; namely, the viewpoint that there is a single "real" structure versus the view that any structure is necessarily man-made. Mischel (1968), arguing for a variant of the second position, had held that Norman's five factors reflect in part "behavioral consistencies that are *constructed* by observers rather than actual consistency in the subject's behavior" (p. 43). This argument is plausible when one notes that semantic consistency was an important criterion in developing the rating scales. Further support for this semantic consistency viewpoint was provided by Passini and Norman (1966), who demonstrated that the same factorial structure was shown by guesswork ratings attempted on complete strangers, and by D'Andrade's (1965) demonstration that an analysis of the degree of semantic similarity among the trait words employed in the rating scales also yielded the same factorial structure.

To summarize, the major contribution of factor analysis is in understanding the relationships among items and scales of personality tests. Usefulness, in any predictive sense, is not an intrinsic property of factorially derived scales (unless, like Cattell, we consider them to be assessing some "real" properties of the organism), but must be demonstrated empirically. The reported empirical validities of factor scales have in general tended to be quite low, with the major exception of those two factors which have been consistently replicated.

OVERVIEW OF THE THREE STRATEGIES IN PERSONALITY TEST DEVELOPMENT

We have discussed three ways in which assessment procedures can be developed in order to obtain responses from an individual that will be meaningful in understanding behavior in the personality domain. The three procedures were carefully delineated and were presented separately for reasons of clarity, although it was not meant to suggest that combinations of methods cannot and have not been employed. Thus, a balanced and sophisticated method might involve the initial selection of test stimuli based upon theoretical or rational considerations, with factor analysis for the attainment of internal consistency, and final refinement based upon clear-cut empirical findings. Unfortunately, this type of test derivation is both time consuming and costly, and has rarely been employed.

One question that can be raised is whether or not there is any clear superiority of one of these three strategies over the others. An empirical answer to this question is provided by the recent study of Hase and Goldberg (1967). These authors took the CPI items and constructed four sets of 11 scales each, developing each set by one of the major strategies of test construction, regarding the rational and theoretical methods as separate approaches. The 11 rational scales were the four rationally derived CPI scales plus seven others developed in the same fashion. The 11 theoretical scales were specifically developed for the purposes of this study using the Murray (1938) need system. The empirically derived scales were the 11 original CPI scales which had been developed empirically. The 11 factor scales were developed on the basis of a special factor analysis of the items done by the authors for this purpose. The predictive validities of these four sets of scales were then compared against 13 criterion measures obtained from 200 college women, such as college achievement relative to ability, an experimental test of conformity, sorority membership, dating behavior, and peer ratings on a variety of personality traits, such as dominance, sociability, and responsibility.

The main finding of this study was that the four sets of scales were equivalent in validity when measured against the 13 diverse criteria. Obtained validity correlations averaged over the criteria were: rational = 0.27; theoretical = 0.26; empirical = 0.26; and factor analysis = 0.26. These four mean correlations were all significantly higher than those obtained from two additional sets of scales which had been devised for control purposes.

Hase and Goldberg conclude that the choice of the particular strategy to be employed in personality test construction is far less critical than is ordinarily believed. Instead, they argue for more concern about and interest in the test stimuli themselves, a point with which we are in full agreement. They also offer the appropriate caution that, despite the clear-cut nature of the findings, they are based upon a single set of self-report inventory items and criteria obtained in a single setting with paid subjects. Thus, there is a need for replication and extension of this most important study.

Summary

In a purely empirical approach to test development, the recognition of rational or theoretical connections would be irrelevant, since the stimuli would be selected solely on the basis of their ability to lead to the desired description or prediction. The empirical approach is not often used alone, but usually in combination with other methods. The *Minnesota Multiphasic Personality Inventory* (MMPI), perhaps the best known of all personality inventories, was originally developed as an aid in classifying psychiatric patients into diagnostic groups. The MMPI is currently scored on 13 scales, most of which represent psychiatric categories. It was derived from an original item pool of more than 1000 rationally selected statements by contrasting the responses of patients in each category with those of normal subjects. Although the MMPI has a number of disadvantages, including item redundancy and the fact that many normals get high scores on the psychiatric scales, there is a large amount of evidence for its research and clinical usefulness. Since clinical interpretation involves *patterns* of scores rather than individual scales, a degree of skill is necessary in its use.

The *California Psychological Inventory* (CPI) is somewhat similar to the MMPI, but was designed to assess significant aspects of normal personality functioning. Its 18 scales, most of which were derived empirically, are grouped into four clusters: poise, ascendancy, and self-assurance; soocialization, maturity, and responsibility; achievement potential and intellectual efficiency; and intellectual and interest modes. A considerable amount of normative information is available for the CPI, and in spite of some redundancy among the scales, it appears to be a fairly useful device.

General problems with the empirical approach include its lack of contribution to theoretical understanding, and a frequent lack of cross-validation information. Nevertheless, the empirical approach in combination with rational or theoretical considerations for the initial selection of the item pool is usually considered to be the most promising today.

In the *internal consistency* approach, complex statistical procedures are used to group items whose responses tend to be related to each other. The personality meaning of these item clusters, or factors, must be determined by other means. Guilford's several factor analytically derived inventories, of which the *Guilford-Zimmerman Tem-*

perament Survey is most representative, assesses ten such variables. In the *Thurstone Temperament Schedule*, developed from similar data, seven factors are thought sufficient to cover the range of normal personality functioning. Cattell's *Sixteen Personality Factor Questionnaire* assesses 16 such factors or "source traits," which Cattell considers to be natural unitary structures, logically equivalent to atomic elements in the physical world. In general, there has been considerable lack of agreement over the number and names of the necessary and sufficient factor traits for describing personality, which is not surprising since the definition of factors is partly arbitrary. However, there does seem to be good agreement that two factors, which Eysenck has named extroversion and neuroticism, are clearly represented in self-report inventories.

Our division of assessment development procedures into three categories has been for convenience of presentation, and any sophisticated device would certainly involve more than one of them in its development. A recent study has suggested that when considered alone, each approach is about as valid as the next, although this finding must await more general confirmation.

5 BEHAVIOR SAMPLES AND BIOGRAPHICAL DATA

It seems reasonable to suppose that the most logical and direct way to study an individual's personality characteristics would be to observe him in real-life situations in which these characteristics are manifested. For example, if we were concerned about a person's ego strength, or about his emotionality, the best indices of these aspects of his personality should be provided by his behavior in situations where he has been subjected to stress or where emotionality would be elicited. When we have carefully identified the behaviors to be observed in such situations, the only assumption needed for accurate prediction is that there is some generality to these behaviors.

If the foregoing reasoning is correct, why have psychologists been primarily interested with tests and other assessment devices where the relationships between the elicited responses and the behaviors of concern are less obvious? Why, for example, have psychologists attempted to use the perception of human movement on the Rorschach as an indication of ego strength and the response to color as an index of emotionality, instead of studying these behaviors directly? In general, the reasons for avoiding the more direct approach to assessment are related to the fact that this strategy is more difficult and complex than it initially appears. We shall now examine some of the problems involved.

DIRECT OBSERVATION

One difficulty of direct observation concerns the representativeness of the behavior observed. There must be a sufficient number of observational situations planned to provide a representative sample, and the observation periods must be long enough to ensure that the observations are not largely a function of some transitory mood or trivial circumstances.

A second difficulty involves possible changes in the behavior under observation due to the observational process itself. In other words, the knowledge that one is being observed or judged often has direct consequences on the behavior under scrutiny. The result could be increased motivation and higher performance, or anxiety and lowered performance, or studied indifference with no apparent performance change. Consider, for example, a student teacher being evaluated by a supervisor sitting in the room, or an assembly line worker who knows that there is a time-study engineer on the line. It can readily be appreciated that the subject's awareness of being observed might produce nontypical behavior at a time when the occurrence of typical behavior is an absolute necessity. Campbell (1957) called these influences "reactive effects of measurement," and Selltiz et al. (1959) used the term "guinea pig effects." An illustration of guinea pig effects was reported by Moos (1968), who studied the behavioral effects of having psychiatric inpatients wear wireless transmitter microphones. In general, the effects were very small, but there was a tendency for some of the more disturbed individuals to show substantial reactions to being observed.

A third difficulty of direct observation involves invasion of privacy of the subject by the observer. This problem is especially important in personality assessment, since many of the behaviors which should be observed, such as affection, aggression, and sexual identification, are typically regarded as personal and private. Problems of invasion of privacy will be considered in more detail in Chapter 9.

Natural Behavior Samples

Despite the above problems, the direct approach to the assessment of personality has enjoyed fairly wide use. One common technique involves the collection of *behavior samples* in natural settings. Natural settings allow considerable opportunity to observe behavior as it really occurs, although serious problems are raised by the guinea pig effect and by other difficulties of arranging for and reporting the necessary observations. One technique for reducing these effects involves *participant observation*, in which the observer is himself actively engaged in a spontaneous fashion with the individual or group under study. Participant observation has been widely used by anthropologists studying other cultures (see Williams, 1967, for a representative overview), and also by psychologists for a variety of purposes. In one interesting example, psychologists joined a "Doomsday" sect that met together to await the end of the world (Festinger, Riecken, and Schachter, 1956). The psychologists, whose professional role was not revealed to the sect, observed and recorded the group behavior before and during the time it became clear that the prophecy would not be fulfilled. Two of the above difficulties are raised by this example: the question of the observer's objectivity in observing and recording data under such circumstances, and the ethical question of invasion of privacy.

Another strategy to reduce guinea pig effects has been to provide for invisible or hidden observation, so that the subject is not aware of the observer's presence. Hidden microphones, "candid cameras," one-way vision mirrors, and electromechanical devices to record subjects' movements in a chair or other piece of furniture represent some of the currently available devices for unobtrusive observation (Webb *et al.*, 1966, pp. 142–170).

Other sources of natural behavior samples may be found in historical records available on individuals; for example, official school records, high school and college yearbooks, medical and dental records, and records of military service. Thus, Barthell and Holmes (1968) were able to demonstrate that the high school yearbook entries of persons who were later diagnosed as either schizophrenic or neurotic differed in expected ways from a control group. Although Schwarz (1970) has raised questions about the adequacy of controls used in this particular study, the utility of the method appears promising.

Although the continual development of sophisticated instruments for obtaining behavioral samples is making this approach more and more useful, the invasion of privacy problem is once again clearly apparent. It is obviously possible to secure prior permission of subjects to obtain the observations; but in such a case, the guinea pig effects might not be greatly reduced. Soskin and John (1963) have reported an interesting example in which married couples, in exchange for an expense-paid vacation at a summer resort, permitted the recording of all of their verbal behavior during that time by means of miniaturized radio transmitters.

We have noted that representativeness of the behavior studied is an important issue in the use of behavior samples. One technique that has been developed to heighten the representativeness of such behavior is *time sampling*, which involves the systematic observation of subjects' behavior according to a prearranged schedule of observations. The interval between observations is established to maximize the representativeness of the ongoing behavior that can be observed and recorded. The observations in a time sample are usually frequent and brief. For example, Barker, Kounin, and Wright (1943), in studying preschool children at play, observed and recorded the behavior of each child for one minute during each five minutes of a one-hour session. Barker and Wright (1955) suggested ways of collecting time samples in order to maximize the usefulness of the obtained data. They also developed a "day record" or complete behavioral log of an individual child by having trained observers accompany him throughout his entire day (Barker and Wright, 1951). Since the observers had been present in the community for some time and had spent considerable time in this type of nonparticipant observation with the children involved, the guinea pig effects were reduced. However, the question of the representativeness of the particular day under study remained.

A further problem inherent in direct naturalistic observation is that it tends primarily to permit the recording of public and frequent behavior, whereas many of the behaviors required for personality evaluation tend to be private and sometimes relatively infrequent. Responsiveness to stress, the handling of anger or sexuality, and reactions to tragedy fit this description and may not be observable naturalistically, even with time sampling.

Controlled Behavior Samples

The difficulties involved in data collection in naturalistic settings have led some investigators to attempt to sample behavior under more closely controlled laboratory conditions. Here there is the opportunity for more careful and thorough observation, as well as the potential for sufficient environmental control to elicit behaviors of special interest. Of considerable importance are the laboratory situations in which the subject is presented with a number of tasks or experiences under conditions more or less similar to real life, and is expected to function with the same degree of effectiveness as he would in real life. These laboratory or controlled naturalistic observations are termed *situational tests* or *work samples*.

Among the earliest situational tests were those employed by Hartshorne and May (1928, 1929) and Hartshorne, May, and Shuttleworth (1930) in their investigation of character, incorporating such traits as honesty, truthfulness, self-control, and persistence. Hartshorne and May assumed that character consisted of a series of responses or habits, and they attempted to measure these responses by sampling them directly. For example, in assessing honesty with money, children were given boxes of coins which had been secretly identified so that the experimenters could later determine which child had a particular box. Since the children were unaware of this arrangement, their honesty in handling money could be determined without their knowledge under relatively naturalistic but controlled conditions. Recognizing that honesty with money might be unrelated to other kinds of honesty,

Hartshorne and May also collected behavior samples involving the possibility of other types of dishonesty. Thus, children were given an impossible task to perform and were then asked to report their own scores. The extended work of these authors involved a wide repertoire of tasks, concerned with the generality of behaviors such as honesty and persistence. Although these and similar tasks have been used in a variety of research studies (for example, Brock and Guidice, 1963), the procedures have neither been standardized nor widely used as routine assessment devices for practical purposes.

Situational tests have also been utilized to assess suitability for military and intelligence operations, with a special emphasis upon determining characteristic modes of responding to stress. The principal feature of this type of assessment has been the intensive study by a highly trained staff of observers of a small group of candidates in a live-in program lasting several days and typically held at a remote and secluded site. These programs have made use of the traditional testing devices previously discussed in Chapters 3 and 4, but particular emphasis has been placed upon observing the candidates' reactions to the novel situation, to the continued pressure of scrutiny and evaluation, and to a series of specially designed stress situations. In one such situation, designed to assist in the selection of military personnel for the Office of Strategic Services, candidates were required to construct a five-foot "Tinker Toy" cube with the aid of two supposed helpers, who were really members of the evaluation team who had been instructed to criticize, ridicule, and otherwise impede the candidate in completing the task (OSS Assessment Staff, 1948). The helpers carefully observed the candidate's reaction to this continual stress and frustration. In another instance, a group of candidates were given the task of crossing a stream and were provided with some materials to build a primitive bridge. They were then observed in their efforts to organize themselves into an effective work group to solve the task. Since the successful candidates operated throughout the world and performed a great variety of tasks, criterion measures were hard to obtain, making it difficult to assess the effectiveness of these particular selection procedures. Nevertheless, the correlations between overall suitability ratings and success in the field, as evaluated by such criteria as judgments by field commanders, ranged from 0.08 to 0.53, varying with the particular group studied and the criteria used (OSS Assessment Staff, 1948, p. 428). Further, it should be noted that the assessment program had a fairly rigorous set of selection standards, which served to decrease any correlation between the observers' predictions and judged criterion performance.

The live-in assessment procedure has also been used for selecting members of the British Civil Service (Vernon, 1950). The situational tasks employed here were based upon a thorough job analysis of the work for which the candidates were applying, and included committee tasks and the handling of routine paper work. There was much opportunity for informal observations of the candidates throughout a three-day period but there were no deliberately stressful situations built into the assessment procedure. With a rather homogeneous group of university graduates, the median correlation between ratings of trained observers and independent on-the-job evaluations collected two years later was 0.41. The median correlation between the more traditional written ability tests and the evaluations was only 0.12, indicating that the trained observers were able to identify significant elements of potential success that were not otherwise detected.

It is important to reemphasize that, in this example, the assessors had a clear understanding of the psychological requirements of the criterion task and were able to arrange for assessment situations to elicit relevant behaviors. Similar positive results have been reported with candidates for United States Army Officer Candidate Schools using leadership performance exercises as the situational task (Holmen et al., 1956) and by Mills, McDevitt, and Tonkin (1966) for selecting police cadets using a "clues" test, a situational exercise in police detection. On the other hand, assessment procedures based upon more traditional psychological tests, including a wide variety of personality tests, have not been so successful in predicting success in psychiatry (Holt and Luborsky, 1958) or in clinical psychology (Kelly and Fiske, 1951; Kelly and Goldberg, 1959).

One technique which is often used in live-in or "house party" assessments is the *leaderless group discussion* (LGD). In this procedure, which originated in the German and British military assessment programs (Ansbacher, 1951), a small group of candidates, typically fewer than 12, is asked either to "discuss something" or to discuss a specific problem, perhaps a topic of current political or social interest. For a management group, the topic might be a management problem such as how to deal with an unsatisfactory employee. Since the procedure is otherwise unstructured and the group members are usually strangers to each other, the situation is rather ambiguous. There is opportunity to observe and rate behaviors like leading and following, social poise and self-presence, and "goal facilitation," which refers to the degree the individual helped the group accomplish its goal through making suggestions or by enabling others to contribute.

Initial participation in an LGD is usually equated with attempted leadership (Bass, 1960, p. 115), since most of the talk is directed at influencing other members either with procedural suggestions or with opinions on the topic under discussion. Attempted leadership, as defined in this manner, could be measured by determining the amount of time spent talking, in terms of total number of responses, rated participation, or total time talked. Other ways of assessing the members of an LGD have included ratings of behaviors such as "motivating others to participate" and check lists of behaviors such as "led the discussion," to be completed by either the participants themselves or external, non-participating observers.

Perhaps the most extensive and formal way of categorizing the various kinds of behavior observable in this and other social interactions is by means of the Bales Interaction Check List (Bales, 1950). In this technique, observers categorize every response made in the group into one of 12 predetermined categories, such as *shows solidarity* (gives help or reward), *shows tension release* (jokes, laughs), and *asks for orientation* (asks for information, confirmation). At the present time, however, the Bales Interaction Check List is more of a research instrument than a functional assessment device.

In general, there is excellent evidence for the reliability of observing LGD behavior. For most of the available methods of quantifying the behavior, the average correlation between any two observers is typically between 0.8 and 0.9 (Bass, 1954, p. 472). There is also sound evidence for the predictive value of LGD behavioral indices. For example, Bass and Coates (1952) reported correlations of 0.40 to 0.45 between LGD scores and ratings of military officers by their superiors. Similar findings have been reported for British foreign service officers (Vernon, 1950), British Civil Service employees (Vernon, 1950), and fraternity and sorority leaders and sales trainees (Bass, 1954).

The LGD procedure is a very good example of the utility of the situational test or work sample approach to personality assessment, particularly in the evaluation of characteristics such as leadership. Leadership involves the behavior of the individual in group settings, particularly his ability to structure, organize, and generally influence the group; and clearly such behavior is elicited and observable in the LGD. It should not be surprising, therefore, that the behavior displayed in the sample does provide information about the individual's behavior in other situations that require similar responses for effective performance.

One portion of a recent study by Gordon (1967) examined the relative utility of several assessment procedures, including individual situational work samples, in predicting failure of Peace Corps trainees to be selected for an overseas assignment. The subjects were 178 trainees in three different training programs, all of whom were subjected to an intensive one-week live-in assessment program. The program included a variety of paper-and-pencil personality inventories of the type discussed in Chapter 4, a foreign language learning task, and four specially devised situational work samples, in which the subject was required to develop a plan to build an infirmary on a South Seas island, describe to a foreign national the American governmental system of checks and balances, discuss American culture with an anti-American, and enlist the aid of an Indian government official in a project to raise poultry. Prior to overseas departure, 74 trainees were rejected as unsuitable, although the personnel making this decision did not have access to the earlier assessment data. In general, each of the various assessment approaches enabled predictions of failure to be made that exceeded chance expectation, but there were no worthwhile differences in efficiency of prediction among the various approaches. Gordon argued that the simplest and most economical method of predicting success in the overseas assignments should be used operationally for screening, in this case, the paper-and-pencil inventories. These issues of cost and efficiency need further careful research involving a variety of criterion situations. The additional question of the relative utility of these procedures for predicting success in overseas assignments is as yet unanswered.

In general, behavior samples appear to be useful in personality assessment both for research and for practical purposes, and especially for selecting job candidates where the job requirements are known. In the latter case, a careful analysis of the criterion performance is necessary to identify the particular kinds of behaviors to be sampled. Since many of the determinants of job behavior are components of the environment, the more closely the environment in which the behavior sample is elicited resembles the real-life environment, the more accurate should be the prediction. This conclusion implies that "tryouts" in the real world would often represent the most accurate job selection strategy, and that would seem to be the case. On the other hand, attempts to identify more general or underlying personality traits such as autonomy or ego strength by means of behavior samples have been much less successful, perhaps because these behaviors are not easily observable and are not closely linked with environmental cues. Also, molar behavior of the type usually observed involved in situational tests gives the observer little or no understanding of the underlying feelings, reactions, and attitudes of the subject; and it is these response dispositions which are considered important factors in making for the trans-situational generality of behavior. Indeed, these are the factors which we have regarded as the core of personality—that is, one's enduring interpersonal characteristics.

Unsystematic Observations

To this stage we have concentrated upon situations where a trained observer studies a subject in some specific type of behavioral situation. Obviously the subject has also been "behaving" in a wide variety of real-life situations where untrained observers have been present. The child's behavior in the classroom, the employee's on-the-job performance, and the patient's behavior on the ward are all observed and should provide useful data for the purposes of personality assessment. The major problem in making use of informal and unsystematic observations is the manner in which these observations are to be collected from the observers and, particularly, the form in which the observations are to be reported.

One approach is to ask the observer of an individual or group to keep an *anecdotal record*. The observer, who will often be a teacher or supervisor, is asked to make notes of whatever behavior in his daily routine contact he regards as "significant." He is encouraged to record exactly what he observed as soon as possible after the observation, and to be as objective and descriptive in his report as possible. Whatever inferences the observer makes should be clearly identified as such. An anecdotal record developed over a period of time provides a rich though nonquantified account of behavior that is unrivalled for developing an individualized behavioral description. It is the consistency and individuality of certain behavioral observations, for example, seeking affection, refusing help, working diligently at a task, or volunteering for responsibilities, that permit the reader of the anecdotal record to construct a personality "picture." The artistic, clinical nature of this process is clearly apparent.

In order to develop greater focus in anecdotal records upon behaviors of particular interest to the investigator, it is possible to utilize the *critical incident technique* developed by Flanagan (1954). This technique asks the observer to consider instances of behavior that are illustrative of a particular personality characteristic. Thus, a supervisor might be asked to observe and record examples of good or poor work performance, or a psychiatric ward nurse might be asked to record all instances of aggression. The observer is again required to record objectively the actual behavioral incidents, and it is the difficult task of the reader to draw inferences from this record. It can be appreciated that the values and attitudes of the observer are clearly a factor in making the observations. For example, a supervisor who regards quantity of output as the most important indicator of good work performance will probably record different critical incidents than would a supervisor who is primarily concerned about quality of product.

Anecdotal data is perhaps more widely used in another context. Potential employers often attempt to ascertain the suitability of a job candidate through *references*—that is, by requesting letters of recommendation or by a telephone inquiry about the applicant. Reference checks are usually of limited use, since they typically consist of positive but vague generalities. One comprehensive study of reference checks made by the United States Civil Service Commission (Goheen and Mosel, 1959) indicated that such inquiries did not even identify disqualifying factors, such as alcoholism, which were readily uncovered by field investigations. Letters which are negative take on particular weight because of their rarity in actual practice. A recent exception to these findings has been the experience of the Peace Corps where, in our personal experience, reference checks have produced considerable frankness on the part of respondents, yielding useful comparative information about applicants. In this area, a significant relationship has been demonstrated between quantified ratings of reference checks and overseas success (Stein, 1966).

BIOGRAPHICAL DATA

Written Methods

In the previous section we discussed observations of current behavior as a basis for personality assessment and prediction. Next we shall consider records of a person's past behavior as a source of personality assessment data.

One approach, which has found favor in personnel selection, is the *weighted biographical data sheet* (England, 1961). In this method it is assumed that personal history items, obtainable from a formal written application blank, have predictive value for success or failure in a particular occupational setting. The items can be *demographic* (such as age, sex, marital status, and number of dependents), *experiential* (such as number of schools attended, age when first married, number of jobs held, and arrest record), or *behavioral* (such as recreational pursuits, hobbies, current reading matter, and consumption of alcohol). Items that correlate with some criterion of success or failure are identified statistically and are given differential numerical weights according to how predictive they are. In operational use, applications are "scored" according to these weights and the applicant is accepted or rejected depending upon whether or not his total surpasses some "cutting score" which has been previously established by empirical means. This procedure closely resembles the development of empirically derived personality inventories like the MMPI.

The weighted biographical data technique was successfully applied to the selection of life insurance salesmen as early as 1919. Using nine personal history items with weights ranging from -2 to $+3$ and a cutting score of $+4$ on the complete blank, Goldsmith (1922) reported that 84 percent of the successful salesmen would have been selected and 54 percent of the unsuccessful ones would have been rejected. During World War II, scores on the Air Force Biographical Data Blank were found to correlate 0.30 with pilot success (Guilford, 1947). More recently, this technique has been successfully used to select unskilled factory workers (Scott and Johnson, 1967), management personnel (Scollay, 1957), and sales clerks (Mosel and Wade, 1951). The criteria used have included job tenure or longevity, productivity, amount of absenteeism, and size of salary. Since these criteria are not always highly correlated, it is important for the investigator to decide which criterion is of primary importance in his particular setting.

Continual cross-validation or rechecking of the weighted application blank appears to be necessary. An interesting study (Hughes, Dunn, and Baxter, 1956) reported that the usefulness of the application blank "disappeared" within two years after it was put into operational use. It was surmised that the field management staff, who knew the item weights, were leading or guiding the applicants so that their blank would "pass" the cutting score. Obviously, this criticism is equally pertinent to any assessment device used for selection purposes.

This approach has recently been used for other kinds of vocational and achievement predictions. Freeberg (1967) has written a positive review of the literature on biographical material as a predictor of scholastic achievement, using grades, nonclassroom achievements, persistence, and curriculum choice as the criteria. Taylor and Ellison (1967) have reported on the successful use of biographical data to predict scientific careers, and Owens and Henry (1966) have surveyed the literature on the successful use of biographical data to predict creativity in a variety of work settings.

Another major application of the biographical or personal history data method is in psychopathology (Robins, 1954). It has long been noted that patients in mental hospitals, especially those diagnosed as schizophrenic, differ in prognosis, with some showing rather prompt and good recovery while others make little or no change. Beginning with the work of Wittman (1941) at Elgin State Hospital, a number of investigators have attempted to identify particular aspects of case history or biographical data that are associated with good and poor prognosis in schizophrenia. Kantor, Wallner, and Winder (1953) and Phillips (1953) provide prominent examples of this approach, although Kantor et al. have included information about current symptoms in addition to case history data. In general, those schizophrenics with good prognosis (who subsequently recover) are found to have been better adjusted prior to the onset of the illness, with less family psychopathology, more satisfactory heterosexual experiences, better vocational adjustment, and more general stability than the group with poor prognosis (who recover very slowly or not at all). The terms *reactive* and *process* schizophrenia have traditionally been used as more or less synonymous with good and poor prognosis respectively. In general, studies relating scores on life history prognostic scales to actual outcome have yielded moderate positive results (Buss, 1966, pp. 224–225; Garfield and Sundland, 1966), and these findings have led several investigators (for example, Rodnick and Garmezy, 1957) to regard as essential the inclusion of a life history measure of prognosis in research with schizophrenic patient populations.

We shall now examine the technique developed by Zigler and Phillips (1960) for using case history data to evaluate the relative premorbid adjustment level of psychiatric patients in general. It is based upon six personal history variables: age, measured intelligence, education, occupational level (unskilled or semiskilled), employment history (usually unemployed, seasonally employed, part-time employed, and regularly employed), and marital status. These variables are used to produce a composite measure of social competence that is significantly related to the type of symptoms shown by the patients. The patients with higher social competence scores tend to show symptoms which can be regarded as "turning against the self," and those with lower scores tend to show symptoms indicative of "avoidance of others" or "self indulgence and turning against others." Since these latter symptoms are typical of schizophrenia, it can be concluded that patients diagnosed as schizophrenic tend generally to have relatively poor premorbid social competence. Zigler and Phillips (1962) have further been able to demonstrate that within schizophrenics, those who exhibit a relatively good level of premorbid social competence are more likely than the poor premorbid patient to show symptoms characterized by "turning against the self." From these findings, they were able to conclude that the reactive–process distinction in schizophrenia might be better regarded as a social competence or social maturity dimension which can be assessed through personal history data, and that this dimension is applicable to all of psychopathology rather than to schizophrenia alone.

In order to obtain a convenient record of personal history data, which is often quite incomplete in mental hospital case records, Briggs (1959) developed the M-B History Record. This is a 175-item written questionnaire to be filled out by a relative or friend who knows the patient well. The items are factual and concern the patient's life history, including such diverse areas as education, food preferences, and marital status. This questionnaire, in a self-administering multiple-choice format which can be mailed out to informants, would appear to be a useful source of personal history data for work with psychiatric patients. A less extensive self-report questionnaire of 20 items was developed by Lanyon (1967a) to measure social competence in normal male college students. Scores on this questionnaire are related to other measures of social effectiveness, including ratings by peers.

The personal history information reported on a biographical data blank, in addition to providing a basis for deriving a score according to a predetermined formula, can be regarded as a behavioral record which can be clinically analyzed. When provided with this diverse array of data, the skilled clinician can develop many hypotheses about the personality characteristics of the respondent, much in the same fashion that skilled clinicians approach a Rorschach protocol. Beside the content of the blank, potential personality information can be provided by assessing aspects such as how neatly the blank has been completed, how completely information has been provided, and differences in how various questions are answered. The applicant for a job who lists under the category of *Health History* the fact that he had "Measles-July, 1937" presumably is rather different in his bodily concerns than the applicants who fail to record this rather trivial event. There are many specific items on the blank that can provide relevant material about the personality of the respondent. The youthful applicant who reports owning an expensive sports car, although his income is modest, has different needs and values from the person reporting that he has several large life insurance policies. At least one commercially available form, the Worthington Personal History Blank (Spencer and Worthington, 1952), is specifically designed to maximize the availability of such data by deliberately minimizing the amount of structure provided for completing the form. For example, there is no information about whether pencil or pen should be used, or how the applicant's name is to be written—whether last name or given name should be written first. It should be noted that there are many other similar sources of written clinical data, including letters, diaries, and other personal documents (Allport, 1961). The obvious problem common to all of them lies in developing adequate methods for evaluating the usefulness and accuracy of the inferences which are drawn by the clinician.

The use of biographical or life history data for personality assessment, especially the weighted application blank, has strong research support, but there are problems inherent in this method that should not be overlooked. The items are subject to falsification, since many are rather obvious in the sense that the "correct" or socially desirable answer can readily be ascertained. The problem of coaching applicants has been previously mentioned, as has the need for cross-validation of the scoring procedure. The clinical use of the data depends heavily upon the skill and acumen of the individual clinician, and this process needs careful checking.

Interviewing

An *interview* can be regarded as a conversation between two people: the interviewer (a trained professional, who is attempting to understand and assess the other) and the subject. The interview is distinguished from ordinary conversation by its purposive and probing nature. Much has been written on this complex and involved subject (Bellows and Estop, 1954; Bingham and Moore, 1959; Fear, 1958; Kahn and Cannell, 1957; Matarazzo, 1965; Sullivan, 1954), and it clearly is beyond our scope to give more than a broad outline of the procedure as used for personality assessment purposes. The role of the interview in personality change or psychotherapy will not be touched upon.

In general, there are two kinds of information available in the interview: that involved in the *content* of the subject's responses and that involved in his *style* or manner of relating to the interviewer. Most interviewers, particularly beginning ones, tend to focus upon the content of the interview. In the intake interview in a social service agency or mental hospital, for example, the interviewer will concentrate upon clarifying the patient's presenting complaints, what he has previously done to alleviate these problems, and what he expects from the present situation. The basic question in an intake interview is why the patient is at the agency. In an employment interview, the focus is upon occupational and educational history, job and personal skills, motivation for the present job and for future advancement, and general suitability for work with the employer. The basic question here is whether the applicant is hirable. In a personal or case history interview the concern is with obtaining a more complete set of data about the individual for a specific purpose, such as research or psychotherapy treatment planning. The emphasis here is upon gathering as much data about the subject as possible.

The purposes of content-centered interviews could be categorized in a variety of different ways, and the above samples are offered simply for illustrative purposes. What is important to note is that one major concern in an interview is with the content of the information supplied by the subject. As with a biographical data sheet, the information supplied in an interview is useful for assessment and prediction, and indeed can be weighted and scored as in the weighted application blank procedure discussed above. If this is the case, however, then why should an interview be employed rather than the less time-consuming and more readily available application blank? For one thing, the interview is less structured and more flexible than the application blank, permitting the interviewer to vary his approach and his questions in order to maximize the possibility of openness and truthfulness. This procedure would obviously not be possible in a highly structured and standardized interview where a predetermined schedule must be followed, such as interviews carried out by public opinion polls. Related to the advantage of flexibility, the opportunity for the interviewer to establish *rapport* or interpersonal warmth before proceeding is frequently recognized as another important reason for preferring the interview. The interviewer also has an opportunity to observe the subject's reactions, both the obvious ones like blushing and long hesitations and the more subtle ones like oblique, noninformative answers, all of which suggest that a fuller exploration of the topic under consideration would be appropriate.

The latter considerations highlight the second purpose of the interview, the opportunity to observe the subject directly in an interpersonal situation. One way of conceptualizing the interview is to regard the subject's total behavior as a sample of his interpersonal skill and his manner of approaching and dealing with others. The less structured interviews, which offer the subject few or no clear directions and permit great latitude in the areas to be covered, clearly provide interpersonal behavior samples. Of course, the interviewer can deliberately play a role in order to evoke responses to particular kinds of "others." He can be deliberately casual and noncommittal, warm and sympathetic, or cold and rejecting. The OSS assessment staff, among others, developed stress interviews where the subject was harassed, criticized, pressured, and otherwise made uncomfortable in order to evaluate his resistance to stress.

It is most important for each professional interviewer to know something about his own social stimulus value and to be aware of the modal type of interpersonal situation he establishes for his interviewees. There is considerable research evidence (Gottschalk and Gleser, 1969; Kahn and Cannell, 1957) that there are large differences among interviewers and that this may be an important variable in clinical practice and research. The use of the interview as an interpersonal behavior sample obviously requires considerable training and experience on the part of the interviewer in order for this technique to be useful for assessment purposes. Recently reported research by Webster (1967) on the manner in which decisions are made during an interview demonstrate how little has been understood in this area.

A major difficulty with the interview is the fact that the interviewer himself is a fallible instrument. There is much evidence about the subtle cues that interviewers provide, cues of which the interviewer himself may be unaware, that tend to guide and bias the outcome of the interview (Kahn and Cannell, 1957). It is also likely that interviewers tend to avoid probing in certain areas, those in which they themselves are anxious (Bandura, Lipsher, and Miller, 1960). These interviewer biases contribute to the general concern that is expressed about the utility of the interview as an assessment device. In a recent review of the utility of the selection interview, Ulrich and Trumbo (1965) concluded that "the bulk of the evidence favors both the structured interview and interviews limited in purpose. Recurring evidence suggests that the interview may be most successful if limited to the assessment of personal relations and career motivations" (p. 100).

Two noteworthy examples of structured and limited-purpose interviews are the Vineland Social Maturity Scale (Doll, 1953, 1965) and the Structured Clinical Interview (Burdock and Hardesty, 1968). The purpose of the Vineland Social Maturity Scale ". . . is to measure the extent to which the person progressively dominates his environment and creates, demands, or justifies his own freedom of action as age increases" (Doll, 1965, p. 12). In administering the Vineland, the interviewer asks the mother of a young child to discuss the child's ordinary social behavior in areas such as eating, dressing, communication, and socialization, with special focus upon his "actual and habitual performance" in these areas. Although the interviewer does take notes during the interview and may probe for additional details, the mother generally does not know that the information she is supplying will be scored against an objective, standardized schedule of normal social development. She is simply asked to talk about her child and his behavior in specific areas. The Vineland yields a social age (SA) and a social quotient (SQ) score, which may be considered analogous to the mental age and ratio IQ scores of the Stanford-Binet Intelligence Scale. Although the standardization of the Vineland is now somewhat dated, as are some of the items, this approach to the objectification of interview data has proven to be a useful one.

The Structured Clinical Interview (SCI) is a technique for evaluating in a quantitative manner the degree of psychopathology present in a psychiatric patient. It consists of a standardized interview schedule on which a trained interviewer observes and scores the patient as the interview progresses, much like a standardized individual intelligence test. The SCI taps ten areas of functioning, including anger-hostility, conceptual disfunction, fear-worry, and incongruous behavior. A measure of overall level of psychopathology is also obtained.

A number of content analysis procedures have been developed to objectify and quantify the data obtained in less structured interviews. They include measures of speech disturbances and silences (Mahl, 1956), verbal content analyses (for example, Auld and Murray, 1955), and time measures, such as average length of subject verbalization (Ulrich and Trumbo, 1965). Although they are not designed to be directly useful for assessment or prediction purposes, these analytic procedures offer promise for providing better understanding of the interviewing process and for ultimately making the interview a more useful personality assessment device.

QUANTIFICATION OF OBSERVATIONS

We have concentrated thus far on a rather wholistic approach to the data obtained in behavioral observations of one type and another, and we have made passing references to ratings and to other attempts at quantifying the data. We shall now examine in greater detail these quantification procedures and some of the inherent problems involved in using them.

A *rating scale* is a form or device by which an observer can record his observations or judgments about the behavior of another person in some predetermined, ordered fashion. Rating scales may be filled out either during or after the observation, and the observations can be complete and wide-ranging or incomplete and circumscribed. In principle, just about any data can be quantified by rating procedures.

although consideration must be given to issues such as interrater agreement and possible rater biases. The form of the rating scale for personality assessment may range from a simple list of adjectives to be checked (Gough and Heilbrun, 1964) to continuous scales of generalized personality traits like dominance-submission and masculinity-feminity. The generally preferred form for making trait evaluations is the *graphic rating scale*. Figure 5-1 shows two illustrative items taken from the Haggerty-Olson-Wichman Behavior Rating Schedule (1930), a commercially available rating scale for recording behavioral observations on school-aged children. These are descriptive scales in

18. Is he shy or bold in social relationships?

Painfully Self-conscious (4)	Timid Frequently Embarrassed (2)	Self-conscious on occasions (1)	Confident in himself (3)	Bold, insensitive to social feelings (5)

13. How does he impress you with his regard to masculine traits?

Is a "sissy" (5)	Slightly effeminate (3)	Has average boy qualities (1)	Very masculine (2)	Entirely masculine. A "buck" (4)

FIGURE 5-1. Illustrative items from the Haggerty-Olson-Wichman Rating Schedule.

that each point corresponds to a presumed behavior pattern; they are bipolar with the two extremes equidistant from some average or neutral position; and they are graphic in that the rater is allowed to mark at any position along the continuum to represent the degree to which the subject possesses the trait. The Haggerty-Olson-Wichman scale was designed to identify maladjusted children, and items suggestive of pathology are given special attention by means of the weight assigned to those behaviors which occur more often in problem children. These weights are given in parentheses below the rating scale. The higher weights, 4 and 5, were given to behaviors most typical of problem children, while a weight of 1 was given to behaviors rarely reported for problem children.

Ordinarily, a range of five to seven points on a graphic rating scale is regarded as adequate to produce a sufficient dispersion of ratings for discriminating among subjects. If there are only a few judges available, a rating technique allows more opportunity for differentiating among subjects than does a dichotomous task such as an adjective check list, on which items such as "aggressive" or "flexible" are either endorsed or not endorsed as descriptive of the subject without regard to different degrees of applicability. Satisfactory discrimination on an adjective check list can be obtained when there are a larger number of judges involved; here the subject's "score" on an item can be the number of times it is checked by the pool of judges.

Graphic rating scales have been developed to tap a large variety of behaviors. Most often they are specially devised by an investigator for his particular purposes, although there are commercially available sets such as the Haggerty-Olson-Wichman Schedule. Some have been especially designed for rating patient behaviors in psychiatric wards. A good example is given by the Wittenborn Psychiatric Rating Scales (Wittenborn, 1955), which are based upon careful research, including factor analysis, and yield highly reliable patient descriptions.

Rating scales tend to produce fairly good interjudge agreement, and they are widely used in personality research because of the paucity of readily available measures of the behaviors or traits under study. There are however, certain kinds of rater errors which are particularly bothersome in rating scales and which should not be ignored. Similar errors are doubtless involved in all personality assessment, but they are seen most clearly in their effects upon ratings. One is the tendency to produce *constant errors* or biases in filling out a rating scale. Thus one rater may rarely or never use low ratings, while another might rarely use high ratings. A related problem is the *generosity* error, where raters generally tend to give subjects highly favorable evaluations. Such ratings are of little value since they do not discriminate satisfactorily between individuals. Another related problem exists when raters have only limited opportunities to observe the subject, and therefore may not have enough data to make certain ratings. Under these circumstances the so-called *halo effect* may become important, where the rater overgeneralizes from the evidence available, especially if it tends to be positive.

A number of procedures have been developed to reduce rating errors. Constant errors can be reduced by statistically transforming each rater's score into some type of standard score which will compensate for his constant error and, to a lesser degree, for his leniency error. Asking for specific behavioral or anecdotal data to support a particular rating is also an effective technique for reducing these errors. The halo effect can be reduced in the same way, especially if there is an opportunity for the rater to use a category like "insufficient data to make this rating." Another technique to reduce rating errors is the *forced-choice* technique (Richardson, 1949; Scott, 1968), in which the rater is forced to choose which of two traits or phrases, which have been closely matched on favorability, is the more descriptive of the subject. A further technique that can be used when there are several subjects to evaluate is to have the observer rank-order the individuals on the trait dimension under consideration. When the group to be ranked is rather large, they can be ordered into a specified distribution along the trait dimension such as a seven- or nine-point forced normal distribution. A "forced" distribution means that the number of individuals to be placed at each of the seven or nine points is specified in advance, and "forced normal" means that these numbers are specified in such a way that the resulting distribution will have approximately the same shape as the normal curve, with relatively few subjects at the most extreme points of the distribution and most of the group in the center. Such ranking procedures, however, are ipsative; that is, they only provide relative data about the group under study, and do not indicate how the group would compare with any other group along some absolute dimension of the trait or how an individual from the group would compare with an individual from another group.

An important use of forced-distribution ranking procedures is the "*Q-sort*" (Block, 1961; Stephenson, 1953). The observer is given a deck of cards, each of which contains a single statement, such as "is basically anxious," or "communicates ideas clearly and effectively." The judge, who may be the subject himself, in which case the Q-sort becomes a self-report measure, is then asked to rank-order the statements from most descriptive to least descriptive of the subject, using a forced normal distribution for the ranking.

The items of the California Q-sort (Block, 1961) have themselves been rated (weighted) by trained clinicians for adjustment, so that the Q-sort for a particular person can be scored individually for adjustment. Another way in which the Q-sort has been used in personality assessment is to ask the subject to sort the cards once as he "actually is" and then again as he "would like to be." The discrepancy between these actual self and ideal self Q-sorts has been widely used in psychotherapy research as a criterion measure for personality change (Rogers and Dymond, 1954), with the expectation that successful psychotherapy would reduce this discrepancy. Marks and Seeman (1963), in another interesting use of the Q-sort, have developed an "atlas" of Q-sort statements that are empirically correlated with various MMPI profiles.

The Q-sort method is a useful technique for both clinical and research purposes, especially for the description of complex or global personality attributes, but several problems should be noted. One concerns the nature of the items involved in a particular Q-sort deck and involves the problem of whether any manageable group of short statements can satisfactorily describe complex behavior or personality functioning. Another problem is created by the assumption that the descriptive statements can be "forced" into a normal distribution without producing biases. A third involves the fact that unless the Q-sort employed offers a comprehensive and unbiased coverage of the personality domain of interest, comparisons among different Q-sorts will not yield results.

Peer ratings are ratings made by the *peers* of the subject, that is, people with the same rank or status, such as classmates or fellow workers. Peer ratings, which are generally based upon extended observation in real-life situations, tend to show a high degree of interjudge agreement, with coefficients of correlation often 0.9 or above. Peer ratings often produce evaluations of the subject which may be rather different from other judgments, a situation which reflects the different values of the peer and superordinate (or subordinate) subcultures. A rebellious college student who leads student protests may be seen as a leader by his peers but as a malcontent and troublemaker by his professors. Obviously, both kinds of information are relevant, but perhaps for different purposes.

One approach frequently used in peer ratings is the *nomination technique*, where each member of the peer group is asked to list or nominate a fixed number of persons who are group members and who are most prominent or visible in particular ways. As part of Peace Corps selection procedures, for example, all the members of a training group would be asked to nominate the five trainees they would: (1) most like to be assigned with overseas; (2) least like to be assigned with overseas; (3) regard as the most successful; and so on. Unpublished research on Peace Corps peer ratings has indicated that they are consistently successful in predicting overseas success. Similar findings of the predictive efficiency of peer nominations have been reported for doctoral candidates in clinical psychology (Kelly and Fiske, 1951), officer candidates (Holmen et al., 1956), and a variety of other occupational groups. A serious problem with using this technique, especially in the context of selection, is the high degree of anxiety about the task and antagonism towards the investigator which may be aroused.

A close variant of the nomination technique is the *sociometric rating*, developed by Moreno (1934), which is used to study the social structure of small groups. Each person in such a group is asked to choose one or more other group members with whom he would like to work, play, sit near, and so forth, and also to choose those whom he wishes to avoid. The patterns of likes and dislikes are then given pictorial representation by plotting them on a *sociogram*. From the sociogram, the small cliques within the group can be identified, as can the leader or "star" and the social isolate.

For young children, nominations can be obtained by the "Guess Who" technique (Hartshorne and May, 1929) where members of the group are asked to "guess who" is the class athlete, the one who plays games best; or who is the class bully, the one who is always annoying or picking on the other children. The number of times each child is nominated under such rubrics constitutes his score on that dimension.

Peer ratings are readily obtainable, and they represent quite a useful approach to personality measurement. In the past they have been employed primarily in research and in personnel selection. For other purposes, such as clinical assessment, they have rarely been used in spite of the important vantage which they seem to offer in understanding individual behavior.

The *semantic differential* (Osgood, 1952; Osgood, Suci, and Tannenbaum, 1957) is a rating technique originally developed as a tool for assessing the meaning of concepts. The individual rates the concept or person on a series of seven-point bipolar adjective scales, such as simple–complicated or cruel–kind. Factor-analytic studies have shown that the majority of the adjective scales which have been employed in these ratings can be summarized in three factors: (1) evaluation (which incorporates adjective scales such as good–bad and kind–cruel), (2) activity (for example, fast–slow and active–passive), and (3) potency (for example, strong–weak and large–small). Wide use has not been made of this tool as a means of clinical personality description; rather, it has been utilized as a research instrument. One good example of research use is Nunnally's (1961) extensive study of public attitudes toward concepts in the field of mental health. Thus, professionals who treat physical disorders received higher ratings on the "evaluative" dimension than professionals who treat mental disorders. Also, the mentally ill were rated by both the public and by general medical practitioners as dangerous, unintelligent, and unpredictable.

Summary

Although the most direct way to assess personality would seem to be through the study of persons in real-life situations, this approach is more difficult than it sounds. Problems involved are the representativeness of the behavior to be observed, possible changes in the individual's behavior as a result of the measuring process itself (guinea pig effects), and invasion of privacy. Despite these difficulties, direct observation of behavior has enjoyed fairly wide use as an assessment procedure.

A common technique involves the collection of *behavior samples in natural settings*. This might be done through participant observation, in which the observer himself is engaged in some way in the behavior under study. Problems of guinea pig effects have led to the development of techniques for hidden observation, including the use of electronic devices, although invasion of privacy still constitutes a problem. In order to ensure greater representativeness of data, periodic or time sampling may be employed. Behavior samples may also be collected in controlled or laboratory settings. Also referred to as *situational tests*, such settings allow for closer control over the behaviors of interest. One technique of note is the leaderless group discussion, in which a small group of people are called upon to discuss a specific topic. An opportunity is thus provided for the observation of interpersonal characteristics such as leadership and social poise.

Unsystematic observations are also employed in assessment. An observer might keep an anecdotal record, in which he notes everything which appears significant in his daily contact with the individual. In the critical-incident technique, note is made of instances of behavior which the observer considers particularly illustrative of the individual's behavior. Letters of reference also constitute unsystematic observations about interpersonal behavior. Problems of the representativeness of the behavior reported are an obvious drawback in this approach.

Considerable use has been made of *biographical data* for personality assessment purposes, particularly in personnel selection. Personal history data provided on a formal job application blank can be examined impressionistically as a basis for forming hypotheses about a candidate. The weighted biographical data sheet provides an empirical approach in which a score is determined from weights assigned to various personal and biographical items. Personal history data has also been used empirically in psychiatric settings to predict the outcome of schizophrenia, and it is likely that such data can also be used to predict the course of other psychopathological processes.

The *interview* is a common means of obtaining biographical data and also provides an opportunity for direct observation. Research on the interviewing process suggests that the manner in which information is collected by the interviewer is not well understood, and that interviews which are structured or limited in purpose are the most likely to provide valid information. Two noteworthy examples of structured or limited-purpose interview schedules are the Vineland Social Maturity Scale, designed for the assessment of retarded children, and the Structured Clinical Interview, a technique for evaluating psychopathology.

How are behavioral observations quantified? Perhaps the most common technique is some variant of the *rating scale,* an approach which can be applied to just about any kind of data. Problems with rating scales include possible rater biases or constant errors, unwillingness to give low or undesirable ratings, and the "halo effect," where a rater overgeneralizes from limited evidence. One method for reducing rater errors is the forced-choice technique, in which the rater is forced to choose which of two descriptions, matched on favorability, is the more applicable. A variant of this technique is the Q-sort, in which the rater arranges a series of cards, each containing a personality statement, in order from least to most descriptive of the individual. Other rating methods include the peer nomination technique, where each member of a peer group is asked to list a certain number of persons who best meet a specific criterion. The semantic differential, another rating procedure originally developed as a tool for assessing the meaning of concepts, also has applicability in personality assessment.

6 RELIABILITY AND VALIDITY

The first five chapters have provided an overview of the nature of personality assessment, its history, and the common methods for performing it. This chapter deals in more detail with two concepts, reliability and validity, which are basic to an adequate understanding of the scope and limitations of different assessment methods.

Reliability, as its name implies, has to do with the reproducibility or verifiability of a measure. To take a very simple example, let us say that yesterday we have measured a child's height as 48.3 inches. Today somebody else measures the same child, and gives his report as 48.4 inches. We doubtless would consider that the two measures are in good agreement with each other; that is, we would consider the initial measurement of the child's height to have been verified or reproduced. The 0.1 inch discrepancy reflects the fact that repeated measurements almost always will be slightly inconsistent or unreliable, while our satisfaction with the result shows that the inconsistency is small enough for the results to be useful to us. Thus, the discrepancy of 0.1 inch is so small under these circumstances that it can be regarded as inconsequential. In other cases of physical measurement, however, where the tolerance levels are quite small, as in an engine cylinder, such a difference would be practically important and a higher level of reliability of measurement would be required.

We should note that reliability is not the same as precision. Precision refers to the exactness with which the measurement can be specified; thus, a measuring procedure which permits us to report to the nearest one-thousandth of an inch would be more precise than one permitting a report only to the nearest tenth of an inch. A mechanical gauge which gave a reading of 2.432 inches would have precision to one thousandth of an inch, but if a second reading gave

2.381 inches, the reliability of the measurement would be nowhere near the precision indicated by the instrument.

The requirement that measurements be made "accurately enough" is also applicable to personality assessment. Compared with the measurement of physical characteristics such as height, personality measurement has always been rather sloppy, that is, somewhat unreliable. Thus, one point of concern affecting any decision to utilize a personality assessment device should be its reliability, and such instruments ordinarily have some index of reliability available for the potential user. We shall return to the matter of reliability in a moment.

In personality measurement there is an additional difficulty, which is not present with the common physical measurements. In common physical measurement there are generally agreed-upon standards against which measurements are made. There is no question that a yardstick (or a meterstick) is appropriate for measuring linear distances, like body height. In personality assessment, however, questions are frequently raised about the legitimacy of the measuring device for assessing or evaluating the dimension under scrutiny. For example, can one really measure depression by counting the number of achromatic color responses given on the Rorschach? In this case, there is not only the question of a reliable count of the number of these responses but there is the further and more serious problem of demonstrating that counting achromatic color responses results in a legitimate measure of depression, in the sense that the markings on a yardstick result in a valid measure of height. (It is interesting to note that the legitimacy or validity of the measuring instruments employed also becomes a problem in physical measurement in cases where very high degrees of precision are required.) Since it is necessary to be able to measure something with adequate reliability before we can determine whether the measure in fact is related to the concept of concern, we shall discuss reliability first.

RELIABILITY

Reliability refers to the repeatability of measurement. In a hypothetical situation where the measuring procedure was completely reliable, it would be assumed that any change in the obtained measure reflected a true change in the attribute under study. Thus, in such a system, an increase of one pound on a scale would indicate that the object has gained exactly one pound of weight; and similarly, an increase in the score on a depression scale indicates that the respondent now is more depressed. Reliability is the more generic term, and the terms *consistency* and *stability* are employed to describe instrument-related and time-related reliability respectively.

Consistency refers to the agreement that is obtained by simultaneously using two or more instruments (for example scales, rulers, or tests). Any measuring instrument or set of instruments may be regarded as being drawn from a large population of such instruments (real or hypothetical) that might have been used to measure this particular attribute. Consistency is usually evaluated by simultaneous testing with another instrument or instruments, hopefully selected randomly from the available population. Although this poses little problem in the measurement of physical dimensions such as height or weight, it raises some difficult problems in personality assessment, problems to which we shall return shortly.

Stability refers to the accuracy of the obtained measurement over time. Obviously, retesting over time may involve consistency as well as stability if another instrument is used to make the second measurement. If the same instrument is used on both occasions, then we have a direct assessment of the stability of the measurement. Failure to obtain complete reliability is thus a consequence of the inconsistencies or errors that are a function of changes occurring in the system over time, or of differences associated with the particular instrument used, or both.

In general, reliability refers to many kinds of evidence which attempt to describe the agreement among measurement operations. Each bit of evidence emphasizes or focuses upon a certain source of disagreement or error and may overlook others. Personality measurement involves taking a sample of behavior at a particular time on a particular day in response to a particular set of stimuli, the responses being recorded by a particular examiner according to a particular system. Some sampling errors are associated with each of these "particulars." The particular occasion is a sample from a period of time and the particular set of stimuli or questions is a sample from the previously mentioned real or hypothetical array of available stimuli. The particular test administrator, observer, or scorer, as well as the scoring system used, are likewise single instances from real or hypothetical populations. It is important to be able to identify how much a particular response or score is likely to change as a function of changes in each of these aspects of measurement. Unfortunately, however, this type of information is rarely available in personality assessment.

Examination of recent textbooks on psychometric theory (for example, Ghiselli, 1964; Horst, 1966; Nunnally, 1967) suggests that experts differ on the philosophical assumptions to be made about the basis of psychological measurement. These differences in philosophy give rise to some differences in defining exactly what is meant by reliability and thus lead to differences in the recommended ways of assessing the reliability of a measure. In this chapter we shall try to steer a middle course through the various approaches, while attempting to avoid inconsistencies as well as issues which are beyond the scope of the book.

We shall begin with the observation that reliability is closely related to the concept of measurement error. Errors of measurement can be considered to be of two kinds—*systematic* and *random*. If we observed the time from a clock which was always five minutes fast, we would be making a systematic error. If on the other hand, the clock was accurate but was always so distant from us that we were unable to read the minute hand precisely, we would be making a random error. Systematic errors can be thought of as associated with correctable mistakes; random errors, which tend to average about the correct or absolute score, can be regarded as the "fuzziness" left in the observation when all the systematic biases have been identified and removed.

To put it another way, random measurement errors are "built into" the measuring device, as when we try to measure to the nearest tenth of an inch with a yardstick marked only in inches, or when we try to assess "depression" with an omnibus paper-and-pencil inventory scale that contains very few items dealing with the reportable clinical aspects of depression that are necessary to cover the concept of depression as it is typically understood. In contrast to these random types of error, which are difficult to avoid, systematic errors are more identifiable and more easily correctable. In a sense, systematic errors are the fault of the test developer or user rather than being inherent in the instrument. We would be risking systematic error if we administered a depression scale to subjects who lived in a different culture (or subculture) from that represented by the available norms, or if we used stressful instructions which were markedly different from those used with the normative population. These potential systematic errors can and should be corrected by developing new norms based on the appropriate cultural group or for the alternate testing conditions.

In their attempts to quantify reliability, psychometric theorists traditionally have concentrated on specifying the contribution of *random* errors to low reliability. Opinions differ on whether and to what extent *systematic* errors also should be considered a source of unreliability of measurement, and hence reflected in a numerical index of reliability. Each of the several commonly used measures of reliability reflects random error; each may also reflect some (but not all) of the sources of systematic error. The most recent revision of the American Psychological Association's *Standards for Educational and Psychological Tests and Manuals* (1966, p. 26), in recognizing this state of affairs, recommends that each investigator make clear exactly what sources of variability in scores are regarded as contributing to "error" in the particular reliability measure he reports.

Let us now consider the common methods for assessing reliability. The traditional index of reliability is the *reliability coefficient*, which can be regarded either as the correlation between the actual test scores and hypothetical "true" scores, or as the average correlation between the actual test scores and all other possible tests measuring the same characteristic. The following practical approaches to assessing reliability attempt to approximate this definition.

As we have implied above, reliability associated solely with random error (errors stemming from the fact that the content of the test is but one sample of the universe of content covering the characteristic of interest) is termed the consistency or internal consistency of a test. This can be assessed in various ways. One method, statistically sophisticated and involving complex assumptions, is by means of the *Kuder-Richardson reliability* formulas (Kuder and Richardson, 1937). The most useful of these formulas involves the percentage of items scored in a particular way, the correlations between the items and the total score, and the standard deviation of the test. These data are entered into a formula which provides a good estimate of consistency, providing the test measures only one statistical factor. The complexities of this approach are beyond our scope here, but are considered in detail in most texts on psychometrics. Another procedure is to divide the test into two comparable halves and correlate one half with the other. The obtained correlation is then "corrected" to its expected value for the full length of the test by what is known as the Spearman-Brown prophecy formula. Such an estimate of consistency, often arrived at by contrasting the odd and the even items in a test, is known as the *split-half reliability* coefficient. A similar method for determining consistency is through the use of similar or *alternate* (or *parallel*) *forms* of the test, if they are available. The correlation between the forms is essentially similar to the corrected correlation between the two halves of the same form. When alternate forms are not available, a common compromise has been the use of a retest with the same form, and the correlation between the two sets of scores is termed the *test-retest reliability* coefficient.

Test-retest and alternate-forms correlations express more than the test's consistency. If the subjects remember some of the items when taking a retest, they might give the same answers purely from memory, which would have the effect of spuriously increasing the correlation. Or, as previously noted, conditions from one testing session to the next might change, giving rise to unknown sources of systematic error. Yet again, the subjects themselves might change in the characteristic being measured. These last two circumstances would both serve to reduce the size of the reliability coefficient.

What particular method of computing a reliability coefficient should be employed in practice? A simple answer is that the coefficient should reflect the different kinds of errors in which the user is interested. Thus, if we wanted to know the test's reliability in assessing a concept, a consistency measure (Kuder-Richardson or split-half) would be appropriate. If we were interested in the test's stability in repeated administrations and under diverse conditions, then test-retest or alternate-forms reliability would be more appropriate. Hopefully, the test producer should provide both sets of data.

What are acceptable limits for reliability coefficients? To answer this question, we must look at the way in which these coefficients can be used practically. This ordinarily is done by means of the *standard error of measurement*, a quantity derived directly from the reliability coefficient and the standard deviation of the obtained scores. Representing the reliability coefficient by r, and the standard deviation by s, the standard error of measurement is the quantity $s\sqrt{1-r}$. To illustrate the meaning and use of the standard error of measurement, let us utilize the Sc scale of the MMPI. Internal consistency estimates (split-half correlation coefficients) for this scale have been reported to be in the neighborhood of 0.91 (Dahlstrom and Welsh, 1960, p. 474). The standard deviation of all MMPI scales is 10 for scaled scores. The standard error of measurement can now be calculated from the above formula to be $10\sqrt{1-0.91}$, or 3. That is to say, if it were possible to carry out the same testing many times over, the Sc scores obtained would average out to be the "true" score, but they would be distributed about this average with a standard deviation of 3.

If a distribution of scores is not markedly asymmetrical, about two out of three scores fall within one standard deviation of the mean. Thus, the chances that the scores obtained in any given test administration is within three points of the "true" score are about two out of three. To put it another way, if a respondent obtains a scaled score of 55 on Sc, the chances are about two out of three that his "true"

score is within three points of 55, that is, between 52 and 58. By
similar reasoning, since about 95 percent of the scores in a reasonably
symmetrical distribution fall within *two* standard deviations of its
mean, the chances would be about 95 percent, or 19 in 20, that our
respondent's true score would be within six points of 55, that is, between 49 and 61.

Suppose the reliability coefficient (split-half) were only 0.75 instead of 0.91, as appears to be somewhat nearer the case with the
D scale of the MMPI (Dahlstrom and Welsh, 1960, p. 474). With
a standard deviation once again of 10, the formula shows the standard
error of measurement to be $10\sqrt{1 - 0.75}$, or 5. In practical terms,
if a respondent obtained a score of 60 on the *D* scale, and we wanted
to establish a range that would be 95 percent certain to include his
"true" score, that range would be 50 through 70. Clearly, the lower
the reliability coefficient, the less reliance can be placed on a score
as an estimate of the "true" degree of the characteristic possessed by
the respondent.

In concluding our discussion of reliability, it is worth noting that
Cattell (1964) has proposed three major ways in which test consistency, the generic term he considers most preferable, might be measured. The first of these is the consistency or agreement of scores over
occasions, that is, changes in the same test given to the same people
at different times. Cattell calls this consistency "reliability." The second type of consistency is across tests (or parts of a test, or, commonly,
single items) and involves the agreement on the same occasion and
the same people over the tests (or parts). This consistency would be
termed "homogeneity." The last kind of consistency is across people
and involves the agreement as to the meaning of scores on the same
test applied at the same time to different sets of people. This third
type of consistency, labeled "transferability" (or hardiness), would
seem to be an especially neglected aspect of reliability in its traditional
sense. The transferability or generalizability of a personality assessment device over subcultures or generations is an important factor
in determining limitations on its use.

Reliability and Projective Techniques

The quantitative scores derived from projective tests often have
low reliabilities when assessed by the above methods. Since the reliability of a measure sets an upper limit on its potential usefulness or
validity, the low reliabilities often have been blamed for the low
demonstrated validities in research investigations of these tests. On
the other hand, it has also been argued that the usual methods for

assessing reliability are not applicable to projective instruments. For example, the split-half method is said to be inappropriate for the Rorschach because it is impossible to divide the ten cards in such a way as to obtain comparable halves. Test-retest reliability has been held inapplicable because a retest is regarded as a different psychological experience from the original test, and because projective techniques are said to be particularly sensitive to slight changes in the subject. Indeed, some proponents of projective tests seem to assume that such instruments are completely reliable and that the observed changes in test responses over time reflect real changes in the individual. Since many of the characteristics tapped by these tests, such as mood or energy level, do fluctuate over time, there is a certain cogency to this assumption. However, any real appreciation of the problems of reliability of measurement must lead to the conclusion that many, if not most, of these fluctuations are a function of the marginal reliability of the instruments.

There are certain measurement problems which contribute to unreliability in any test, but which tend to be particularly troublesome with projective devices. One problem has to do with test construction. In general, the stimulus materials used in projective tests have not been chosen with any thought toward ensuring that the various scoring categories would be adequately represented by the stimuli. It is often true, as with the TAT, that scoring systems were not developed until some years after the stimulus materials were selected. In the TAT, the examiner even has a choice as to which stimulus he will employ. This haphazard development of scoring categories has contributed to low reliabilities. Ratio (and difference) scores, as used in the Rorschach, are particularly vulnerable to low reliabilities. Holtzman, in developing the HIT, took care to select stimulus cards for their specific contribution to certain scoring quantities and, as a consequence, the reliabilities of most of the HIT categories are satisfactory.

A second problem involves standardization of instructions. Directions for the administration of the Rorschach and a number of other projective instruments are not standardized, and thus the examiner can significantly influence the subject's responses. For example, Gross (1959) administered the Rorschach to 30 patients, and for 20 of them he gave social reinforcement after every human content response by saying "good" or by nodding his head. The reinforced patients gave significantly more human content responses than the remaining 10 patients. The importance of such subtle examiner differences, differences of which the examiner himself may be unaware, should be clear to the reader.

Even more vexing is the problem that subjects are permitted to give a varying number of responses, of varying lengths. The latter portion of a long response or set of responses is probably different in psychological content from a short response. Short responses on the Rorschach or TAT often tend to contain mainly "popular" or banal material. Also, variability in response length makes statistical comparisons extremely difficult.

There is also the problem of scoring. In some tests, such as the MMPI, scoring is mechanical. That is, little or no subjective judgment of the categorization of a response is involved. The same is true for some of the scoring categories in tests like the Rorschach. Here, for example, determining total number of responses given involves little or no judgment, once the data have been collected. Similarly, measuring the height of a figure drawing, or its total area, is a rather mechanical procedure. But by far the majority of scores derived from projective tests involve some subjective judgment in their determination. For example, does this Rorschach response involve color or human movement? Does this TAT story reflect the need for achievement, or affiliation, or both? In Rorschach tests, unreliability of scoring is aggravated by the fact that the several scoring systems available (Toomey and Rickers-Ovsiankina, 1960), although not identical, are similar enough that psychologists often tend to overlook the differences.

The question of scoring reliability is simply one of interjudge or intrajudge agreement, but it must be remembered that unreliability of scoring contributes to overall test unreliability. Murstein (1963, pp. 144–146) has presented a summary table of scorer reliabilities for characteristics scored from the TAT. The median scorer reliability of the 45 studies where reliability was reported as a correlation was 0.74. With scorer reliabilities as low as this, the problems of achieving acceptable levels of test reliability are indeed large. It is possible, however, to achieve higher scorer reliabilities. Feld and Smith (1958) reviewed a group of studies that used the TAT scoring system devised by McClelland and his coworkers (McClelland, Atkinson, Clark, and Lowell, 1953) and reported them to have a median reliability of 0.89. Such high reliabilities require care and effort and are the exception rather than the rule.

Reliability of Global Interpretation

Too close an involvement with the above approaches to reliability determination involves a danger of missing what is, for practical purposes, the main issue involved in reliability. Tests are techniques for gathering information about personality and, usually, for making predictions about future behavior based on personality functioning. Thus, our ultimate concern with reliability should be for the reliability of the use to which the test is put. That is, if the Rorschach is employed to provide a comprehensive description of global personality functioning, then the issue is the reliability of the global descriptions, not the reliability of individual scoring categories.

What is involved in assessing global reliabilities? The procedures would be similar to those discussed previously. For example, split-half reliability would be assessed by comparing the interpretations made by examining comparable halves of the test, test-retest reliability would involve the comparison of interpretations made from two different administrations of the test, and interjudge reliability would be determined by comparing the interpretations made of the same test material by different judges. Interexaminer reliability could also be assessed in a similar fashion.

In order to make global personality descriptions which can be statistically compared with one another in this way, some common descriptive framework for personality is required. One typical procedure is to employ a series of rating scales or dimensions which are relevant to the test and to the kind of descriptive information required. Interpretation is then made by having the examiner assign scores or positions on these scales to the subjects following a study of the test protocol. A similar procedure would be to have the examiners answer a number of true-false or multiple-choice questions about the subject. Another common method is the use of the Q-sort technique. A typical Q-sort would consist of 100 cards, each containing a personality statement. The examiner is asked to study the test protocol and then to sort the descriptive statements into nine piles, representing equal intervals from least descriptive of the subject to most descriptive of him. The number of cards to be placed in each pile is determined in advance, so that every judge provides the same distribution of cards. In all the above techniques, rank correlation or percentage agreement methods can be applied to determine a numerical index of reliability. (If one wishes to determine reliabilities involving a single examiner, the number of test protocols being judged should be sufficiently large that the examiner will not be able to remember, or guess, which ones came from the same subject.)

One kind of global approach to assessing reliability, the matching technique, has been especially recommended (Holzberg, 1960). An application of this approach would be to have several examiners prepare a personality description from each of several Rorschach protocols, and then have another group of examiners attempt to match the descriptions belonging to each of the original subjects. A major problem here is that correct matchings often can be made through using obvious cues, such as highly idiosyncratic responses, that are not particularly relevant to personality. This disadvantage is particularly important where the examiners are given a series of test and retest protocols to match, but it is of less concern if they are to match personality descriptions which are prepared in a standardized format.

The kind of reliability established for any assessment procedure should be appropriate for the use to which the procedure is to be put. If predictions about specific events are to be made, it is the reliability of these predictions which should be examined. If global personality descriptions are sought, it is their reliabilities which are at issue. Although there will often be more basic sources of reliability to consider (such as scorer reliability), on which the ultimate reliabilities may depend, it is the reliability of the procedure-in-use that is the question of ultimate interest.

VALIDITY

In Chapter 3 we introduced the general notion of the *usefulness* of a test or assessment procedure, meaning the extent to which it permits us to understand and predict some of a person's nontest behavior. We have also used the word *validity* as more or less synonymous with usefulness. We will now explore the concept of validity in greater detail.

The American Psychological Association's *Standards for Educational and Psychological Tests and Manuals* (1966) considers the validity of a procedure to mean the degree to which it is capable of achieving its aims. It has long been recognized that since different tests may have different types of aims, an approach which would be appropriate for demonstrating validity in one test might well be inappropriate for another. Three approaches to the assessment of validity are generally recognized, each being specific to a particular set of aims for a test: *content, predictive,* and *construct* validity. This three-fold division in the purposes of a test is somewhat artificial, and generally it is necessary to demonstrate that a test possesses validity in more than a single way. Obviously, the establishment of validity requires much more than just the acceptance, by either the target person or the test user, of the personality description or prediction yielded by the test instrument. Forer (1949) clearly indicated the fallacy of such "testimonial" or "personal" validity in a study which demonstrated a uniformly high degree of acceptance by a sample of undergraduates of a single, identical personality description. Naturally, the students were unaware that they all had received the same feedback.

Content Validity

Content validity involves showing that the content of the test is representative of the behaviors in which we are interested. Content validity has special relevance for achievement and aptitude tests, where the responses to the test items presumably are samples of the behaviors of concern. Personality assessment by means of behavior samples and situational tests, as discussed in Chapter 5, also involves content validity by the direct elicitation of the relevant responses. For example, suppose we wished to develop a test of leadership, and we arranged for a series of behavioral samples which required the respondent to display behaviors characteristic of his responses to situational leadership demands. If these behavioral situations are a representative sample of leadership situations in general (or of some clearly identified subset of situations), and if the amount of artificiality introduced by the testing situation is minimized, we would have a valid test of leadership (or an aspect of it) simply by virtue of the fact that the *content* of the test is a representative sample of the behavior of interest. In a sense, the content validity of a test for a particular purpose is the same as the subjective evaluation of the criterion itself. If, however, the aim of a test is to predict behavior under somewhat modified real-life circumstances, such as leadership in combat, then more than content validity is required.

It sometimes is argued that paper-and-pencil personality inventories are valid simply if they appear to have content (or face) validity; that is, when they are rationally derived. Thus the presence on a depression scale of items referring to the experience of mood disturbance, loss of motivation for daily activities, and psychomotor retardation would be taken as reasonable grounds for the usefulness of the scale. But the clinical behaviors of depression cannot be sampled by the marking of an IBM true-false answer sheet. It is the nontest or real-life correlates of these marking responses that are of interest to us, and these must be demonstrated. Fortunately for test developers, we have already seen that rationality (or content validity) of a scale appears to be a necessary though not a sufficient condition for its usefulness.

Predictive Validity

In personality assessment, because of its practical orientation, we often are most concerned with predictive validity in its various forms.

Predictive validity refers to "the accuracy with which we can make guesses about one characteristic of an individual from another characteristic" (Ghiselli, 1964, p. 338). The test or assessment measure is called the predictor, and the characteristic we are guessing at is known as the criterion. A straightforward numerical index of predictive validity is given by the correlation between predictor and criterion. Predictive validity is central to the criterion groups approach to test construction. It would be the appropriate type of validity to be demonstrated if, for example, we wished to use a patient's average elevation on the MMPI scales at the time of his admission to psychiatric treatment as an index of the length of time he would be hospitalized. The correlation between average elevation and days of subsequent hospitalization would be an index of the validity of average elevation as a predictor of hospitalization.

It is important to ensure that the criterion measure does not become "contaminated" with the predictor, otherwise the correlation may be spuriously high. That is to say, the overall elevation of the patient's MMPI profile in the previous example must be given no part in determining the length of his hospitalization. This means that both in the original criterion research and in the subsequent practical use of the predictor extreme care must be exercised in maintaining the confidentiality of the predictor scores. Otherwise such scores become "self-fulfilling prophesies."

There are as many different predictive validities for any given test as there are criteria to predict. The fact that average MMPI elevation might be found to predict length of hospitalization does not ensure its success in predicting likelihood of rehospitalization, even though both criteria might be considered measures of "success of treatment." Moreover, the fact that average elevation is found to predict length of hospitalization in one particular location and with one particular population does not automatically mean that it will be successful in another location. In the latter case, cross-validation with the new population should be carried out. The procedures involved in cross-validation and the dangers of a failure to do so have been discussed in Chapter 4. Cureton (1950) provided an appropriate and amusing illustration of this point. As a general rule, predictive validity should be demonstrated for every use to which an assessment procedure is to be put.

Predictive validity does not refer necessarily to prediction in the future, although it may. It is logical, and often useful, to consider prediction to a *concurrent* event, and also *postdiction* to an event that has previously occurred but cannot be measured directly without considerable effort. For example, let us say we wished to determine the nature and degree of the interpersonal needs of a group of college students. One method would be to have trained observers follow them about for a period of time, gathering information from real-life situations. Another would be to arrange a series of situational tests. A third approach could be to administer a paper-and-pencil inventory, or have them judge themselves on a variety of rating scales. The inventory or self-ratings would represent attempts to make an economical determination of certain characteristics of the students which exist at that particular time. Validity then would be determined by arranging the more lengthy and costly behavior sample and situational test procedures, for which content validity has presumably been demonstrated, and using them as the criteria with which to compare the paper-and-pencil procedure. If these behavior samples or situational measures were available only at some future time, then we would again have future prediction.

Construct Validity

Construct validity is a term introduced by the American Psychological Association's (1954) "Technical Recommendations for Psychological Tests and Diagnostic Techniques," and elaborated by Cronbach and Meehl (1955), to provide a label for a method of demonstrating validity which had been used to some extent prior to that time, but without a complete understanding of the logic and implications of the method. It is relevant where there exists no single definitive or tangible criterion for the quality, trait, or characteristic which is to be assessed.

Cattell (1964) pointed out that validity can be dimensionalized in a number of ways. One way involves the concrete versus the abstract or the particular versus the conceptual dimension. Frequently we are interested in the correlations between scores on a test and such particular or concrete criteria as the number of psychiatric hospitalizations or the number of traffic offenses. Predictive validity studies of this nature have considerable appeal because they are immediately useful and do not require much methodological or theoretical sophistication.

Often, however, we are interested in the validity of relationships involving constructs or abstract terms, such as ego strength, anxiety, or extroversion, for which there are no single commonly accepted measures. While we can demonstrate the predictive validity of a psychiatric hospitalization scale or a criminal recidivism index by means of a single correlation, it is far more difficult to demonstrate the construct validity of an anxiety scale or for a measure of any other generalized, abstract concept in the psychological domain. What is necessary for construct validity is the gradual accumulation of supporting evidence garnered from a variety of research findings, arranged to demonstrate a *network of relationships* among the measure in question and other relevant concepts. The nature and strength of these relationships should be predictable both from the theory or theories in which the concept is embedded and from the generally understood meaning of the concept. Thus, to establish construct validity of a measure of anxiety, as the term is generally understood, one might set out to demonstrate positive relationships between the measure and behavior in temporary stress situations, most forms of psychiatric difficulty, physiological indices such as palmar sweating and heart rate, and certain other behaviors typically regarded as related to anxiety. In addition, it should be demonstrated that *no* relationship exists between the measure and certain characteristics that are presumed to be independent of anxiety, such as height or intelligence. Establishment of construct validity for an instrument best might be thought of as a continuing program in which the meaning of the construct is gradually sharpened and reified by the nature of the relationships into which it is found to enter, and by which the meaning of the construct may become clarified as unexpected relationships are discovered. In the last analysis, since there is no single coefficient or specifiable group of coefficients that, a priori, are acceptable as clearly "demonstrating" the construct validity of a measure, judgments about the degree of construct validity possessed by the device must necessarily be subjective.

The notion of "construct validity" itself has been seriously questioned (Bechtoldt, 1959; Sarbin, 1968) on the grounds that it contributes nothing to our theoretical understanding of human behavior or to the accuracy and utility of our practical work. One central issue in the objections to construct validity is the danger that the postulated attribute or construct will be taken for a *real* entity, rather than a convenient explanatory fiction. Sarbin (1968), using the construct of anxiety as the focus of his discussion of this problem, cogently pointed out the pitfalls involved in assuming that such mental states or traits as anxiety exist. The major danger, of course, is an involvement in searching for a verbal answer to questions like "What is anxiety?," a question which cannot meaningfully be answered. Sarbin argued that our attempts to construct scientific fictions or "myths" are a function of our language system and verbal habits, and that these tendencies need careful attention and control. Nevertheless, much of current research literature involving personality assessment techniques purports to involve construct validation, and so the knowledgable reader should be aware both of what is involved and of the problems inherent in this approach.

Incremental Validity

When tests are used as the basis for prediction in a clinical situation, the determination of the usefulness of the test is not as simple as determining the accuracy of prediction—that is, the predictive validities. As Sechrest (1963) has explained, tests such as the Rorschach are often ". . . interpreted after interviews, reading of case reports, conferences, and the like. It seems clear that validity must be claimed for a test in terms of some *increment* in predictive efficiency over the information otherwise cheaply and easily available" (p. 154). Meehl (1959) had earlier spoken of the "increment in valid and semantically clear information transmitted" (p. 114), and, as early as 1957, Cronbach and Gleser (1957, second edition 1965) discussed the same topic at length in regard to personnel selection.

Since the notion of evaluating the usefulness of a test according to its incremental validity in that particular situation seems so obvious and relevant, it may seem surprising that most of the diagnostic tests commonly used in clinical practice show poor incremental validity. This is partly because clinicians are not generally oriented toward constantly evaluating the efficiency of their behavior. The reader is reminded of Hathaway's (1959) estimate that if clinicians were to evaluate their testing activities from an efficiency viewpoint, more than 40 percent of these activities would be abandoned. Research which has evaluated different assessment procedures in terms of their incremental validities will be discussed in Chapter 8.

Hits and Misses

The predictive validity of an assessment device traditionally has been expressed in terms of a correlation coefficient between the predictor score and the criterion. If the criterion involves a hit-or-miss situation, such as whether a parolee will or will not violate his parole, predictive validity is sometimes more appropriately expressed in terms of the percentage of times the prediction was correct.

Working within the framework of hits and misses (or percentage correct) makes it possible to demonstrate the importance of taking into account the *base rate* of an event, that is, the proportion of times the event occurs in the population of interest. Let us use the example of parole violation. Suppose we know from past experience that 30 percent of our potential parolees are likely to violate their parole. The base rate for parole violation is thus 30 percent, or 0.30. If we were to predict the future behavior of parolees from this information alone, we would do best if we predicted that *no* parolees will violate the conditions of their parole. Since 30 percent will in fact be violators (though we have no way of knowing which 30 percent), we will be wrong 30 percent of the time. That is, we will be 70 percent accurate in our prediction. Suppose now that we have developed a test which has been shown to identify potential parole violators with 65 percent accuracy. Even though the test enables us to do better than the completely chance rate of 50 percent, we would be ahead in terms of predictive accuracy to predict directly from the base rate of 70 percent. Incidentally, once we know that the base rate of nonviolators is 70 percent, the "chance rate" of assignment is really higher than 50 percent. If we randomly assigned *any* 70 out of 100 prisoners to the "nonviolator" category, we would be correct 70 percent of the time, or 49 times. Likewise, randomly assigning the remaining 30 to the "violator" category would result in 9 correct placements. Thus, in making a chance 70/30 assignment, we would be correct 49 plus 9 or 58 percent of the time. Some psychologists would go one step further and consider that "chance" should be identified with the base rate of 70 percent. A detailed analysis of the use of base rate data in evaluating predictive accuracy has been provided by Meehl and Rosen (1955).

In the above analyses we have ignored the relative costs of the alternate outcomes. To be more precise, we have taken for granted that both kinds of possible errors—failing to identify violators and mislabeling nonviolators—would be equally costly. In practice, it is likely to be the case that an error in one direction would be more costly than an error in the other. For example, we could imagine that the cost of placing on parole a criminal who later violates his parole may be more costly, all values considered, than refusing parole to a person who would not have violated it. Analyses of the problems of taking into consideration values of alternate outcomes have been made by Arthur (1966), Buchwald (1965), Cronbach and Gleser (1965), and by Rimm (1963).

Utilization of base rate data provides insight into the danger of using automatic cutting scores on tests regardless of the population being considered. For example, Hathaway (1956b) reported that on the K-corrected Sc scale about 60 percent of schizophrenic patients in his psychiatric cross-validation group achieved a T score of 70 or greater, whereas only 2 percent of the normal cross-validation subjects scored in this range. Suppose the scale is used for diagnosis in a clinic where approximately half the patients are schizophrenic and the other half are "normal." Simple calculation (Meehl and Rosen, 1955) will show that calling schizophrenic all patients who score 70 or more will

TABLE 6-1
Percent of Patients Diagnosed Schizophrenic or Normal by the
Sc Scale, Using a Cutting Score of 70, where 50 Percent are
Actually Schizophrenic and 50 Percent are Actually Normal.

T Score	Actually Schizophrenic	Actually Normal	Total
T score 70 or more (diagnosed schizophrenic)	30*	1	31
T score below 70 (diagnosed normal)	20	49*	69
Total	50	50	100

* Correctly diagnosed

result in 79 percent of all patients being correctly diagnosed. The calculation is portrayed in Table 6-1. Further, of those patients diagnosed schizophrenic by the test, 30/31 or 97 percent are in fact schizophrenic. Most of the errors made will be in the direction of mislabeling schizophrenics as nonschizophrenic, so that a *lower* cutting score (for example, 65) would raise the overall diagnostic efficiency. The main point is that the use of 70 as a cutting score assures that almost all patients labeled schizophrenic by the test are, in fact, schizophrenic. The *Sc* scale, in practice, is not quite so successful as portrayed here, because some of the 50 percent who are normal will achieve high *Sc* scores owing to other disorders.

Now suppose we were to give the test to apparently normal college students. Let us assume that about one percent of these students are schizophrenic. If the same cutting score of 70 is used, the test will diagnose 2.6 percent of them as schizophrenic. This situation is represented in Table 6-2. In other words, most of the students scoring 70 or more on the *Sc* scale are *not schizophrenic*. Conceptualizing the prediction in terms of hit-and-miss and base rates makes it clear that although the predictive accuracy is much higher for college students (97.6 percent) than for patients (79 percent), the test entirely fails in its function when used with the population for which it was not intended. This, however, is not to deny that the high *Sc* scoring college students would tend to be different in some way or other from the lower scoring students, and these differences can be ascertained from specific validity studies conducted on college students.

The above example on the danger of using automatic cutting scores

TABLE 6-2
Percent of Students Diagnosed Schizophrenic or Normal by the
Sc Scale Using a Cutting Score of 70, where 1 Percent are
Actually Schizophrenic and 99 Percent are Actually Normal.

T Score	Actually Schizophrenic	Actually Normal	Total
T score 70 or more (diagnosed schizophrenic)	0.6*	2.0	2.6
T score below 70 (diagnosed normal)	0.4	97.0*	97.4
Total	1	99	100

* Correctly diagnosed

also points up another problem of predictive accuracy, that of predicting events which occur infrequently. Thus, Table 6-2 suggests that it would probably be wasted effort to try to employ the Sc scale for the efficient identification of the few schizophrenics among a college population. The problem of predicting infrequent events has been dealt with in detail by Rosen (1954), using suicide as the infrequent event of interest. Estimating the suicide rate among psychiatric patients as 0.0033, and assuming a "correct" prediction rate of 75 percent, Rosen presented hypothetical data to show that even if the cutting score on a suicide detection index were raised so high that only 2.5 percent of the actual suicide cases were correctly identified, more than 98 percent of those patients called "suicide" would have been incorrectly labelled. Needless to say, the same problem is present, though often unrecognized, in attempting to identify potential suicide patients by clinical or subjective judgment.

Since the necessity for identifying patients who are potentially suicidal exists regardless of the difficulty of the prediction, ways of dealing with the potential of suicide must be found. Rosen pointed out that since hospital administrators take the attitude that suicide should be prevented at almost any cost, the usual procedure is to err on the side of safety, by identifying an enormous number of "false positives." Thus, almost any patient who shows signs (whether clinical or on a psychometric index) regarded as suicidal will be treated as a potential suicide risk. Also, some improvement in psychometric prediction would result from the careful collection of detailed data over a number of years, in order to permit more precise classification and the identification of certain subgroups of patients for whom suicide might be relatively more frequent. Such data have in fact recently been published by Farberow, Shneidman, and Neuringer (1966), and have been utilized by Diggory (1969) in a cost analysis of suicide prevention.

Selection Ratios

In discussing predictive and concurrent validity, we have assumed that predictions or decisions are to be made for every client examined. That is, we have had to make a decision for every person involved. Under some circumstances, we shall have a slightly different problem—that of *selection*. Here, an assignment does not have to be made for everybody. Suppose we are asked to select 10 schizophrenic patients from a ward of 200. Let us say we know from past experience that there are about 100 schizophrenics on the ward, although we do not know exactly who they are. Our chances of performing this selection successfully by administering a test for schizophrenia and selecting the 10 highest scores are quite high, even if the predictive validity of the test is mediocre. The reason for this is that we are not going to make a prediction for the majority of the patients. All we have to do is to make a prediction about the few patients about whom we are most likely to be correct—that is, those with extreme scores.

The *selection ratio* is defined as the number of people to be selected compared to the total number considered. In the above example, this ratio is 10 to 200 or 0.05. The smaller the ratio, the more successful the selection will be, given the same predictive validity for the test. Another factor which influences accuracy of selection is the proportion of suitable patients in the group being considered, that is, the base rate. In the above example, the base rate is 100 to 200 or 0.50. Tables are available (Taylor and Russell, 1939) to indicate the expected accuracy of selection, given a specific predictive validity, base rate, and selection ratio. In the above example, suppose the schizophrenia test had a predictive validity correlation coefficient of 0.4; the Taylor-Russell tables show that we would most likely have successfully identified 8 schizophrenics out of 10. Suppose, however, that there were only 20 patients to select from, still assuming that half are really schizophrenic. The selection ratio would now be 10 to 20 or 0.50, and the Taylor-Russell tables indicate that our most likely selection would be 6 schizophrenics out of 10, or only slightly above the chance selection of 5 out of 10.

Selection ratios are important where many people are competing for a few openings. Under such circumstances, a test with fairly low predictive validities can be used to provide fairly accurate selection. This situation often arises in the selection of a person to fill a desirable job from among many candidates, and it would also arise where there are limited treatment services available, such as psychotherapy, and many patients desiring treatment.

Summary

Reliability has to do with the repeatability of a measure. Reliability across presumably equivalent forms of a measuring instrument is called *consistency*. *Stability* refers to reliability over time. Lack of reliability, or measurement error, can be either systematic or random. Systematic errors, or biases, can be corrected for or allowed for. Random error can be regarded as stemming from the fact that the content of a test is simply one small sample of the universe of content covering the characteristic of interest. A number of different practical techniques are available for assessing reliability, and which one is used should depend on what sources of unreliability are to be assessed. The Kuder-Richardson formulas assess only random error and give an estimate of the internal consistency of a test. Split-half reliability also gives an estimate of random error; alternate-forms and test-retest reliabilities estimate varying degrees of random and systematic error. For practical use of reliabilities in determining the accuracy of a test score, the standard error of measurement can be determined from the reliability coefficient and the standard deviation of the obtained scores.

The special problems associated with determining reliabilities of some projective tests have often led to the inappropriate conclusion that reliability considerations should not apply to them. These problems stem from several sources: the fact that the tests were not constructed with the reliability of scoring categories in mind, the lack of standardization of instructions for administering and scoring the tests, and the subjective aspects of scoring. One approach has been to concentrate on the reliabilities of the various uses to which the test results are to be put; that is, the reliability of global interpretations. This approach, in spite of a number of difficulties, is probably the most appropriate for projective techniques.

Validity may be considered as the degree to which an assessment procedure is capable of achieving its aims. Since different tests may have different kinds of aims, an approach that is appropriate for demonstrating validity in one test or situation may be inappropriate for another. Content or face validity is claimed for a test whose content is a representative sample of the behaviors of interest. Predictive and concurrent validity refer to the accuracy with which guesses about a certain characteristic of the individual, the criterion, can be made from another characteristic, the predictor. Construct validity is relevant where there exists no definitive criterion for the characteristic which is to be assessed, so that it is desirable to demonstrate a network of relationships between the measure of interest and a variety of relevant concepts.

In a clinical situation, the simple predictive accuracy of a test is less important than its incremental validity. Incremental validity is the degree to which a test improves the accuracy of the prediction above the level achieved without the test. It is suspected that if closer attention were paid to incremental validities, much present-day routine clinical testing activity would be dispensed with.

As can be demonstrated when accuracy of prediction is evaluated in terms of hits and misses, it is important to know the base rate or frequency of the event of interest in the population. It is also important to know the cost or value associated with making an incorrect decision in one direction or the other. If the problem is one of selection rather than prediction, that is, if a prediction does not have to be made about every subject on whom information is available, then the selection ratio also becomes a factor in determining predictive efficiency.

7 RESPONSE DISTORTIONS

Responses to personality assessment procedures are influenced by other variables beside the personality characteristics of the respondents. Although an individual's personality characteristics are generally assumed to be the major determinants of his response, we now know on the basis of both research and theory that these responses are complex products of a number of psychological, sociological, linguistic, and other variables, many of which have nothing to do with the purposes for which the assessment procedure was designed. For example, personality test responses may be influenced by a conscious desire to appear well-adjusted, or by the obviousness of the "correct" answers to various items. Responses may also be influenced by recent prior experiences, such as viewing a dramatic motion picture film. As a further example, there are subcultural differences in the use of evaluative words such as "often" and "very," which may affect test answers. An understanding of how these systematic irrelevancies, typically termed response biases, response sets, or response styles, affect the responses to personality assessment devices is necessary both for improving our effectiveness in utilizing our current instruments and for developing new ones. In our discussion we shall employ the generic term *response distortions*.

Cronbach (1941, 1942, 1946, 1950) was the first to direct attention to response distortions. He was concerned with the distorting effects of generalized tendencies for students to guess when in doubt on true-false classroom achievement examinations. The concern about response distortions was later extended by Cronbach and others to personality measurement instruments, first to those of the self-report variety and then to the Rorschach, TAT, and others. Some critics have even tended toward the extreme position that answers to personality tests reflect little else but response distortions, and that any efforts to use these

tests for assessing the underlying response tendencies typically subsumed under the rubric of personality are doomed to failure. Another
view, one with which we are in accord, is that response distortions
themselves are consistencies in behavior which sometimes permit useful
inferences about the personality of the persons who evidence them.
The major issue here, and throughout our discussion of personality
assessment, is the degree to which inferences made from responses
to assessment devices can be shown to have an empirical basis. Responses which are not related to any nontest behaviors of interest constitute, by definition, *error variance* and strong efforts must be exerted
to eliminate or to substantially reduce them. On the other hand, responses which are related to personality-relevant behaviors should be
studied and understood, no matter what they are called or what brings
them about.

There are two kinds of response distortion. The first, *response
style* (Jackson and Messick, 1958), refers to the tendency to distort
responses in a particular direction more or less regardless of the content
of the stimulus. Examples of response styles are the tendency to answer
"true" a disproportionate number of times on true-false inventories,
and the tendency to choose a particular numbered alternative, such
as alternative "C," in a multiple-choice task. On the Rorschach, the
tendency to respond to the whole blot or the color rather than the
shape of the blot would also be an example of response style. Since
the content of a test stimulus is usually a powerful determiner of
the response that will be given, the influence of response styles will
become greater as the content becomes more ambiguous. Thus, we
have the interesting situation that with instruments whose stimulus
content is relatively ambiguous, such as the Rorschach and the TAT,
response styles have been deliberately assessed and have been regarded
as important indices of personality factors, while with self-report questionnaires, at least until recently, response-style parameters have been
treated largely as error variance.

The second kind of response distortion, *response set*, refers to the
". . . conscious or unconscious desire on the part of the respondent
to answer in such a way as to produce a certain picture of himself.
In this traditional usage, an individual may have a set to dissimulate,
to malinger, to appear aggressive, to fake good, to get the job, etc."
(Rorer, 1965, p. 133). As distinct from response styles, which may
be regarded as relatively "contentless," response sets are largely determined by the stimulus content: the clearer or less ambiguous the content, the more susceptible it is to the influence of response sets. Since
tests like the Rorschach and the TAT are more ambiguous in stimulus

content than the self-report personality questionnaires, it has been assumed that the former are less susceptible to the influence of response sets than the latter, but research evidence to be discussed later in the chapter indicates that this assumption is not well supported.

It should be recognized that a particular response or pattern of responses could be evoked by either a response style, a response set, or some simultaneous interaction of both a set and a style. Thus "defensiveness" could refer both to the response set of generally revealing very little about oneself and to the response style of choosing the "cannot say" or "uncertain" category on questionnaires which included such a choice. A well-designed program of personality assessment would include provisions for dealing with both aspects of response distortion.

In the remainder of this chapter we shall consider to what extent response styles and sets interfere with personality assessment and to what extent we may capitalize on them to enhance the assessment procedure. We shall first examine what is currently known about the role of response styles in assessing personality, starting our discussion with acquiescence.

Acquiescent Response Style

The response style that has been the most thoroughly researched is that of acquiescence, or the tendency to respond "true" in a true-false questionnaire. In its most extreme form an acquiescent response style would lead to a "true" response to all items, regardless of content, including such items as "I murdered my mother." It would also lead a respondent to answer affirmatively to two contradictory statements, for example "I am happily married" and "I am unhappily married." Fortunately, extreme instances are rarely encountered and concern about acquiescence has been mainly directed toward its influence on ambiguous items like "I often worry about unfulfilled responsibilities." On this item, a positive response may result from the fact that the respondent does indeed behave in that fashion; but it may also mean that he is uncertain about this behavior and his response has been determined by an acquiescent response style. Whenever personality questionnaires contain many relatively ambiguous items on which the majority of the keyed responses are in the same direction, the scores are open to the influence of an acquiescent response style.

Much ingenious research has been conducted in an effort to evaluate the influence of acquiescence. One popular approach has been to develop an alternate form of a personality questionnaire, one that contains reversals of the items in the original questionnaire. For example, if the original item was "I am nervous," then the reversed item might be "I am not nervous," or perhaps "I am calm." If both forms of the questionnaire were administered to a group, and if individuals responded consistently to the *content* of the items, the resulting correlation between the two forms should be high and negative, approaching in value the reliability of the original form. To the extent to which an acquiescent response style influenced the responses, this correlation would be reduced.

A number of item-reversal or direction-of-wording studies have been conducted in an effort to demonstrate that acquiescence exerts a strong effect on scores on the California F Scale, a measure of authoritarian personality tendencies (Adorno, Frenkel-Brunswick, Levinson, and Sanford, 1950). Although in many of the studies item-reversal forms have indeed yielded lower correlations with the original form than has retesting with the original form, Rorer (1965) and others have pointed out that exact reversals of inventory items are extremely difficult to write and that the lower correlations obtained are probably due to the differences in item wording. As an illustration of this point, the reader might consider whether either of the two alternatives given above to the sample item "I am nervous" is the exact logical reversal of the original.

Because of this problem of item wording, Rorer (1965) concluded that acquiescence as a response style is "of no more than trivial importance" (p. 129). He underscored the significance of an observation made by Wiggins (1962) in regard to a study (Couch and Keniston, 1960) where subjects were asked to rate their agreement or disagreement to personality items on a seven-point scale. Wiggins observed that the subjects' responses were pretty well confined to the middle part of the scale and that the majority of the subjects gave approximately equal proportions of "agree" and "disagree" responses. On the other hand, Campbell, Siegman, and Rees (1967) concluded that acquiescence, as evaluated by direction-of-wording studies, has a "dependable, albeit often small . . . effect" (p. 293), particularly for the California F Scale and for some of the MMPI clinical scales, Hysteria (*Hy*), Psychopathic Deviate (*Pd*), Paranoia (*Pa*) and Hypomania (*Ma*). They insist that this effect is not as important as some critics have claimed, but they do feel that it is significant enough not to be ignored in test construction and analysis.

Some researchers have attempted to demonstrate that extroversion or expressiveness (one of the two principal factors yielded by factor-analyses of personality questionnaires) is actually best described as acquiescence. Two somewhat different lines of reasoning have stemmed from this position: (1) that the factor is therefore trivial, and (2) that acquiescence itself is the important personality variable. Couch and Keniston (1960) offered support for the latter position by demonstrating that high and low scorers on their Overall Agreement Score represented opposites on a hypothetical personality continuum, which they labeled "stimulus acceptance" versus "stimulus rejection." Block (1965) questioned the adequacy of these conclusions on the grounds that the Overall Agreement Scores themselves were inadvertently biased because of the content of the items and that it was the content, not acquiescent response style, which led to their results. In order to disentangle the confounded effects of content and style, Block constructed acquiescence-free MMPI scales by eliminating items from the scales until they were balanced for "true" and "false" keying. A series of factor analyses of responses to these modified (and presumably acquiescence-free) scales produced the same factorial structure as had been obtained with the original scales, leading Block to conclude that acquiescence was not a significant variable in the factor structure of the MMPI and that the structure was therefore determined by item content.

Studies have also been made of the relationships among the various measures of the acquiescent response style and how these measures are related to nontest behavioral indices of an "acquiescent personality." Although some positive relationships have been reported, most of the findings have been negative. For example, Mogar (1960) found a relatively low correlation between two reversed forms of the California F Scale, and no relationship between either form and an independent criterion of authoritarianism. Husek (1961) developed a reliable measure of acquiescence by having subjects "agree" or "disagree," supposedly by mind reading, to statements about which the experimenter was thinking but never verbalized. However, this measure was unrelated to a variety of other personality trait measures.

Why have many measures of acquiescence, especially the total number of "yes" responses to an inventory, been found to be significantly correlated with such personality dimensions as extroversion or stimulus acceptance? Rorer (1965) suggested that, due to our language structure, we characteristically ask certain kinds of questions in certain ways. To ask these questions in a "reversed" form would be awkward and clumsy. In other words, it is a structural characteristic of our English language that the items assessing certain behaviors ordinarily will be written to be keyed for a "yes" answer.

It is quite reasonable to conceptualize a personality characteristic or underlying response predisposition of acquiescence, or agreeableness, which could be tapped by the content of the items rather than by response style. Thus, Norman (1963c) identified such a dimension in the five factors that he regarded as basic in his factor-analytic study of personality structure. However, it seems fair to conclude that stylistic measures of acquiescence have not provided a very useful means for tapping the personality variable of acquiescence. In general, the conclusion drawn by Rundquist (1966) seems to be defensible: that the role of acquiescence response style in personality assessment is a minor one, but nevertheless it is important enough not to be ignored.

Deviant Response Style

Another style or mode of responding to personality test items that has attracted considerable interest is that of making atypical or unusual responses. There are certain modal or usual responses to personality test items that are given by the general population; for example, an affirmative response to the inventory item "my father was a good man," the response of a "a bat" to Card V of the Rorschach, or the drawing of a clothed figure on the Draw-a-Person test. It is presumed that variations or deviations from these usual or modal responses to test items are indicative of some general tendency towards deviance.

This position has been formally articulated by Berg (1955, 1957, 1959) as the Deviation Hypothesis: "Deviant response patterns tend to be general; hence those deviant behavior patterns which are significant for abnormality and thus regarded as symptoms are associated with other deviant response patterns which are in noncritical areas of behavior and which are not regarded as symptoms of personality aberration" (1955, p. 62). Berg, who is the chief proponent of this argument, has insisted that the Deviation Hypothesis involves and characterizes deviance both in the direction of pathology and in that of giftedness and creativity. Thus schizophrenics and research scientists are both presumably deviant in showing certain responses to test items which distinguish them from each other and from the general public. It is important to note that, according to the Deviation Hypothesis, the content of the test items is irrelevant. Thus, the test items can be content-free, such as the preference for simple geometric designs. All that is necessary is that the stimuli will evoke response patterns, some of which can be identified as deviant on a clear-cut statistical basis. Berg (1959, p. 89) has suggested that the stimuli should be relatively unstructured since ambiguity of structure heightens the operation of stylistic factors, and he has emphasized the need only for empirical validity.

We have noted that the relative ambiguity of such instruments as the Rorschach is quite likely to evoke differences in response style, and thus deviant response style should be an important consideration in the interpretation of these instruments. Rorschach himself initially noted (1942, p. 23) that most responses to his inkblots are determined by the form of the blot, and "in order to avoid subjective evaluation," he developed the "definite range of normal form visualizations"—the so-called good form or F+ responses—based upon the actual responses given by 100 normal persons. Rorschach noted that good form perception was disturbed by various psychopathological states, especially schizophrenia, and he stated that "the more stable the emotions, the better the form visualization" (p. 31). The evaluation of form level accuracy of perception in Rorschach responses by means of the frequency of occurrence of these responses has been more thoroughly studied and reported by Beck et al. (1961) and by Hertz (1951). In contemporary Rorschach interpretation (cf. Allison, Blatt, and Zimet, 1968), the form level as determined by frequency tables and by the examiner's judgement and clinical experience is considered to be an important index of the general level of deviance or psychopathology to be attributed to the subject.

In order to demonstrate the direct application of the Deviation Hypothesis, Berg developed the Perceptual Reaction Test (PRT) (Berg, Hunt, and Barnes, 1949). This consists of a series of simple geometrical line drawings and the subject checks either "like much," "like slightly," or "dislike much," for each design. In summarizing a series of studies in which the PRT was used to distinguish between groups of normals and psychiatric patients, Berg (1959) concluded that the meaningless designs of the PRT are just as effective as stimuli for differentiating the groups as are stimuli involving traditional verbal content (that is, the personality questionnaire).

The Deviation Hypothesis has been severely criticized by a number of students of personality measurement (such as Rorer, 1965; and Sechrest and Jackson, 1962, 1963), on much the same bases as others have criticized the concept of an acquiescent response style. First, Sechrest and Jackson have reported that there is little evidence to support the generality of deviant response tendencies even on content-free "noncritical" assessment devices. Second, in typical studies of the Deviation Hypothesis it is not possible to decide whether the individual's responses are due to a deviant style or to the subtle item content. As Rorer (1965, p. 139) has noted, since reliable scales of deviance have been established, for example, on the PRT, and since the subjects are not responding simply to a particular response alternative, then on logical grounds they must be responding to the item content, at least in part. Third, studies by Norman (1963b), Duff (1965), and Goldberg and Slovic (1967), summarized in Chapters 3 and 4, have clearly shown the importance of item content in personality assessment devices of the questionnaire type. Finally, it should be noted that the Deviation Hypothesis is extremely general, predicting only that deviance on one response measure will be correlated with deviance on some other response measure in some unspecified direction. For the Deviation Hypothesis to be practically useful, and more than trivial in its importance, greater specificity is required; that is, it must be specified precisely what deviations in behavior would be predictable from particular patterns of deviation on assessment devices such as the PRT.

Response Style: Comment

It seems rather safe to conclude that the distorting influence of response styles in personality assessment has been overemphasized, as has the necessity of regarding stylistic factors as major personality variables in themselves. In self-report questionnaires, the possibility that response style may significantly affect test-takers' responses can be reduced by taking steps to ensure that each scale contains a comparable number of items keyed "true" and "false," and by integrating the "cannot say" and "uncertain" responses (where they are permitted) directly into the scoring scheme.

Several lines of evidence suggest that stylistic factors have been overemphasized even in projective techniques and that here, too, content variables may be more important than stylistic ones. First, following an evaluation of personality assessment based upon a variety of Rorschach scoring categories, Zubin (1954) concluded that response content showed greater promise than stylistically based formal scoring categories. An example can be found in the work of Elizur (1949), who developed a quantified and highly reliable content scoring scheme for manifest anxiety and hostility in Rorschach protocols that appears to have good validity. More recently, Zubin, Eron, and Schumer (1965), in their discussion of the Rorschach, have concluded that "content approaches offer some promise, and the validity picture is not dim" (p. 237). A second line of evidence is exemplified by Murstein (1965), who concluded that, of the various projective stimuli used in assessment, sentence-completion tasks, which are the most content-oriented of these stimuli, have the greatest demonstrated usefulness. This position is supported by research reviews of the Bender Visual-Motor Gestalt Test (Billingslea, 1963) and of projective drawings (Swensen, 1957, 1968; Roback, 1968); the reviews concluded that these

less content-oriented projective instruments have very limited usefulness for personality assessment other than as screening devices.

Social Desirability Response Set

We concluded above that response styles (content-free distortions
of responses to personality assessment devices) are relatively minor
variables in most of our efforts to evaluate personality. The situation
is rather different, however, when we consider response *sets*, the tendency to systematically "slant" responses to personality assessment
items. The reader should recall that our definition of response set includes both the deliberate efforts by the subject to bias his answers
in a particular direction and also his subtle, unconscious tendencies
to make biased responses.

The most ubiquitous of all response sets is that of defensiveness,
or the set to "fake good." One recent approach to understanding this
problem has been through the study of a special case of defensiveness,
the *social desirability* response set, or the tendency to give what the
individual regards as socially desirable responses rather than straightforward responses which would more accurately reflect his personality.
To anticipate our conclusion with regard to social desirability response
set, we shall find that persons who respond in a socially desirable
fashion "naturally" or unconsciously are probably reflecting their personality characteristics accurately, and that it is the conscious, deliberate attempts to make oneself appear socially desirable that constitute
an important source of response distortion. We shall use the term "social desirability" to refer to the natural production of socially desirable
responses, and the term "defensiveness" for the deliberately biased
efforts in this direction.

The initial research on social desirability as a response set in
personality assessment was reported by Edwards (1953). He obtained
college students' ratings of a variety of self-report inventory items
on a nine-point scale, according to how desirable they regarded the
behavior involved in each item. He then asked another group of students to take these same items as a self-report personality assessment
device, and found a very high positive correlation (0.87) between the
frequency of endorsement of each item by the second group and the
mean social desirability ratings of the first. In other words, these college
students were, to an overwhelming degree, responding to the items
in what they perceived as the socially desirable direction. Edwards
(1962, 1964a, 1964b) went on to demonstrate that a person's scores
on the MMPI scales were so highly correlated with his social desirabil-

ity ratings of the individual items that his actual MMPI profile could be predicted moderately well from these ratings. Following Edwards' lead, several recent factor-analytic investigations of the MMPI (Edwards and Heathers, 1962; Edwards and Diers, 1962; Jackson and Messick, 1962) have interpreted the high correlation between social desirability ratings and the primary factor loading of the MMPI (that is, the factor typically labeled "ego strength," or "anxiety" when scored in reverse) as an artifact of social desirability response set rather than a measure of adjustment level. Although the research on social desirability has been primarily conducted within the framework of self-report personality questionnaires, there is no reason to believe that responses in projective approaches to personality assessment may not also be related to their social desirability. In one of the few studies that have attempted to investigate this phenomenon, Reznikoff (1961) reported insignificant correlations between the social desirability ratings of a series of common TAT themes and their frequency of endorsement, and concluded that social desirability is not an important source of variance in the production of the TAT themes. However, until more information is available, no definite conclusions should be drawn on this matter.

The conclusion that social desirability response set is the most basic, or even a very important, variable influencing responses on personality questionnaires has been seriously challenged on a number of grounds—methodological, empirical, and theoretical. Norman (1967), for example, has noted that the statistical designs used by Edwards, and hence his results, "are basically irrelevant to the problem under consideration" (p. 276). A number of investigators have offered evidence that there are important differences in the correlations obtained between general or grouped social desirability ratings and frequency of endorsement of MMPI items and the correlations between *individual* social desirability ratings and the same frequencies of endorsement; further, this difference is most marked for psychiatric patients. Taylor (1959) has shown this to be the case, obtaining correlations of 0.79 and 0.36, respectively, for a group of schizophrenic patients. These results suggest that individuals whose own social behavior is not socially desirable will be less influenced by the social desirability characteristics of an item than will persons whose behavior is more desirable. Indeed, it should be noted that the most important criticism of psychopathological behavior in general is its social undesirability.

Another empirical demonstration that social desirability is not a distorting factor in responses to personality inventory items was reported by Heilbrun and Goodstein (1961a). Recognizing that each pair of statements in the EPPS had been matched on social desirability on a group basis (see Chapter 3 for further details on the development of the EPPS), but that conceptions of what is socially desirable differ from person to person, these authors asked subjects to rate the EPPS statements for social desirability. Then, for two of the EPPS scales, they rematched the item pairs uniquely for each subject on the basis of his own social desirability ratings, thus providing a personalized version that controlled for individual differences in social desirability. Each subject's scores on the regular versions of the two scales were also obtained. The validities of the two regular scales were slightly poorer than those of the personalized scales, suggesting that the EPPS procedure was not completely successful in eliminating the influence of social desirability on inventory responses.

Yet another important line of refutation of the importance of social desirability response set is provided by the factor-analytic studies of Block (1965). Using a procedure similar to that involved in his study of acquiescence response style, Block modified the regular MMPI scales by eliminating items so that their scores were free of any influence of social desirability. A series of factor analyses of these desirability-free scales produced factor structures that were essentially the same as those produced by factor analysis of the original MMPI items, strongly indicating that social desirability response set did not account for any significant response variability on the MMPI.

A cogent argument against regarding social desirability as a response set at all is the theoretical argument that social desirability is an important predictor variable. Normal individuals ordinarily behave in normal, that is, socially desirable ways—indeed, this is what is typically meant by "normal." And as we noted earlier, social undesirability of behavior is perhaps the most important criterion of psychopathology. That psychopathological persons tend to admit being psychologically disturbed by their responses to questionnaire items, such as those on the MMPI, is an easily demonstrable fact; and that their disturbed behavior is socially undesirable is also immediately obvious. As Heilbrun (1964) has noted, the tendency to make socially undesirable responses to personality questionnaires would seem to be sufficiently related to the production of nontest undesirable behavior that a prediction from one to the other is possible. The conclusion that the production of socially desirable behavior is a correlate of adjustment or psychological health seems inescapable, and this conclusion precludes the relegation of social desirability to the category of response distortion.

Defensiveness

A serious problem in the evaluation of personality is the tendency of persons to *deliberately* slant or bias their responses to personality assessment devices. Although the following discussion will center on the problem of defensiveness, or the deliberate efforts of persons to present a favorable or well-adjusted picture of themselves, similar comments could be made about the efforts of individuals to slant their responses on other personality attributes, such as extroversion or persistence. Meehl and Hathaway (1946), in reviewing past efforts to deal with the problem of defensiveness in personality assessment, pointed out that most developers of personality tests (especially tests of the self-report inventory type) were aware of these problems but could offer no effective solution. Indeed, it is the obviousness of the problems connected with personality inventories that accounts in part for the popularity of the projective approaches to personality assessment, because it is widely believed that the projective approach obviates or at least sharply reduces these problems. We shall shortly examine this belief in some detail.

Evidence on the prevalence of defensiveness as a problem in personality assessment comes from a variety of sources. First, normal-appearing personality test profiles are often obtained from psychiatric patients and other deviant individuals who should not produce normal profiles. Second, there is much evidence that a variety of subject groups, such as college students and psychiatric patients, can alter their personality test responses upon request, especially on self-report questionnaires, in order to make a good (or better) impression. It is worth noting that even college students, who ordinarily produce rather normal personality questionnaire profiles, can produce more favorable profiles under "fake good" instructions. This is especially true on inventories with largely obvious items, that is, where the social desirability of responses is quite apparent. For example, Fosberg (1941), using the Bernreuter Personality Inventory, was able to show that the correlation between scores obtained under normal instructions and those secured under "fake good" instructions was quite modest (0.11), clearly indicating how a defensiveness set can affect inventory responses of this sort.

On the other hand, there is considerable evidence to suggest that t is not possible for disturbed individuals, especially psychiatric patients, to completely simulate a normal profile, particularly on inventories that involve items that are more subtle, that is, where the social desirability of the responses is not quite so apparent. In one investigation of this aspect of the problem, Grayson and Olinger (1957) demonstrated that only 11 percent of a group of psychiatric patients could fake a normal MMPI profile. While some patients responded to these instructions by producing more deviant profiles, others simply produced a different pattern of abnormality on their profiles. Further, Canter (1963) has demonstrated that the ability to "fake good" is itself related to the relative adjustment of the individual. Using groups of alcoholics and applicants for employment, Canter found that the better adjusted subjects were the more successful in producing "fake good" profiles on the California Psychological Inventory. A recent study by Lanyon (1967b) has suggested that these findings might also hold in the simulation of pathological profiles. In this study, well-adjusted college students were shown to be superior to poorly adjusted students in their ability to simulate an MMPI pattern suggestive of psychopathic personality.

There is a strong belief on the part of some psychologists that projective techniques, especially the Rorschach, are not susceptible to this kind of conscious dissimulation. This position received some support from an early series of studies by Fosberg (1938, 1941) in which subjects were at various times instructed to make the worst possible impression, to make the best possible impression, and to respond in a straightforward, natural manner. Although Fosberg regarded his results as indicating that the Rorschach was indeed resistant to faking, his statistical procedures have been criticized as faulty (for example, Ainsworth, 1954). Also, several later studies (Carp and Shavzin, 1950; Feldman and Graley, 1954; Henry and Rotter, 1956) have provided evidence contradicting Fosberg's conclusions. These latter studies strongly suggest that the Rorschach is in fact vulnerable to faking in both the good and bad directions; they further suggest that normal subjects may be more capable of distorting their responses than psychiatric patients, and that it is somewhat easier to "fake bad" than to "fake good."

Research on dissimulation with other projective instruments, although quite sparse, tends to support these conclusions. For example Weisskopf and Dieppa (1951) showed that subjects could successfully dissimulate in both positive and negative directions in producing TAT stories, and generally were more successful at "faking bad," a conclusion also supported by the more recent work of Kaplan and Eron (1965). In a study using Rosenzweig's (1945) Picture Frustration Test Schwartz, Cohen, and Pavlik (1964) found that instructional sets to be defensive or to be frank produced predictably different responses from their subjects. Similarly, Meltzoff (1951) was able to show that responses to sentence completion stems could be distorted in both "fake good" and "fake bad" directions.

The above studies support the conclusion that the problem of defensiveness on projective devices for personality assessment is a serious one. It is particularly interesting to note that, in their clinically oriented guide to Rorschach interpretation, Phillips and Smith (1953) devoted an entire section to the problems involved in interpreting guarded or defensive Rorschach protocols. Not surprisingly, their characteristics of defensive protocols—fewer responses than expected, a reduction in response determinants other than form, and an increase in the number of popular responses—correspond approximately to those characteristics isolated subsequently by Henry and Rotter (1956) in an experimental study of this problem.

Combating Defensiveness

The conscious and deliberate efforts of some test-takers to slant their responses (especially in the positive direction) to personality assessment devices of both the inventory and projective varieties constitute a serious problem. Perhaps the simplest and most direct approach in dealing with the problem is to appeal for the cooperation and honesty of test-takers in making their responses. But this kind of candor and willingness for self-disclosure involves a fairly complex set of attitudes, and may not be as easily obtainable as we would hope. It seems safer to assume that defensiveness will probably be a significant factor in most personality evaluation situations, and to make attempts to evaluate or control it by other strategies.

While students of projective techniques have tended to rely upon subtle clinical signs of dissimulation, workers interested in self-report questionnaires have attempted a variety of other approaches to reducing these problems. One common approach is the use of *detection* devices. Thus, a number of inventories have included special scales in an effort to assess the degree to which the test-taker is attempting to slant his responses. For example, the verification scale of the Kuder Preference Record (Kuder, 1951) and the lie scale of the MMPI give a score indicating the number of times the individual has responded to certain items that are infrequently answered in this fashion. The verification scale is primarily aimed at identifying subjects who are responding randomly, while the lie scale attempts to identify persons with naively defensive attitudes that would suggest a strong "fake good" set. A typical item from the MMPI Lie scale is "I do not always tell the truth." Those individuals who answer more than a few such items in the naively defensive direction are typically regarded as having "faked good," and their protocols are usually considered invalid for either clinical or research use. The *F* scale of the MMPI, which represents an effort to identify those subjects who are responding in an atypical manner, contains items which are rarely answered in a particular direction. Because rare responses are usually also socially undesirable or psychopathological, the *F* scale also serves to identify persons who are attempting to "fake bad." There is a fair amount of research evidence showing that such scales are to some degree effective in identifying dissimulation (for example, Gough, 1947; Cofer, Chance, and Judson, 1949).

Since detection scales offer the psychologist little alternative but to ignore those profiles which clearly indicate dissimulation, some effort has been expended in the development of *correction* devices. Here an attempt is made to assess the degree of defensiveness present in a protocol and then to correct the profile accordingly. The *K* scale of the MMPI, developed empirically to correct for the more subtle aspects of test-taking defensiveness, is a good example of a correction device. Such scales are sometimes termed "suppressor" scales, in accordance with their presumed function of suppressing or correcting for the effects of dissimulation. It has been pointed out in Chapter 4 that the *K* scale was developed by comparing the responses of normal persons with those of psychiatric patients whose scores on the clinical scales were in the normal range, and who could thus be assumed to be "faking good." High scores on this scale are obtained by answering "true" to items such as "I have never felt better in my life than I do now." The raw *K*-scale score is used directly as a corrective variable and is added, in different fractions, to the respondent's scores on five of the clinical scales (*Hs, Pd, Pt, Sc* and *Ma*). The use of the *K* scale in this way has been shown to increase the discriminatory power of these scales, particularly in the crucial middle range of score values (Dahlstrom and Welsh, 1960, pp. 50–52). At the same time it should be recognized that suppressor scales are not likely to result in much improvement unless the predictive validity of the original scales is rather high in the first place (Norman, 1963a). Another significant point is that the optimal fractions of the *K* scale to be added can be expected to differ according to the population of interest. Heilbrun (1963) has reported a revised set of *K* correction fractions for improved validity of the MMPI among college students.

It should be noted that scores on suppressor scales such as the *K* scale themselves have interpretative value, especially in normal populations. For example, both Smith (1959) and Heilbrun (1961) have been able to demonstrate that, in a normal population of college students, the K scale is better regarded as an index of psychological health or adjustment than as a measure of defensiveness.

Another widely used approach to the control of defensiveness is through the development of forced-choice items, with the items matched in pairs (or triplets) for social desirability. Each item in the pair is keyed empirically, or by some other means, as a significant predictor of a behavior of interest. The EPPS, described in Chapter 3, employs this approach. There are a number of problems still unsolved in the forced-choice procedure. First, there is the requirement that the subject choose one of the alternatives, although neither of them may be descriptive of his behavior. We thus have no information about the absolute strength of his preference or of the personality characteristic underlying it. Second, the items in a pair, although matched in a general way for desirability, often still differ enough that faking is possible. For example, Dicken (1959) administered the EPPS twice to a group of college students, once under normal instructions and once with a set to make a good impression by scoring high on one of several of the EPPS personality characteristics. Not only were the subjects successful in their attempts to fake good, but the instructional set also produced a variety of other significant changes in the obtained EPPS scores. Third, and perhaps most important, the use of the forced-choice format may eliminate some of the critical predictive variance of the instrument. As we noted earlier, efforts to eliminate social desirability may reduce the predictive power of the instrument while they are reducing the influence of defensiveness. A recent review by Scott (1968) of studies comparing the validities of forced-choice and single-stimulus tests reached the more neutral conclusion that the validities achieved with the two approaches did not differ, and that there was no conclusive evidence for the advantage of the forced-choice approach in controlling defensiveness. Thus, it would seem that the forced-choice technique has not proved to be as advantageous a technique for personality questionnaires as had been initially anticipated.

Still another technique that has been advocated as a control for defensiveness is the use of subtle items, that is, items with empirically demonstrable predictive or concurrent validity but with little or no face validity. We have already seen, however, that subtle items tend in general to be less valid or useful than the more obvious items. Norman (1963a), who proposed a complex method for controlling dissimulation by carefully eliminating the most obvious items in his scales, came to a similar conclusion, that the use of such scales "constructed for use in one setting with one class of respondents, may not generalize widely" (p. 240).

All the above methods of attempting to handle defensiveness have some merit and all have their strong supporters. At the same time, each of these methods has some clear-cut limitations and none is a completely satisfactory procedure for handling defensiveness in responding to personality questionnaires. There are two further approaches, each involving some built-in controls, which have not yet been well explored but which seem to offer some promise. The first, initially discussed by Buss (1959) and by Buss and Durkee (1957), involves the phrasing of items in such a way that neither a true nor a false response would be regarded as particularly undesirable. For example, rather than asking the question "Sometimes I lose my temper," to which an affirmative response would be socially undesirable, we would rewrite the item as "I am afraid that I sometimes lose my temper" or "Sometimes I cannot help losing my temper," or "I am concerned about losing my temper," all of which are phrased in a less undesirable manner. From Buss's studies, it would appear that this kind of phrasing can do much to reduce problems of defensiveness. A second new approach involves a more dramatic departure from our typical conceptualizations about personality assessment. Instead of regarding personality in terms of traits or typical behaviors, we might think of personality in terms of *abilities* or maximum performance. Thus a measure of dominance might involve a situational test where the subject would be required to respond as dominantly as possible and would be evaluated on his actual performance in meeting these task expectations. For a test of maximum rather than habitual performance, the problem of faking or defensiveness becomes somewhat irrelevant. Wallace (1966, 1967) has explored some of the implications of this approach to personality assessment and we shall discuss it more completely in Chapter 10.

Summary

Response styles have been defined as tendencies to select disproportionately some response category independently of the content of the test stimulus. Acquiescence, the most widely studied response style, is the tendency to overrespond "yes" on true-false inventories. In an attempt to determine the degree to which acquiescence style distorts inventory responses, several research strategies have been used, including examination of the correlations between scores on original scales and "reversed" scales, factor-analytic studies, and comparison among various measures of acquiescence. The evidence seems to indicate that acquiescence does not exert an important distorting influence on inventory responses, and that previous conclusions to the contrary have not taken into account the contribution of item content. Deviant response style, the tendency to give responses in a deviant direction, has received somewhat less attention than acquiescence and we have concluded that this style is likewise of little practical importance in personality assessment.

Response sets have been defined as distortions produced by the respondent for the purpose of giving a certain picture of himself. Social desirability, or the natural tendency to respond in a socially desirable direction, may not be such a distorting factor as was once supposed, but may instead reflect actual (socially desirable) characteristics of the respondent. Deliberate efforts to make a good impression by consciously distorting answers, however, pose a serious problem for the validity of assessment devices that has not been adequately resolved. A variety of efforts to combat defensiveness include detection scales such as the lie scale of the MMPI, correction scales, and built-in controls such as the forced-choice technique and the use of subtle items. However, these solutions also have their problems. Contrary to popular belief, projective techniques are also quite vulnerable to respondents' efforts to slant their responses, although it appears to be somewhat more difficult to deliberately make a good impression than to make a bad one.

8 PROBLEMS OF APPLICATION

We have surveyed many of the major procedures and devices involved in contemporary personality assessment and have attempted to explain their underlying rationale and their actual development. In this chapter we shall discuss how the various devices are actually used in practical situations, some of the issues and problems involved in their use, and some proposed alternatives for contemporary practice.

Because psychologists have been engaged in personality assessment for many years, it would be reasonable to suppose that there have evolved fairly standard assessment strategies for use in any particular situation. For example, there ought to be a relatively standard approach to the evaluation of executive potential, or psychopathology, or leadership in particular situations. Unfortunately, this is not the case. There tend to be rather substantial differences among actual practitioners as to which instruments are the most useful in a given instance, and as to what should be done with the responses once they are obtained. In general, the behavior of psychologists in making decisions about assessment strategies seems to be governed more by tradition and superstition than by relevance or evidence. Commenting upon this state of affairs, Meehl (1956) has taken the position that assessment devices ought to be chosen "on the basis of their empirically demonstrated efficiency, rather than upon which one is more exciting, more 'dynamic,' more like what psychiatrists do, or more harmonious with the clinical psychologists' self-concept" (pp. 264–265). Hathaway's (1959) similar criticism has already been mentioned.

CLINICIAN VERSUS ACTUARY

The many problems involved with how the scores derived from the chosen assessment instrument or instruments should be used have recently been of great interest for research-minded assessment psychologists. The reader may wonder why such problems exist, especially for those instruments with demonstrated empirical validity, that is, with known predictive usefulness. In making a specific prediction, one might presume that the size of the validity coefficient (the known correlation of the test score with the behavior to be predicted) should permit us to make a straightforward prediction, by assuming a simple linear relationship between score and behavior. However, most contemporary assessment devices are multiphasic, so that they yield more than one score, and each of these scores has a different predictive relationship with the criterion behavior. The practitioner thus is faced with the decision of how these several scores should be combined into a single predictive statement. Another aspect of this problem is that in any given situation most contemporary psychologists will want to use several different assessment devices, and these devices yield a melange of scores and responses that require integration before any predictions can be made. Still another problem is the fact that many times the accumulated validity data involve a criterion situation that is somewhat different from the one now confronting the psychologist, so that existing validity coefficients are not directly applicable. How psychologists ought to go about using assessment data, how the scores ought to be combined, and how a specific prediction or decision should be made, have been the subjects of rather heated controversy, which has been crystallized around comparisons between the *clinical* and *actuarial* modes of operation. We shall first consider the topic of *prediction* and then discuss personality *description*.

Clinical Versus Actuarial Prediction

In most practical situations, the professional psychologist has at his disposal an enormous amount of data, such as test scores, interview impressions, and biographical information, and he is asked to make one or more predictions from these data. Will this patient improve in intensive individual psychotherapy? Should this manager be promoted? Should this delinquent be paroled, or should he be imprisoned? In such situations, the psychologist's task is to integrate the available data and make a single overall prognostic or diagnostic decision. The reader may note that the same problem exists for the physician who is attempting a physical diagnosis or treatment regimen, the stockbroker advising a client whether or not to buy a stock, the potential better at the parimutuel window, and so on.

In the *actuarial* approach to prediction, the predictors (cues, scores, responses, data) are first quantified and then are combined according to a set of rules that have been empirically determined, and that are to be scrupulously followed. On the basis of previously completed research, each of the obtained predictors is given some quantitative weight, and these predictors are then combined into a "best-fitting" actuarial model. The model may be a simple linear regression equation, or a more complex configurational one. The important consideration is always that the actual process of decision making in the actuarial mode follows predetermined rules in a strictly mechanical fashion, requiring no human judgment once the procedure is established.

The *clinical* approach to prediction, in contrast to the actuarial approach, permits the practitioner to assign his own weights to the predictors and to combine these predictors in a subjective fashion. The clinical approach refers to instances in which the psychologist (or the physician, or stockbroker, or what have you) uses his judgment or "intuition" in order to make what he feels are the appropriate adjustments in the given circumstances.

Examples of the two approaches are as follows. A clinical psychologist may note that a particular patient is depressed, rather agitated, somewhat seclusive, and preoccupied with themes of alienation and death. From these observations, he concludes that the patient is potentially suicidal and recommends that he should be watched carefully. This type of procedure, based largely upon the informal accumulated experience of the clinician and his private conception of what is involved in suicide, is called the clinical (or case study) method of prediction.

Alternatively, the psychologist might observe the patient's age, his marital status, and certain MMPI test scores. He then consults an actuarial table, which gives the statistical frequency of suicide in persons as a function of such characteristics, and obtains a figure indicating the probability of suicide by that particular patient. This type of procedure, where the prediction derives solely from prior statistical data, is called the actuarial (or statistical) method of prediction.

One of the early attempts to develop an actuarial prediction procedure for personality-related events involved the prediction of the likelihood that prisoners would violate their parole (Hart, 1923; Burgess, 1928; Glueck and Glueck, 1930). In the most comprehensive and influential of these studies, Burgess (1928) utilized the case files of over 3000 parolees and was able to identify 21 factors in pre-parole history that were related to parole success. Burgess then "scored" each of the 3000 case histories by assigning one point for every predictive factor that was present, yielding a "likelihood of nonviolation" score which could range from 0 to 21. Burgess was able to demonstrate that only 1.5 percent of those with scores of 0 or 4 were violators. The intermediate scores yielded corresponding intermediate results. These data appear to offer strong support for an actuarial approach to the prediction of parole success, although we shall see later in this chapter that Burgess's failure to deal with the problem of *base rates* flaws his conclusions and raises questions about the practical usefulness of the scores. Nevertheless, the actuarial approach has been successfully applied to a wide variety of other problems, including the prediction of academic success in various educational programs, and response to different kinds of institutionalization and therapeutic treatments.

Note that the distinction between clinical and actuarial methods does not imply anything about the nature of the data utilized. Case history data, interview impressions, and formal personality assessment scores can be used in both the actuarial and the clinical approach. In the former case, these data are quantified and interpreted according to established rules, while in the latter case the interpretation is subjective and left to the assumed skill of the clinician. As Gough (1962) has written,

The defining distinction between clinical and actuarial methods is instead to be found in the way in which the data, once specified, are combined for use in making the prediction. If the procedures, however complex mathematically, are in principle such that a clerk, or a machine, or anyone else could carry out the necessary operations and that the result would be the same in all instances, then the method is actuarial or statistical in the sense here being discussed. If the combining is done intuitively, if hypotheses and constructs are generated during the course of the analyses, and if the process is mediated by an individual's judgment and reflection, then the method is clinical (p. 530).

Thus, quantified responses to the ambiguous stimuli of projective techniques are a perfectly legitimate source of data for actuarial prediction. For example, Klopfer et al. (1951) developed an "ego strength" measure from the Rorschach, involving a weighted score of the number of human movement, animal movement, and inanimate movement responses, plus the use of shading, color, and form determinants. On the basis of these scores, a therapeutic prognostic index was possible. Further, Daston and Sakheim (1960) developed a Rorschach index

for predicting attempted or successful suicide, and Piotrowski and Briklin (1961) developed a Rorschach prognostic index for schizophrenics.
In each of these cases, it was the objectification of the data which
permitted the application of the actuarial method.

It should be obvious to the reader that the relative efficiency of
the clinical and the actuarial approaches can be directly compared.
Burgess (1928) compared his actuarial results with clinical predictions
made by two prison psychiatrists and concluded that the overall advantage lay with the actuary. Meehl (1954) was the first to draw attention
to the fact that, although the two approaches arouse strong partisan-
ship and affect, the question of their relative accuracy is, in the final
analysis, a straightforward empirical one. After a rather full discussion
of the logic involved in the two approaches, Meehl (1954) summarized
all of the studies then available that attempted a direct comparison.
These studies, not all of which are relevant to the personality domain,
tended to fall into three categories: success in training, parole violation,
and recovery from psychosis. Meehl's conclusion was that "in all but
one . . . the predictions made actuarially were either approximately
equal or superior to those made by a clinician" (p. 119).

Meehl noted several qualifications: (1) too little was known about
the skill of the clinicians involved in making the predictions, (2) some
of the actuarial predictions were made on the data from which the
original prediction rules had been derived (that is, the prediction rules
were not cross-validated), and (3) the predictive efficiencies for individual clinicians were rarely reported, so that it usually was not possible to determine the performance of the most accurate clinicians. Nevertheless, Meehl did conclude that the studies favored the actuary over
the clinician. He further noted that, in favor of the clinician, some
clinical predictive activity (for example, during psychotherapy) cannot
in principle be duplicated by statistical procedures. On the other hand,
the time saved by employing actuarial rather than clinical procedures
is an important factor in favor of the actuarial method.

Meehl (1965) has more recently summarized the state of the
controversy as follows:

Monitoring of the literature yields a current bibliography of some fifty
empirical investigations in which the efficiency of a human judge in combining information is compared with that of a formalized ("mechanical,"
"statistical") procedure. The design and range of these investigations permits much more confident generalization than was true on the eighteen
studies available to me in 1954. They range over such diverse substantive
domains as success in training or schooling, criminal recidivism and parole
violation, psychotherapy (stayability and outcome), recovery from psy-

chosis, response to shock treatment, formal psychiatric nosology, job success or satisfaction, medical (nonpsychiatric) diagnosis, and general trait ascription or personality description. The current "box score" shows a significantly superior predictive efficiency in about two-thirds of the investigations, and substantially equal efficiency in the rest. . . . It would be difficult to mention any other domain of psychological controversy in which such uniformity of research outcome as this would be evident in the literature (p. 27).

Has clinical prediction *ever* been shown superior to actuarial? The single study (Hovey and Stauffacher, 1953) which Meehl (1954, p. 108) considered to show the superiority of the clinician was later discovered by him to contain a statistical error which nullified this conclusion (Meehl, 1959a). A more recent paper by Lindzey (1965) attempted to demonstrate one clinical situation, the prediction of homosexuality from TAT protocols, in which clinical predictions were superior to an actuarial approach. In the first part of this study using noninstitutionalized homosexuals, both the clinician and the actuary (using 20 objective TAT indices combined in an after-the-fact fashion) obtained a high degree of success in predicting homosexuality. In the second portion of the investigation, when the results were applied to a prison population, the clinical method was reported to be substantially more effective than the actuarial. However, Goldberg (1968a) reanalyzed Lindzey's data and concluded that no reliable evidence of the clinician's superiority was presented.

A number of psychologists have disputed the correctness of Meehl's conclusions about the proven superiority of the actuarial method. In a detailed critique, Holt (1958) argued that, in defining the problem as clinical *versus* actuarial prediction, Meehl had encouraged competition and controversy rather than attempts to understand the relative contributions of these two approaches. Holt described the process of prediction as involving several steps; a study of the criterion, choice of intervening variables, choice of measures of these variables, data collection, and data combination. Clinical or statistical approaches can be used at any of these steps, so that a prediction process should be characterized as "more clinical than statistical," or "more statistical than clinical." Holt used the term "sophisticated clinical prediction" to describe a procedure employing all the above steps but retaining the clinician as a prime instrument, and "naive clinical prediction" for a procedure in which the clinician does not make a systematic effort to collect the necessary preliminary information before making his predictions. Most of the studies of clinical prediction reviewed by Meehl (1954) were, according to Holt, studies of the naive clinical method, and thus could not be expected to show what an experienced clinician could do if he were really to put his mind to it. Holt emphasized his view that there were prediction problems where it would make best sense to employ a more clinical approach, and also problems where a more actuarial approach would be the method of choice. Thus, for any problem, an attempt should be made to find the optimal combination of the methods.

The most recent review of studies comparing clinical and statistical prediction methods is that of Sawyer (1966). Like Holt (1958), Sawyer felt that an important part of the question has been neglected, namely, how the data are collected—whether a clinicial or a mechanical *measurement* procedure is employed. This neglect, according to Sawyer, has resulted in an incomplete picture of the issues involved in the clinical-statistical controversy. By Sawyer's criteria, data collection would be statistical or mechanical "if rules can be prespecified so that no clinical judgment need be involved in the procedure" (p. 181). All self-report, biographical, psychometric, and clerically obtained data would be regarded as statistical data. Information gained in interview or observation, on the other hand, would be regarded as clinical data, since it involves subjective judgment. Allowing additional categories for composite methods. Sawyer classified 45 studies which compared the prediction of behavioral outcomes according to both the mode of data collection and the mode of combination of data. In spite of methodological problems and equivocal results in many of these studies, Sawyer was able to conclude the following: (1) clinical combination of data was inferior to mechanical, no matter how the data were collected; (2) the type of synthesis between clinical and statistical methods which had been suggested by Holt (1958) did not appear promising; and (3) the clinician may serve a useful function in the data *collection* process "by providing, in objective form, judgments to be combined mechanically . . . that is, by assessing characteristics that otherwise would not enter the prediction." Thus, "improvement should result from devising better ways for the clinician to report objectively the broad range of possibly relevant behavior he perceives" (p. 193).

The reader might question why the clinician may be able to identify important predictors but not be able to utilize them in making predictions as consistently as the actuary. The clinician is simply not as reliable as the formula or the computer. Humans have their "bad days," they are influenced by boredom and fatigue, and they can be distracted by interpersonal and environmental circumstances. All of these human foibles interfere with the consistency with which the clinician can apply his expertise. These effects tend to be reasonably "random" and they add error to the clinician's judgments, attenuating their accuracy. On the other hand, formulas, computers, and statistical tables ordinarily are not subject to such errors, a fact which almost certainly helps account for their greater accuracy.

The Clinician as Hypothesis Builder

A safe conclusion to be drawn from the foregoing discussion is that once *empirical* relationships have been established between cues and criteria, the clinician can profitably be supplanted by an actuarial model of the phenomenon to be predicted. This suggests that an important role for the assessment clinician, perhaps his most important role, is the identification or discovery of new predictors or cues that will enhance predictive accuracy.

An example of the role of the clinician as a hypothesis generator can be found in the work of Meehl and Dahlstrom (1960), who developed a set of rules for discriminating between the MMPI profiles of patients who, independently of the MMPI, had been unequivocally diagnosed as either neurotic or psychotic. Meehl and Dahlstrom initially used their clinical judgment to sort the profiles, and then wrote a series of sequential, mechanical rules which attempted to duplicate their clinical judgment. Kleinmuntz (1963), using an essentially similar approach, was able to develop a computer program for distinguishing between the MMPI profiles of normal and maladjusted college students.

But even the hypothesis-generating role of the clinician can in principle be supplanted by the computer. Goldberg (1965), using the same MMPI profiles as Meehl and Dahlstrom (1960), compared their rules with a wide variety of other potentially discriminative rules and indices, some based directly on clinical experience, and some which were more or less arbitrary and had no known clinical significance. One of the more interesting findings was that it was one of the latter rules—the linear combination of scores $(L + Pd + Pa - Hy - Pt)$—which proved to be the best discriminator between neurotics and psychotics. In principle the Goldberg procedure, that is, the empirical development of hypotheses, could be extended to any predictive situation. The efficiency of an assortment of different hypotheses or indices—indeed all possible indices which could be generated—thus could be examined by a computer, bypassing the need for the clinician even to generate hypotheses. This nontheoretical approach precisely corresponds to the empirical approach to test construction discussed earlier in Chapter 4, and embodies both the same advantages and the same disadvantages.

Clinical Versus Actuarial Description

The failure to demonstrate the superiority of clinical over actuarial prediction led some clinicians to turn to personality *description* as an area in which the clinician's special abilities should be more clearly apparent. For example, Halbower (1955) compared the accuracy of personality descriptions generated by clinicians from patients' MMPI profiles with descriptions which were generated from MMPI profiles by actuarial procedures. First he identified, and defined by specific rules, four MMPI "types" which were relatively common in his patient sample. For example, the "code 13" type was defined by the following rules: Hs and $Hy \geq 70$; $D < Hs$ and Hy by at least 10 scale points; either K or $L >$ both $?$ and F; $F \leq 65$; and scales Pd, Mf, Pa, Pt, Sc, Ma, and Si all ≤ 70. To construct "cookbook" or actuarial descriptions of each profile type, he selected at random nine patients whose MMPI profile fitted the type. Each patient's therapist then completed a 154 item Q-sort which involved the ranking of personality descriptive statements from "most like the patient" to "least like the patient." The mean of the five most similar Q-sorts was designated as the actuarial description of that type. To compare the accuracy of these cookbook descriptions with those made clinically, two additional patients fitting each MMPI profile type were selected, and the therapists' Q-sorts were again used as the criterion. Not one of the individual clinicians' readings of an MMPI profile correlated as strongly with the criterion as did the cookbook reading. Halbower repeated the comparison using patients drawn from a different population, and achieved identical results.

The possibility that more accurate patient personality descriptions could be obtained from an MMPI cookbook than from a clinician led Marks and Seeman (1963) to develop a relatively comprehensive cookbook for describing the majority of psychiatric patients. Using MMPI profiles from the psychiatric patients of a midwestern medical center, they were able to develop 16 different profile types which accounted for 78 percent of the patients in their sample. The authors reported much normative information about their profile types (including other psychometric information, case history details, presenting symptoms, diagnosis, and course in treatment), expressing the data in terms of percent of occurrence and giving a comparison with patients in general.

A similar handbook of MMPI profile interpretations was developed by Gilberstadt and Duker (1965). They developed 19 profile types, using a similar approach to that employed by Halbower and by Marks and Seeman. Based upon a careful reading of the case histories of the male psychiatric patients that fitted each of these profile types, Gilberstadt and Duker reported the most likely diagnosis and an extended clinical personality description of each type. They also reported a list of complaints, traits, and symptoms that statistically differentiated each type from patients in general.

A third MMPI interpretive cookbook was developed by Drake and Oetting (1959) for describing college students. Basing their analyses on the three highest and two lowest MMPI scales of the profiles of more than 4000 college students who had sought counseling, they identified statistically nearly 700 different patterns. They then examined the counseling case materials and independently compiled a list of problems, descriptive phrases, and other items descriptive of these individuals. The cookbook lists the various code patterns, their frequencies, and the personality descriptions that were significantly associated with each pattern.

Several research efforts have been made to evaluate these cookbooks. One might expect that such research efforts would have been directed toward determining the adequacy of these cookbook descriptions in other populations (cross-validation), but this has not been the case. Rather, the research to date has been concerned with determining the percentage of patients in other samples that can be covered by the rules. Huff (1965) reported that the Marks and Seeman classification scheme covered only 28 percent of his sample of 149 psychiatric inpatients, while Sines (1966) found that only 17 percent of more than 1000 patients could be included. Likewise, Klett and Vestre (1967) found that the Gilberstadt and Duker rules covered only 28 percent of their psychiatric hospital samples. Payne and Wiggins (1968), using both the Marks and Seeman and the Gilberstadt and Duker rules, were able to classify 49 percent of their patients, this figure rising to 74 percent when any one rule was permitted to be relaxed.

It is noteworthy that almost all of this work on the actuarial description of personality has involved the MMPI. Perhaps one of the important reasons for the relatively limited generalization of the cookbook categories is the fact that the MMPI is not an optimal instrument for yielding a comprehensive personality description. Thus, the MMPI item pool has been shown to contain much redundancy (Block 1965, p. 120), and studies such as that of Sines (1959), to be discussed below, have shown that other sources of information (such as biographical data) might well be more effective than self-report inventories.

Some General Considerations

There are a number of general points to be made about actuarial and clinical approaches as applied both to personality prediction and description. First, it should not be forgotten that any instrument of demonstrated predictive usefulness (validity) can be used in either a clinical or an actuarial manner.

Second, little is yet known about the degree to which actuarial or cookbook descriptions can be generalized from the original sample upon which they were constructed. Certainly, the research reported above on two MMPI cookbooks that describe psychiatric patients suggests that some caution may be necessary, as does Goldberg's (1968a) critique of Lindzey's (1965) findings with the TAT. At the same time, the ultimate contribution of actuarial techniques to clinical psychology will depend upon their generality, since the time and effort required to develop such cookbooks can only be justified when the results can be broadly applied.

Third, there is a general issue pertaining to the clinician of exceptional predictive skill. In studies which have reported the success rates of individual clinicians, it is common to find that some clinicians are consistently more accurate in their predictions than others. It has therefore been advocated that more effort should be directed toward identifying such clinicians and having them train others. Goldberg (1970a), on the other hand, argued that it would be more useful to employ the most accurate clinicians in the development of actuarial formulas that would then supplant the clinicians altogether. His research evidence gives strong support for this position.

Our final comment concerns the relative economy of the clinical and actuarial procedures. Although one advantage claimed from actuarial over clinical methods is the ultimate savings in time, there will be situations in which the clinical method will be more economical, especially if the two methods yield roughly comparable accuracy. Such a situation was described by Johnston and MacNeal (1967), who compared methods of predicting length of stay in a psychiatric hospital. Here, actuarial prediction from case history and behavioral variables was about as accurate as clinical prediction made by the professional staff while handling their routine professional assignments. Since the clinical approach involved considerably less time and effort than the actuarial, it would appear that the clinical approach was clearly the method of choice.

THE PROBLEM OF BASE RATES

The term *base rate*, or the relative frequency of an event (disorder, symptom, behavior) in the population of interest, was introduced in Chapter 6, and examples were presented showing the importance of knowing the base rate of a disorder before making a prediction about its presence or absence for a particular individual. Although the intelligent understanding and use of base rate information would greatly increase the effectiveness of personality assessment in practical situations, psychologists have been relatively slow to accept the importance of base rates and to incorporate this information into their clinical work.

The matter was first brought to prominence by Meehl and Rosen (1955) in their discussion of the hit-and-miss validity of predictive devices. Meehl and Rosen pointed out that the more the base rate diverges from 0.5 (i.e., a 50/50 division in the population), the greater will be the difficulty in prediction. In some cases, the overall hit-and-miss success rate will be *lower* if the test is used than if all persons were simply regarded as belonging to the more frequent category. For example, in Table 6-2 the hit rate (correct diagnosis) was only 97.6 percent, as compared with 99 percent if everybody were to be called "normal."

Despite some shortcomings with the Meehl and Rosen paper (cf. Karson and Sells, 1956), it served to initiate an emphasis on this important area. There is much yet to be learned about integrating a knowledge of base rates with the clinical use of personality assessment devices. However, certain points are known to be of particular importance.

The greatest interest is usually in the overall *usefulness* of a test, and not necessarily in its hit-and-miss success rate. Referring again to Table 6-2, for every 1000 subjects tested, a cutting score of 70 on the *Sc* scale would identify a group of 26, but only 6 of them would actually be schizophrenic (that is, "true positives"). However, we might well be willing to accept this state of affairs if we plan to employ much more extensive and costly procedures for a further evaluation of the 26 thus identified. The benefit would be that we are saved the expense of evaluating the entire 1000 in this manner. The price we pay consists of (1) failing to identify 4 pathological persons—the "false negatives;" and (2) the cost of the screening procedure. Buchwald (1965) has presented calculations to show how, given the relative values of the different available courses of action, one can determine whether or not the use of a particular test would be justified.

With regard to those situations in which the hit-and-miss success rate *is* of foremost interest, Cureton (1957) has shown that for a valid predictor, it should always be possible to find a cutting score that will result in a greater overall proportion of correct predictions than would result from "using the base rate," that is, by regarding every-body as belonging to the more frequent category. Thus, if the cutting score in Table 6-2 were to be raised to, let us say, 100, the result might well be as depicted in Table 8-1. Here, the success rate is 99.1 percent, a very modest improvement over the base rate of 99 percent, but an improvement nonetheless. However, it is doubtful whether a cutting score of 100 would be useful in practice, because the great majority of the actual schizophrenics would not have been identified as such by the test. (We recognize that it *would* in fact be possible to devise a situation where the base rate could never be exceeded no matter what cutting score was employed—for example, if the variabil-ity of scores in the less frequent condition was substantially smaller than the variability of scores in the more frequent condition. The point is, however, that hit-and-miss success rates can be manipulated simply by altering the cutting score.)

In making a particular prediction, it is probably that no single test will be uniformly optimal for all population base rates and relative outcome values. Satz (1970) has provided an excellent illustration of this point, reporting hit-and-miss percentages for the prediction of brain

TABLE 8-1
Hypothetical Percentage of Patients Diagnosed Schizophrenic or Normal by the *Sc* Scale, Using a Cutting Score of 100, where 99 Percent are Actually Schizophrenic and 1 Percent are Actually Normal.

T Score	Actually Schizophrenic	Actually Normal	Total
T score 100 or more (diagnosed schizophrenic)	0.2*	0.1	0.3
T score below 100 (diagnosed normal)	0.8	98.9*	99.7
Total	1.0	99.0	100.0

* Correctly diagnosed

disease from five neurological tests and one neuropsychological test. Three different hypothetical base rates for brain disease are then considered (0.8, 0.5, and 0.2). The data clearly show that two of the tests that gave a relatively poor showing on overall percentage hit-and-miss figures were in fact the most effective when the base rate for brain disease was as low as 0.2. These tests, which made almost no "false positive" errors (calling normal persons brain-diseased) but correctly identified only a moderate percentage of the actual brain-diseased patients ("true positives"), proved most likely to be correct when the great majority of the subjects were *not* brain-diseased.

In conclusion, let us refer back to the actuarial work of Burgess (1928) on parole violation. In his sample, 28.5 percent of all the parolees violated their parole; or, to put it a different way, the base rate for parole violation was 28.5 percent. Thus, we would have been correct 71.5 percent of the time if we had predicted that all parolees would be nonviolators. Gough (1962) reanalyzed Burgess's data and demonstrated that, if optimal cutting scores had been used (those that would give the greatest number of placements in the correct groups of violators and nonviolators), the overall predictive accuracy would have been 76 percent, only 4 percent greater than the accuracy of predicting that all the parolees would be nonviolators. Whether or not the use of the actuarial data would have been justified in this setting (as opposed to following the base rate and predicting that there would be no violation at all) would depend on the relative costs associated with each kind of predictive error.

COMPARISONS AMONG SOURCES OF ASSESSMENT INFORMATION

It may only be a slight exaggeration to say that many psychologists, when assigned a task in personality or clinical assessment, administer to the respondent a standard battery of psychological assessment instruments, and that they usually follow the same procedure *no matter what* information is being sought or what question is to be answered. Part of the reason for their behavior undoubtedly lies in the type of request sometimes made of them. Frequently the hospital psychologist receives a referral "for psychologicals," in much the same way that the patient would be referred "for urinalysis" or "for chest X-rays." Thus, using a preestablished battery of assessment instruments becomes a habit. A moment's thought will indicate at least two deficiencies in this approach. First, every patient is different, so that the task of finding things out about one patient will never be quite the same as finding them out about another. Second, for any given assessment task (whether or not we include the particular patient as part of the definition of the task), there will be one particular combination of instruments and procedures that is optimal for the task.

Although much folklore exists in regard to determining which instruments are most appropriate for a particular assessment task, there is little research evidence of any type in this area. Several studies have been carried out, however, to evaluate the different contributions of various assessment instruments to making a traditional clinical psychodiagnostic evaluation of psychiatric patients. One such study was done by Kostlan (1954). Kostlan collected four kinds of information from each of five male psychiatric outpatients: social case history, the Rorschach, the MMPI, and the Stein (1947) sentence completion test. In order to compare the relative utility of each kind of information in providing an accurate personality description, 20 clinicians, all of whom had at least two years of psychodiagnostic experience, were presented with different combinations of three out of the four kinds of data. Their analyses were then compared with those of criterion judges, using a lengthy checklist of personality descriptive items. The surprising finding was that clinicians who did not have access to a social case history gave personality descriptions which were no more accurate than those made on the basis of "minimal data" alone (age, occupation, education, marital status, and reason for referral to the clinic)! It was also found that the "minimal data" permitted descriptions which were better than chance, and that the most accurate descriptions were those based on combinations which included both the social case history and the MMPI.

Another study was carried out by Sines (1959), who utilized clinical psychology graduate student trainees as judges. Sines first obtained biographical data on a structured self-report questionnaire from each of 30 patients. Each patient was then interviewed and tested with the Rorschach and the MMPI by one of five trainees, with counterbalancing of the order in which these three kinds of information (interview, Rorschach, and MMPI) were obtained. The trainees performed Q-sort personality descriptions of each patient, first using the biographical data alone, and again after each new kind of information was added. Comparisons were then made with a criterion Q-sort description, so that it was possible to compare, for example, the accuracy of a personality description made from the biographical data sheet alone with the description made from that source plus any one or more of the three additional sources of information. According to Sines' report, the clinicians formed specific descriptions fairly quickly, and the descriptions changed little with the addition of data over and above the biographical data sheet. The interview was the only device which appeared to result in an increased accuracy of description.

The most extensive study of the ability of clinical psychologists to make traditional psychiatric diagnoses from assessment instruments was carried out by Little and Shneidman (1959). The instruments involved were the MMPI, the TAT, the Rorschach, and Shneidman's (1951) Make-a-Picture-Story test, each instrument being considered singly. Forty-eight psychologists—12 who were considered expert with each of the four tests—made a diagnosis about four subjects. The subjects were selected (unknown to the judges) to include one subject each with a psychotic, a neurotic, and a psychophysiological disorder, and one normal or nonpsychiatric subject. Additional personality descriptions were also sought from each of the judges. For criterion purposes, psychiatrists made diagnoses from extended case history data for each of the subjects. Although the results of this study are complex, findings of note were the disappointingly low agreement of the test judges both among themselves and with the criterion diagnoses, and the generally low validities (if such a term is appropriate in the present context) of the test judges' interpretations.

A final study comparing personality descriptions from several sources of assessment data was that of Golden (1964), who attempted to determine whether descriptions based on clinical tests increased in accuracy as a function of the number of tests employed. Thirty experienced clinical psychologists were asked to judge five of the patients utilized in the Little and Shneidman study. After reading the minimal data sheet and again after reading each of the Rorschach, MMPI, and TAT protocols, the judges were asked to complete the Little and Shneidman personality questionnaire for the patient. The judges' responses were then compared for accuracy with those of highly experienced professionals who had access to extensive case history data. Golden reported that a better-than-chance personality description could be provided from the information contained in the minimal data sheet plus any one of the tests, but that the accuracy of description did not increase significantly as more tests became available.

What conclusions can be drawn from these studies? For one thing, the studies rather consistently demonstrate that, as sources of data for psychological prediction or description, personality tests do not fare as well as case history data. There is also the suggestion that a single test adds about as much to the case history data as do a number of them, and that it does not much matter which test is utilized. To the extent that this is true, the economics of professional time and effort would favor self-report inventories such as the MMPI. Some criticism can be leveled at Sines' study, and to a lesser degree also to Kostlan's, for using relatively inexperienced diagnosticians, although it will be shown below that the relationship between clinical experience and diagnostic acumen is largely an open question. Also, whatever weaknesses are implied in this criticism, it must be noted that the studies did tend to mirror actual clinical practice in the tests used and in the level of *some* clinical workers.

In defense of the clinician's rather poor showing in the previously reported studies, several points can be raised. (1) These kinds of comprehensive personality descriptions are no longer requested on the near-universal basis that was once the case. The reasons for this state of affairs probably have to do with efficiency and with the limited use made of such descriptions, as illustrated by Meehl's (1960) report that psychotherapists do not find them particularly useful when they begin therapy with a patient. (2) The studies were concerned with general personality descriptions, and not with the assessment and prediction of specific traits and behaviors. We might expect the clinicians to show a higher level of predictive accuracy when dealing with specific behaviors. Little research has been reported, however, comparing the differential usefulness of various instruments and techniques in helping the clinician to make specific predictions. (3) Systematic attention should be given to determining the unique advantages of each of the major assessment instruments and techniques, with the aim of eventually using them only for these unique purposes. (4) It should be emphasized that the use of biographical data seems especially promising for predictive purposes.

Our comments point to the need for developing greater specificity and precision in our choice of assessment instruments, analogous perhaps to the development of disease-specific tests in the field of medicine such as the Schick and Wasserman Tests, which can be contrasted with the earlier reliance upon general signs such as increased body temperature and irregular pulse. A good example of the importance of specificity can be seen in the birth and development of the MMPI— an omnibus instrument for the assessment of psychopathology. Over the years, this instrument has been pressed into service for a great variety of assessment tasks beyond the one for which it was devised. However, an examination of the research literature (for example, Lanyon, 1968) clearly shows that its most valid discriminations are made with psychiatric patients, which is precisely the use intended for it.

CLINICAL ACCURACY AND EXPERTISE

One sensible assumption is that professional psychologists, by virtue of their specific training and experience, would be more accurate in their judgments and predictions about other people than professionally naive persons. Let us review the research evidence on this question.

First we shall consider the accuracy of judgments based upon or utilizing interpersonal cues. We are referring to the cues available to all of us in our dealings with other people: content and style of speech, manner of dress, and all those other subtleties that are regarded as contributing to our *intuitive* impressions about other people. Much of the research on clinical judgment based upon interpersonal cues has been summarized by Taft (1955) and by Vernon (1964). It would appear from their summaries that the ability to judge others is neither entirely general nor entirely specific. That is to say, there is no such person as a uniformly accurate judge of others, although there is some degree of generality to this ability. It is not related to age (in adults) nor strongly to sex, although there is a slight difference in favor of women. The ability to successfully judge others is positively related to intelligence, artistic and dramatic interests, good emotional adjustment, and social detachment, and is negatively related to authoritarian attitudes. Also, judgments are more accurate when the judges are motivated to make accurate judgments and when they come from cultural backgrounds which are similar to those of the persons being judged. There is also substantial though not completely consistent evidence that experienced clinical psychologists may be no more accurate in making judgments based upon interpersonal cues than are clinical psychology graduate students, and that neither group may be as accurate as certain groups of nonpsychologists, such as physical scientists and perhaps personnel workers.

If the experienced clinician is no better able than the inexperienced clinician to make so-called intuitive judgments about persons, what about ability to use formal assessment instruments? Goldberg (1968b) summarized a large variety of relevant research studies and concluded that here too, the amount of general professional training and clinical experience of a psychologist is *not* systematically related to his ability to make accurate judgments from clinical psychological assessment instruments. Among the tests utilized and predictive tasks involved have been the Bender Visual Motor Gestalt Test to identify brain pathology (Goldberg, 1959), human figure drawings to discriminate between psychiatric and normal adolescents (Hiler and Nesvig,

1965), and the MMPI to discriminate between psychiatric and medical patients (Oskamp, 1962).

Rather than dwell upon the details of these and similar studies, let us try to explain their findings and explore their implications. As noted previously, one important issue in clinical judgments and predictions is the low consistency of clinical judgment among clinicians (that is, low interjudge reliability) who are using different sources of data, and even when using the same data. For example, in their study of the reliability of clinicians using four data sources (MMPI, Rorschach, Wechsler-Bellevue Intelligence Scale, and a simple vocational history), Goldberg and Werts (1966) concluded that the "judgments of one clinician working from one data source bear no systematic relationship to those of another clinician working from another data source, even though both judges are ranking the same patient on the same trait" (p. 199). Little and Shneidman (1959) found that their clinicians did not agree among themselves on the judgments made either from different data sources or from the same source. In this context, it is noteworthy that Oskamp (1962) did find a positive relationship between accuracy of judgment and the amount of specific experience his judges had with the MMPI. This finding might result from the fact that the MMPI signs for making the discriminations required by Oskamp were reasonably clear-cut in the research literature; hence experienced MMPI workers would probably know of them, and thus have a specific advantage over the inexperienced judges.

The finding that there is a great deal of unreliability even among experienced clinicians in their judgments suggests that predictive accuracy could be increased if clinicians were aware of the most predictive cues and used them in their predictions. Oskamp (1962) provided data to support this contention by showing that otherwise naive undergraduates who were given relevant training in the MMPI soon increased their judgmental accuracy to that of the most experienced judges. On the other hand, Goldberg (1968b) reported that judges only demonstrated a stable increase in their ability to discriminate psychotic from neurotic MMPI profiles if they were given the values for a valid actuarial index for making this decision. Simply informing them of the existence and nature of the index only resulted in a temporary increase in accuracy.

Goldberg (1968b) reported another kind of training for increasing clinical predictive accuracy, involving immediate feedback about accuracy of prediction, which was even less successful. Naive (undergraduate), middle (graduate), and expert (experienced doctoral level) judges were trained over a 17-week period in discriminating between psychotic and neurotic MMPI profiles. In this period, more than 4000 training profiles were shown to the judges, who made a decision for each and were provided with immediate feedback about their accuracy. The judges also saw another 6000 test profiles. The only group to show more than a negligible increase in accuracy as a result of this training were the naive judges, although the level of accuracy they reached was still substantially below that of the middle-level and expert judges, and even they were still below the ceiling of accuracy provided by actuarial prediction.

Sechrest, Gallimore, and Hersch (1967) also studied several methods of improving clinical accuracy in naive (undergraduate) judges, who were asked to predict the traits of anxiety and pleasantness in subjects from their sentence-completion responses. These authors showed that providing immediate feedback after each judgment did result in superior performance, but there was also some evidence to indicate that this superiority may have been due to enhanced motivation rather than to any specific information imparted.

The above findings suggest several tentative generalizations that might be made regarding the relationship between accuracy of prediction and clinical training. (1) It would seem that a major source of inaccuracy is simply lack of information about the valid cues or predictors for the behavior to be judged. It would appear that general clinical experience by itself is not sufficient, nor even experience with a particular assessment device as a measure for general personality description. What appears to be necessary is some awareness of the specific cues or "signs" that are predictive of the behavior under scrutiny. (2) Inexperienced judges who are provided the correct signs will improve their accuracy *if* they use the signs, but some motivation may be necessary in order to have the judges continue to use the signs. (3) In the absence of previously developed empirical signs, it is possible for judges to develop and "learn" signs by repeatedly making judgments and receiving feedback about the accuracy of these judgments, but once again they must be motivated to do so. (4) If specific empirically developed signs or cues are available, then they are probably better used in an actuarial rather than a clinical manner.

A very much related issue concerns the relationship between the amount of information available to the judge and his accuracy of prediction. Again, the commonplace notion is that the more information or data the clinician has available, the more accurate will be his prediction. Indeed, this rationale typically underlies the use of a "battery" of tests with a patient in order to make a comprehensive personality description. The previously discussed studies of Golden (1964), Kostlan

(1954), and Sines (1959), however, strongly suggest that this notion is erroneous. In attempting to predict success in the VA training program in clinical psychology, Kelly and Fiske (1951) found to their dismay that predictions based upon credentials and objective test data were "better than those made at the end of the program on the basis of all tests, procedures, and observations!" (p. 404). They suggested that providing the clinician with too much information might confuse him in his efforts to sort out the relevant cues or signs and assign optimal subjective weights to them.

Turner (1966) reported rather similar results, using only a single personality assessment device, the Rorschach. In this study personality predictions were made about patients by clinicians who had varying amounts of the Rorschach protocol available to them as follows: (1) free associations to the blots only; (2) free associations plus a marked location chart showing which areas of the blots were involved in the responses; (3) both of the above plus inquiry information to help pinpoint the formal variables which determined the response; and (4) all of the above plus a summary scoring sheet (psychogram) of all of the scoring results. The results showed that there were no increases in accuracy as a function of increased data for either experienced or inexperienced clinical judges.

The major point which emerges once again, from these studies, is that it is important to identify the relevant sources of information for the particular descriptive or predictive task at hand, and that in routine practical situations, attention should be directed toward collecting only the data that are relevant. While there is always the hope that extended data may contain further potentially useful predictors, uncovering such predictors is a different task from routine practical assessment. On the basis of these conclusions, we should not be surprised to learn that certain aspects of personality assessment may be considerably simpler than we had earlier believed. In this connection, Peterson (1965) demonstrated that the two major personality dimensions of maladjustment and introversion–extroversion could be assessed as reliably by simple ratings as by more complicated measures such as personality inventories. Similarly, it has been shown that a combination of a few biographical facts, such as whether or not the patient has ever been married, is of substantial predictive usefulness in the prognosis of schizophrenia. In summarizing his work in clinical inference, Hathaway (1956a) concluded that ". . . the power of a few items as sources of generalization is greater than is usually expected. It is also suggested that inaccuracy enters when the percipient (or clinician) attempts to use additional data that are often less reliable" (p. 249).

One practical implication of this position would be the avoidance of the rather complex and extensive battery of assessment devices typically used for personality description, as well as those predictive indices which involve the collection of large amounts of data. Such an index is the Hospital Proneness Scale of Freedman, Rosen, Engelhardt, and Margolis (1969). Although this index did significantly differentiate clinic patients who eventually did or did not require hospitalization, it necessitates the administration of the Rorschach, the Porteus Maze Test, the TAT, and the MMPI. It is virtually certain that this rather direct prediction could be accomplished in a more straightforward and less complex fashion. A new assessment instrument that takes advantage of these findings is the Psychological Screening Inventory or PSI (Lanyon, 1970). This 15-minute instrument was designed in an attempt to utilize the inventory technique to its best advantage, while avoiding its inherent limitations. The five scales provide certain specific information that is easily obtained by the inventory method and that holds promise of being useful in decision making in mental health screening situations, such as physicians' offices, community clinics, and reformatories. Such a device might be employed either to replace more lengthy psychological evaluations or as a screening instrument where none was formerly used.

A further issue that has concerned personality assessment investigators is the relationship between clinicians' accuracy of judgment and their degree of confidence in that judgment. Another surprising and disconcerting finding of the Kelly and Fiske (1951) study was that the confidence of judges in a prediction was *inversely* related to the accuracy of that prediction. Somewhat more comforting was Oskamp's (1962) report that, in discriminating between MMPI profiles of psychiatric and medical patients, confidence in any judgment was negatively related to the general clinical experience of the judge. Similarly, Goldberg (1959) reported that inexperienced judges were more confident than experienced judges in their predictions of organic brain pathology from the Bender Gestalt test. In another study by Oskamp (1965), the judges' confidence levels increased as more information about the patient was made available but, as noted elsewhere, the accuracy of judgments did not increase. Oskamp (1962) also found that judges could be successfully trained to improve the appropriateness of their confidence judgments.

It appears from these studies that the relationship between the amount of information available to judges and their confidence in these judgments is a complex one, in which the evidence is somewhat equivocal. One fairly consistent finding is that experienced judges tend to place less confidence in their own judgments than do inexperienced judges.

A clear warning that seems to be implicit in the findings is that we should not be beguiled into confidence simply on the basis of having available a considerable amount of information. A clear understanding of how to use the available information for descriptive and predictive purposes is required.

THE PROCESS OF CLINICAL JUDGMENT

Thus far we have been concerned with the *outcome* or consequences of the clinical judgment process, that is, with the effectiveness or accuracy of judgment. Interest has recently developed in the actual *process* of clinical judgment, that is, the question of exactly how the clinician operates.

In the dispute over clinical versus actuarial modes of prediction, Meehl (1959a) suggested that one potential advantage of the clinician rests in his ability to combine the available data in a complex, configural way that cannot easily be reproduced mathematically. We shall now examine the available evidence to determine how correct Meehl's assertion might be, and also to see how this configural process would compare in accuracy of prediction with a simple additive or linear process.

In order to determine whether clinicians utilize simple additive combinations of data in making predictions, or whether they employ complex configural combinations, it is necessary to make elaborate statistical analyses of the data available to the clinician. Basically, these analyses involve some measure of the amount of "nonlinearity" utilized by the judge in his decision making, and several methods for doing this have been developed (Hoffman, Slovic, and Rorer, 1968; Hursch, Hammond, and Hursch, 1964). One fairly consistent finding (Hammond and Summers, 1965) has been that it makes just as much sense to call the clinical judgment process "linear" as to call it "nonlinear." Using a different statistical procedure, Rorer, Hoffman, Dickman, and Slovic (1967) and Hoffman, Slovic, and Rorer (1968) were able to show that some judges *do* utilize configural combinations of signs in their judgments, but that in general, the contribution of these "nonlinear" elements is negligible when the contribution of the "linear" elements to the judgment is determined. Among the judgment tasks examined in these studies was the decision, based on behavioral data, of whether to give a weekend pass to psychiatric patients, and the differential diagnosis of malignancy of a gastric ulcer from X-ray data. These data tend to argue against Meehl's (1959a) position that clinical judgment typically involves the configural combination of data.

We shall now turn to the question of the relative accuracy of these two modes of data combination.

Consistent with their belief that the optimal method for combining data for predictive purposes is configural in nature, Meehl and Dahlstrom (1960) evolved, from their clinical experience, an elaborate series of sequential rules which successfully discriminated among the MMPI profiles of psychotic and neurotic patients. Goldberg (1965) later compared the percentage accuracy of these configural rules with that of 29 uninstructed clinical judges, and more than 100 actuarial signs, rules, models, and tables, using a new sample of patients. He found that a number of simple, linear combinations of scales were able to make the discrimination as accurately as the more complex Meehl-Dahlstrom rules. In a further analysis of the Meehl-Dahlstrom rules, Wiggins and Hoffman (1968) used multiple correlation techniques to determine which of three "mathematical models" best described the judgment process used by each of the 29 clinical judges in discriminating the psychotic and neurotic profiles. They reported that although a configural or nonlinear model distinguished 16 of the 29 judges, the superiority over a linear model was small. In other words, what most judges use when making complex predictions can be as well described by a single additive combination of weighted signs as by a more complex configural combination. Although we are not necessarily arguing that a simple linear model *explains* the behavior of the clinician in making a prediction, it seems clear that the linear model duplicates (or improves upon) the *results* of the clinicians' behavior. One reason for this (Goldberg, 1970b) could be simply that equations are perfectly reliable, whereas human clinicians are not.

Obviously, research in the process of clinical judgment has just begun. Yet such research is essential if we are to understand this critically important process and train others in it. An additional point of concern brought out in the studies mentioned previously is the fact that the judges differed widely in the signs which they utilized and in their methods for combining them configurally. Improvements in accuracy will certainly occur as the sources of this variability can be identified and eliminated.

Summary

Psychologists have recently begun to show an interest in studying and comparing various aspects of personality assessment procedures in order to find out which are the most useful. Most of this research has been done on comparisons of actuarial (mechanical, statistical, clerical) and clinical (subjective, intuitive, experiential) procedures for prediction. Meehl, who brought this research area before the public eye in 1954, concluded that, whenever it was possible to formulate them, mechanical predictive rules were generally equal or superior in accuracy to the subjective predictions of clinicians using the same data. Subsequent research has not changed this conclusion, although it has suggested that a useful function of the clinician is in quantifying his behavioral observations; that is, in the domain of measurement rather than prediction. Actuarial techniques have also been applied to the description of personality, and "cookbooks" are available to yield personality descriptions of patients who possess certain types of MMPI profiles. Ultimately, the importance of actuarial procedures in personality assessment will depend upon their generality; that is, the extent to which descriptive or predictive rules derived on one population are valid for another. The reader is again reminded that in assessing the usefulness of an actuarial sign for prediction or description, it is essential to take into consideration the base rate of the sign, or its frequency of occurrence in the population being considered.

Other aspects of the accuracy of personality assessment have also been studied. Whenever various data sources have been compared for their contribution to a valid comprehensive personality description, biographical information has been shown to be at least as powerful as the commonly used clinical tests. Further, it appears that there is a definite ceiling to the amount of data which it is worthwhile to collect, and that the validity of the resulting assessment is not increased by adding more data; in fact, the validity may even be lowered. Another fairly consistent finding is that general training and experience in clinical psychology does not seem to make a judge more accurate, either in making interpersonal judgments or in judgments from test materials. A possible explanatory factor is the lack of reliability among clinical judges; this underscores the importance of identifying the particular cues that are relevant in making the judgments. A clinician's confidence in his judgments may sometimes increase even though his accuracy does not; however, it appears that specific training could rectify this difficulty. Another important factor in the learning and making of more accurate judgments is the need for high motivation on the part of the judges.

Research on the assessment process, though scanty, suggests the following: (1) optimal judgments can be made as well from simple linear combinations of data as from complex configurational combinations, and (2) the actual judging behavior of clinicians can in most instances be described about as well by mathematical models which are linear as by configurational models.

9 CRITICISMS OF PERSONALITY ASSESSMENT

Psychological tests, including those used for personality assessment, have been criticized for as long as they have existed. Some of these criticisms undoubtedly have arisen from the vague resentments that many of us feel toward being evaluated, especially by examinations of any kind (Amrine, 1965, p. 859). Other criticisms have been based on misunderstandings. For example, Dahlstrom (1969) has pointed out that some government employment application forms require the applicant to sign a statement that his answers are true to the best of his knowledge. The applicant could easily become confused if he is also administered one or more personality tests as part of the application procedure. Self-report personality inventories usually instruct the respondent that there are no right or wrong answers, and either that he is to give his own opinion of himself, or that he is to give the most appropriate response. Most projective devices are even more ambiguous, and require the respondent to give his initial, unqualified impression. All such responses are treated simply as behaviors and not necessarily as "true" or factual information. With such conflicting instructions and attitudinal sets, one can easily understand why respondents could become confused as to whether or not there are supposed to be "right" answers, and also how cautious they should be about their responses. Incidentally, such contradictions point up the importance of having the personality tests administered by, or at least supervised by, qualified professionals, who can make certain that the respondent understands the nature of the task.

Most of the current criticisms of personality assessment are not so easily disposed of. The last decade or so has seen a gradual buildup in public sentiment against psychological testing, feelings which culminated in 1965 in two congressional hearings. The House Special Subcommittee on Invasion of Privacy of the Committee on Government

Operations conducted an inquiry ". . . because of a large body of evidence that certain activities and operations of federal agencies were being carried out concerning which serious questions could be raised. . . . There is the matter of psychological or personality testing of government employees and job applicants by federal agencies. Many federal workers are subjected to extensive tests on their sex life, family situations, religion, personal habits, childhood, and many other matters" (Gallagher, 1965, p. 955). The other inquiry was conducted by the Senate Subcommittee on Constitutional Rights of the Committee on the Judiciary, which made its investigation for similar reasons (Ervin, 1965). The testimony involved in these inquiries was reported in the November, 1965, issue of the *American Psychologist*, and covered a much wider variety of issues than the avowed purposes of the hearings, showing that there was a broad range of dissatisfactions and criticisms voiced by a variety of different people, including a number of psychologists. There might also be some truth in Dahlstrom's (1969) suggestion that psychological tests were to some extent used as a scapegoat for the public's concern and anxiety over the development of "an increasingly precise psychotechnology."

Whatever the reasons for the congressional hearings, they served the purpose of forcing psychologists to face many criticisms of psychological tests and testing practices which had previously been minimized, avoided, or denied. The hearings also had the effect of spurring psychologists to initiate reforms which will undoubtedly be beneficial to both the public and the profession of psychology. Another positive outcome of the lengthy debates and soul-searching generated by the hearings was the clarification of some complex ethical and moral issues in regard to psychological testing in general. In this chapter, we shall deal with some of them that are particularly relevant to personality assessment.

Criticisms of personality assessment might be grouped roughly into two kinds. In the terminology of the popular critic Martin Gross (1965), personality tests have been criticized as *inaccurate* and also *immoral*. Messick (1965), a prominent researcher in personality assessment procedures, formulated the criticisms in a somewhat related manner, saying that "some tests are poor in quality and that tests are often misused" (p. 138).

Out of the flurry of defenses offered on behalf of personality tests, a reasonable viewpoint on their use can be delineated (for example, Anastasi, 1967; Messick, 1965). The *use* of personality tests in the past has certainly been inaccurate and immoral in some instances. Other uses have been both accurate and moral. It remains to sort out the accurate uses from the inaccurate, and the moral from the immoral. We shall discuss these two areas under the headings of *usage* and *moral issues*.

THE USAGE OF PERSONALITY ASSESSMENT DEVICES

Problems in the use of personality tests are of two kinds. First, there are the problems involved in the misuse of a valid test; for example, a test which has been shown to be valid for one purpose is used for another. Second, there are the problems involved in using a test that has no clearly demonstrated validity for any purpose. We shall deal first with the problems involved in using tests which do have established valid uses. In these cases, the criticism would seem to be more appropriately directed at the test users than at the test itself.

Improper Usage

The improper application of otherwise valid tests has probably been, and undoubtedly will continue to be, among the worst of all the abuses of personality assessment technology. In a sense, all such abuses should be considered to be a result of inadequate understanding by the test users of the nature of the test and the critical issues involved.

Use in Personnel Selection. One obvious and serious misuse of personality tests has been their employment by untrained users and in inappropriate circumstances for personnel work in industry. This indictment applies particularly to the use of tests intended for use in psychiatric settings, such as the Rorschach and the MMPI. Some possible reasons for this practice are as follows. There is the need of personnel managers to identify persons with potential emotional disturbances. There is also the fact that the personnel manager's formal academic training in personality measurement is quite likely to have stressed these instruments and their validity in identifying psychopathology, whereas in practice he is more often concerned with assessing aspects of normal personality functioning, especially those related to job success and management potential. Further, some personnel men may be indirectly motivated by a desire to gain some of the status of professional psychologists, or to engage in the psychological voyeurism that is legitimized in that profession. It is noteworthy that a basic cause of the 1965 congressional hearings was the use of the MMPI by the State Department in a limited, though routine, manner. It is this kind of misuse of personality measures in personnel selection which led Gross (1962, 1965) and Alex (1965) to claim that all personality tests are invalid, and to imply strongly that this was true in virtually all situations. Thus, Gross (1965) stated: "The results of many careful experiments that have attempted to validate personality testing have all proven the tests to be worthless" (p. 959).

In response to this criticism, it must be agreed that abuses of personality tests certainly do occur. One direction for professional psychologists to take in counteracting them is to restrict the use of such tests to persons qualified to use them properly. In other words, legal and ethical restrictions could be established for both the use and the distribution of personality test materials, with a concurrent public information campaign to inform society of what it is reasonable to expect from such devices. A step in this direction was the publication of the American Psychological Association's (1966) *Standards for Educational and Psychological Tests and Manuals,* an outgrowth of the 1954 "Technical Recommendations for Psychological Tests and Diagnostic Techniques." Another step was the formulation of ethics for testing practices, as published in the APA's "Ethical Standards of Psychologists" (APA, 1963) and the related *Casebook on Ethical Standards of Psychologists* (APA, 1967). Forehand (1964) has discussed some of the difficulties which would result from the elimination of the use of personality tests in making practical decisions. His discussion clearly indicates that many of the problems raised by Gross might in fact be intensified if tests were to be eliminated.

Mention should be made of the various volumes of the *Mental Measurements Yearbook* (for example, Buros, 1965) and the unwitting role they have played in aiding the test critics. Examination of these volumes will show that there are an enormous number of personality assessment devices available for use, most of them unvalidated in any more than a rudimentary way. The vast majority of these tests, fortunately, are little used in practical situations. For the relatively few tests that are more widely used, the status of their validity, although far from what we might hope, tends to be somewhat better. These yearbooks, however, unwittingly provide abundant ammunition for those who wish to attack personality tests, since they imply (correctly, but misleadingly) that almost all existing published tests have little or no demonstrable validity. A more accurate characterization would be that the validity of some of the more widely used tests, such as the Rorschach, TAT, and MMPI, when employed by adequately trained persons under appropriate conditions, can be satisfactory.

The problem of faking on personality tests is another focus for criticism, one that becomes especially important when tests are used in personnel work. The practical question is whether any valid information can be elicited from a respondent if he does not wish to reveal himself. Our earlier discussion of the faking problem in Chapter 7 led us to a tentative answer that the validity of information gained under these circumstances is doubtful at best, although the evidence is by no means all in. Lovell (1967) has reached a similar conclusion, and has reasoned on this basis that personality tests should therefore not be used at all in personnel selection situations. On the other hand, Dahlstrom (1969), while agreeing with the conclusion, suggested that personality tests ethically *could* be used in personnel situations, since the respondent is protected by having the opportunity to protect his privacy (through faking) if he so desires. Again, we would regard this area as one requiring more attention by professional psychologists.

Failure to Consider Base Rates. A serious area of concern that seems to have been overlooked by the lay critics of personality tests is the problem posed by base rates, an issue discussed earlier in Chapters 6 and 8. The failure to recognize and understand this complex, technical issue by unsophisticated critics should not be surprising, since many professional psychologists are also unaware of its importance.

At the risk of boring the reader, let us again consider how the failure to take base rates into account may result in the misuse of an otherwise valid test. A clear example of this problem is offered by Seeman (1969) in his reanalysis of the results of Hall and LaDriere (1969), who reported that the number of "conceptually inadequate" responses given on the Similarities subtest of the Wechsler Intelligence Scale for Children had diagnostic usefulness in the detection of cerebral pathology. Seeman noted that, if it was assumed that approximately 25 percent of children seen in child guidance clinics were actually cerebrally damaged (almost certainly an overestimate) and the actual cutting score recommended by Hall and LaDriere was employed, accurate diagnoses would be made only 37 percent of the time and inaccurate ones would be made 63 percent of the time, even though there is no question about the "validity" of the "conceptually inadequate" sign. Thus, the failure to take into account the frequency of occurrence of the event to be predicted could result in an unwarranted application of an otherwise valid predictive sign. Once again, the ultimate choice of whether or not to use the sign should depend on the relative costs and values involved.

Discrimination Against Minority Groups. There are a number of other criticisms of personality testing that, although not so obviously connected with insufficient technical understanding of testing problems, can be indirectly linked to it. One is the issue of racial and other forms of discrimination through the use of tests. Most of the complaints that tests result in unfair discrimination against certain minority groups have until now been made in regard to the use of ability tests, but there is no reason to suppose that personality tests are free of discriminatory "biases." There is little question, for example, that there are racial and socioeconomic group differences in responses to most personality assessment devices, differences that *could* result in systematic bias against persons from other than white middle-class backgrounds. Deutsch, Fishman, Kogan, North, and Whiteman (1964) have discussed many of these issues with regard to the use of ability tests with culturally deprived children. An interesting point made by Brim (1965), also with respect to ability tests, is that minority groups should be favorably rather than unfavorably inclined toward the use of properly constructed tests, because tests provide an objective standard for assessment. In fact, this is one clear way to identify unfair discriminatory practices.

On the other hand, it should be noted that the social values underlying the personnel use of personality tests relate to their ability to identify and eliminate unconventional and difficult persons, and the validity of personality tests for accomplishing such a purpose is also a measure of their "bias." The resolution of this dilemma would appear to involve a reconsideration of the underlying social values rather than an attack upon personality tests. In general, the issues with regard to personality and other tests and discrimination are difficult and complex, and the best current insurance against unfair practices is a thorough understanding of the underlying social, psychometric, and ethical principles by test users.

The Experience Controversy. One aspect of the argument concerning use of personality tests by technically unsophisticated persons is more controversial than those discussed above. We are referring, in the context of clinical diagnosis, to claims that expertise with such instruments as the Rorschach requires more than just training with that instrument, but rather intensive experience plus a comprehensive theoretical understanding of both general personality theory and the rationale of the particular test. It follows from this position that many studies which have failed to demonstrate validity for these clinical instruments are inadmissible as evidence because inexperienced clinicians were employed in the study. The issue is not one of marginal versus moderate training (as was the case when the personnel uses of tests were discussed) but moderate versus elaborate training.

There is little research evidence on this question of the necessity for prolonged and intensive training, and the evidence that does exist is inconsistent. On the positive side, Goldberg (1959) demonstrated that an expert in the Bender Gestalt test did much better in diagnosing presence or absence of brain damage than did a number of other judges. However, in the extensive study of psychiatric diagnosis conducted by Little and Shneidman (1959), in which care was taken to select the country's leading practitioners of the tests studied, results were unimpressive. It may be significant that Goldberg's Bender Gestalt expert spent some 20 hours on the 30 protocols in order to achieve his result, and this would be consistent with our conclusion offered in Chapter 8 that the motivation of the judges plays an important part in their clinical accuracy. But even if it can be consistently demonstrated that highly trained clinicians are superior to those with minimal training, the question remains as to whether their superiority would be sufficient to justify the effort and expense of the additional training.

Unwarranted Applications. Personality tests are widely used, albeit ethically and in good faith, for purposes for which they simply were not intended and for which they are inappropriate. For example, it is not uncommon for psychologists to make an estimate of a respondent's intelligence from his TAT stories or his Rorschach protocol. In a similar vein, the far-reaching attempts which have been made to extend the use of the MMPI can be seen from a scrutiny of Lanyon's (1968) collection of the mean MMPI profiles of a large variety of subject groups. It can also be clearly seen from this collection that the more psychopathological were the subjects, the better the discriminations that could be made among their profiles. For example, the MMPI was almost completely ineffective in differentiating good and poor automobile drivers. On the other hand, there are wide and obvious differences between psychopaths and neurotics. As noted earlier, this should surprise nobody, since the MMPI was built for the specific purpose of making the latter type of discriminations, and not the former kind. A similar comment can be made about the TAT, which was devised to describe personality needs and traits, not psychopathology. Strong cautions against using it for the purpose of psychiatric classification should be observed in light of Eron's (1948) normative study, which showed relatively few differences between the TAT responses of college students and those of schizophrenic patients.

Another kind of unwarranted application of personality tests that should be mentioned is the routine development of careful psychodynamic formulations on patients in clinical settings. Although such formulations might be of use in lengthy psychodynamically oriented treatment—though even this has been questioned (Meehl, 1960)—the value of such a procedure in most settings, which depend on other kinds of treatment approaches, is obscure. This point was made by Hathaway (1959) and has been recently developed further by Breger (1968).

Unwarranted Criticisms. Some of the criticisms of personality testing that have been set forth by popular writers (for example, Gross, 1962; Whyte, 1956) can be attributed to the naivete of the critics, who do not appear to understand the psychometric principles involved. Many of the complaints made by Gross (1962, Ch. 5) about the MMPI fall into this category. For example, it was inexplicable to him that a correction score such as the K scale could improve validity, or that a high score on the Sc scale should not invariably indicate schizophrenia. Another such criticism concerns the admissibility of subtle items. Thus, Gross found it somehow inequitable that a person who denies belief in the second coming of Christ should be, to use his term, penalized on the depression scale, and he was unable to comprehend the argument that the depressive patients in the original criterion group did in fact differ from the normal groups in their responses to this item. Hathaway (1964) has gone to considerable pains to explain and illustrate some of these psychometric points which may not be obvious to the layman.

Generalized Test Invalidity

We shall now turn to those criticisms which are more appropriately directed at the tests (or their authors) rather than at the users. We shall concentrate upon those problems of validity that result from test development procedures that do not pay adequate attention to the usefulness of the test in some or other specific respect.

The Criterion Problem. We shall first discuss the problems that occur if a personality assessment device is developed without regard to any clear-cut criterion. It will be remembered from our earlier discussion that when the empirical approach to test construction is used, the test developer has a clear idea of what dimensions of personality he wants to assess, and he tries to make these dimensions operational by specifying definite criterion groups or by some other clearly described procedure. If correctly applied, the rational and theoretical approaches to test construction also include a clear idea of what dimensions or attributes of personality are to be assessed (expressed in either rational or theoretical terms) and reliable methods of defining these dimensions. In all of these cases there are relatively clear-cut definitions which lead to criteria against which the test can be evaluated. Problems begin for personality assessment when there is no clear-cut specification of the criterion—what we are trying to assess.

The problem of criteria has been particularly acute with some of the projective devices and rationally based inventories, but it is by no means absent even for instruments with originally specified criteria. One example is the MMPI scales. The scales were constructed in order to predict patients' assignment to psychiatric diagnostic categories, and the criteria originally employed were the diagnostic categories to which the patients had already been assigned. Hathaway (1959) and Meehl (1959b) have both pointed out that since psychiatric diagnosis is relatively unreliable, and to some extent arbitrary, one might seriously question why so much attention should be given to these nebulous categories. That is, why attempt to develop an instrument which is concerned, from the first, with predicting an event that is arbitrary and unreliable? The ceiling for the predictive accuracy of such scales is set by the reliability of the criterion diagnosis, so that no further improvement in the instrument is possible beyond this level of accuracy.

There are at least two ways to resolve the dilemma of improving a test when no adequately clear-cut referent or criterion exists for what is being assessed. One, proposed by Hathaway (1959), would be to give the assessment result equal status with the criterion. Looking at the issue of psychiatric diagnosis in this light, a patient could then be called schizophrenic from his Rorschach or MMPI record just as validly as from a psychiatric examination. Incongruities among various sources of data would be resolved by clinical judgments. Another way to resolve the problem would be to employ factor-analytic procedures and then to adopt factor scales as "basic" psychological variables, recognizing that the initial construction had been based on fallible data. The merits of this procedure were examined in Chapter 4.

In general, persons engaged in developing techniques of personality assessment have paid far too little attention to the specific aims of their assessment procedures, and to the development of adequate criteria for what is to be assessed. With respect to the assessment of specific behaviors, Holt (1958) wrote:

First, if we are to predict some kind of behavior, it is presupposed that we acquaint ourselves with what we are trying to predict. This may be called job analysis or a study of the criterion. Perhaps these terms sound a little fancy when their referent is something that seems so obvious to common sense. Nevertheless, it is surprising how often people expend a great deal of time and effort trying to predict a kind of behavior about which they know very little without even thinking that it might help if they could find out more (p. 2).

This shortcoming was initially pointed out 25 years ago by Toops (1944), who suggested that comparable amounts of time should be given to developing the criterion and to perfecting the assessment instruments. Similiar warnings and criticisms were offered by Taft (1959) and by Stern, Stein, and Bloom (1956). These writings discussed two large-scale personality assessment studies, the OSS study (OSS Assessment Staff, 1948) and the VA assessment study of training in clinical psychology (Kelly and Fiske, 1951; Kelly and Goldberg, 1959), respectively. Neither of the studies was particularly successful in its aims because of inability to specify clearly in advance the nature of the criterion behavior. A more sophisticated approach to a complex assessment problem was used by Laurent (1962), who wished to employ personality and other data to select management trainees with the greatest potential for success. In order to cope with the criterion problem, Laurent first developed a composite criterion for "success" by factor-analyzing a variety of available measures of success, such as position level and salary history. The resulting primary factor was adopted as a criterion of overall success and could be used as the target for the predictions.

The above studies deal with complex or multiple assessment projects, but similar criterion problems are encountered in developing instruments to assess individual personality characteristics. Many researchers fail to demonstrate predictive validity for projective devices because the tests were constructed without reference to reliable and easily definable criteria. Rather, each investigator is free to choose whichever dimensions of personality he is interested in investigating. The resulting melange of investigations has produced largely negative findings, but there can never be the "definitive" study if there is no definitive criterion.

This discussion perhaps can best be summarized by referring to Ebel's (1964b) viewpoint, in which tests that are clearly proposed to be a short-cut method for avoiding more elaborate methods of behavioral assessment are distinguished from those that are not. For the "short-cut" tests, the criterion for test construction must be the "more elaborate method of assessment," and validity is assessed by the correspondence between the two measures. In such cases, the criterion scores would be produced by a measurement procedure that is superior in important ways (for example, more comprehensive, more reliable) to the test, so that the test is a poorer but more convenient measure of the comprehensive method. In personality assessment, the major problem is usually that a "more elaborate method" for evaluating personality functioning does not exist at this time. It is also true, however, that appropriate criteria could sometimes be developed in the manner utilized by Laurent (1962).

Much more fundamental criticisms have been raised by Mischel (1968, 1969) and Peterson (1968), who have questioned the basic assumptions implicit in almost all contemporary personality theories and also in traditional personality assessment techniques. Mischel's (1968) survey of the currently available research evidence on the consistency and generality of personality traits led him to conclude that there was little evidence for the existence of stable enduring personality traits or states. The most positive evidence suggests that only 10 to 12 percent of the relevant variance can be accounted for by the evidence for such traits; that is, the intercorrelations among measures of these traits at best tend to average about 0.30 or 0.35. He noted, however, that the most stable and generalized traits are those in the cognitive area (intelligence) and the stylistic dimensions of personality (for example, tempo, field dependence–independence).

Mischel explains our *perception* of continuity in personality by the fact that the human mind functions "like an extraordinarily effective reducing valve that creates and maintains the perception of continuity even in the face of perceptual observed changes in actual behavior" (1969, p. 102). He has further noted that the notion of personality traits pervades our language and our concepts about human behavior generally, not only our psychological jargon, and thus plays a critical role in how all of us conceptualize our own behavior and that of others. Still another issue raised by Mischel is that the inferences generated from traditional personality tests to the underlying hypothesized psychodynamics have rather low reliability and are of little value for making behavioral predictions or writing behavioral prescriptions for individuals under professional care. In Mischel's view, much more attention should be given to situational and idiosyncratic determinants in understanding and predicting interpersonal behavior.

Illusory Correlation. Another serious problem which involves the validity of certain assessment procedures specifically applies where tests are interpreted by common sense or by an accumulated fund of clinical information, as is the case with much interpretation of projective drawings and, to some extent, with the Rorschach and similar instruments. The problem was identified by Chapman (1967) and labelled "illusory correlation" (Chapman and Chapman, 1967). It may be because of illusory correlation that certain tests with doubtful empirical validities continue to be used and are supported enthusiastically by diagnosticians.

The Chapmans had observed that, when college students were shown a series of word pairs carefully arranged so that all possible pairings were presented equally often, they systematically but mistakenly reported that certain words tended to occur together more often than was actually the case. Specifically, the illusion was produced that words with high associative strength for each other (for example, table and chair, hungry and food) had occurred together more often than words with low associative strength. The Chapmans characterized this effect as "analogous to the well-known Muller-Lyer illusion, in that there is a widely shared systematic error of observation that is not dependent on the observer's having some exceptional prior experience or training" (Chapman and Chapman, 1967, p. 194).

Reasoning that this illusory correlation might also occur in clinical test interpretation, the Chapmans had college undergraduates observe a series of human figure drawings. On each drawing was arbitrarily written two contrived personality symptom statements which were said to describe the person who produced the drawing. There were six such symptom statements, and each was attached to several different drawings. This observational experience was purportedly designed to teach the subjects the relationship between drawings and symptoms. The subjects, thus having "learned" about figure drawings, then were given a written list of the six personality symptom statements and were asked to list under each symptom statement the drawing characteristics which they had observed to be related to it. The correct response in each case was, of course, that there was no systematic relationship between the personality symptom statements and any drawing characteristic whatever. As expected, however, the subjects tended to list as related to each personality symptom those drawing characteristics which had high associative strength for the symptom. For example, the subjects overwhelmingly reported a connection between the personality symptom of suspiciousness and the drawing characteristic of atypical eyes, even though their "learning" experience had provided absolutely no basis for such a connection. Further investigation produced the following critical finding: that the "personality interpretation" given by the naive undergraduate subjects corresponded closely to the interpretations given by experienced clinicians! Thus, there are indications that some of the "clinical lore" used to interpret projective tests is spurious, and presumably is perpetuated for the same reasons that it originally occurred—because such interpretations "make sense" or are "intuitively correct" although the empirical evidence for these relationships is not present. Chapman and Chapman (1969) have recently extended this avenue of inquiry to certain aspects of the Rorschach, with somewhat similar results. An extended account of the several Chapman studies may be found in a recent summary article (Chapman and Chapman, 1971).

It cannot be concluded that illusory correlation accounts entirely for the discrepancy between the positive claims made by many practicing clinicians for validity of the figure drawing technique and similar tests, and the meager empirical evidence that is available in their support. Nevertheless, the strength of the Chapmans' findings is a potent condemnation of relying solely on one's "experience" in test interpretation, no matter how confident one might be.

MORAL ISSUES IN USING PERSONALITY ASSESSMENT DEVICES

The criticisms to be discussed under this heading do not apply only to personality assessment. They are relevant to many other aspects of psychology, including the experimental use of human subjects, as well as to many aspects of other social sciences, such as economics, education, and law. We are referring to situations in which an individual feels personally threatened with regard to either his personal rights and needs, or his social and civil rights. The threats are often so subtle that the person may find it difficult to articulate his reasons for feeling concern or threat, and he may even explicitly deny that threat is the real cause for his actions. These concerns are the bedrock of the criticisms which have become identified with the term "invasion of privacy."

Dahlstrom (1969) has distinguished two meanings for the concept of invasion of privacy. The first involves the issue of *confidentiality*, where there may be "certain facts about a person that he would prefer to keep secret (that are) in danger of being revealed to someone who could then use them against him" (p. 268). The second is concerned with *inviolacy*, and involves a person's unwillingness to have another person impose upon him in a significant way. In Dahlstrom's words, "They consider any intrusion upon their activities as a violation of their private pattern of living" (p. 268). Anastasi (1967, p. 297) has made a similar distinction.

Before considering these two aspects in detail, let us first examine reasons why the invasion of privacy has become such a socially sensitive issue. Willingham (1967) listed six possible contributing or underlying influences. (1) The first is the concern for individual dignity and privacy that has been sensitized by the civil rights movement. Thus, identification of personal characteristics may facilitate socially invidious comparisons. (2) Second, and ironically incompatible with the first, are the demands for social equality, for social scientists to make careful studies and comparisons of social groups, so that the inequalities can be investigated and changes can be initiated. The third and fourth influences, both technological, are (3) the greatly increased availability of research funds and (4) the development of a highly sophisticated computer technology. Complex and extensive research projects are not only tempting for the researcher, but are seen as mandatory if behavioral scientists are to maintain an image of competence and respectability in the scientific community. (5) The fifth factor, also ironic, is the social scientists' greater need for involvement in socially meaningful research. These efforts might be seen as a reaction against criticisms leveled at much behavioral research in the past, that this research has been irrelevant to the real problems now confronting society. (6) The public has become highly sensitized to invasion of privacy in a number of areas which are not necessarily psychological in nature, but it has failed to make discriminations among them. Thus, some of the resentments against the use of electronic eavesdropping devices, the large-scale accumulation of personal credit histories, and the collection of personal data in the Federal census, have spread to psychology in general and to personality assessment in particular.

Let us now return to our examination of the major complaints about invasion of privacy as they apply to personality assessment. We will do so under the two headings suggested by Dahlstrom, although the two categories will be seen to overlap to some extent.

Confidentiality

Problems relating to confidentiality are present not only with personality assessment data, but with any personal information revealed to a clinical psychologist or counselor, and for that matter to a physician, lawyer, or minister. The latter professions, however, have a long professional history and frequently are protected by legislation which sanctifies information disclosed to them as part of their professional practice.

It seems unnecessary to state that a person has a right to withhold from you whatever information he wishes, unless he has entered into a contract (actual or implied) with you to the contrary. If, in addition, he has reason to believe that you will employ the information against his best interests, he would indeed be foolish to disclose it. The issues, however, are more complex than that. It may seem strange to us now that, at the height of the public controversy over personality assessment, it was often seriously suggested that *all* personality tests should be outlawed! This failure to distinguish their many legitimate and apparently humanitarian uses from their abuses attests to the amount of emotion invested in the issues.

Under what circumstances have people been asked to provide personality information which might be used against them? Perhaps the most blameworthy practice, discussed earlier in the context of validity criticisms, has been the use of psychopathologically oriented assessment devices in the context of personnel selection. The confidentiality problem has arisen here in two ways. First, tests like the MMPI include questions pertaining to sexual and religious practices, information which has little apparent relation to job suitability, but which presumably could afford much opportunity for personal embarrassment and the exercise of prejudices. This is especially true of many of the so-called subtle items. Second, and perhaps more important, the respondent may be revealing information of which he is not aware, and which he would not choose to reveal were he given that choice. The person who is asked to respond to the Rorschach inkblots faces just such a possibility.

What are the ethics of the situation? Rather different views have been proposed by Dahlstrom (1969) and Lovell (1967). It should be remembered that the use of personality tests in a mental health or a counseling setting is not at issue. In those instances, the client is seeking professional help for his own problems, and the outcome of the intervention is clearly understood to be for the client's own benefit. Lovell referred to this type of situation, where there is no conflict of interest between assessor and respondent, as the *client function* of personality testing. Whenever a potential conflict of interest does exist between assessor and respondent, such as in personnel selection, tests are being used in a *personnel function*, and it is this use that has caused concern. Here, Lovell has argued that the use of personality tests is inadmissable on three counts. First, on ethical grounds, it has no place in a free society. Second, on scientific grounds, it is doubtful that adequate validity is possible under these conditions, because of the difficulties of obtaining subject cooperation. Third, on grounds of community service, the public will be best served in the long run if personality tests are not used in this manner.

Dahlstrom (1969) drew attention to a similar dichotomy, initially proposed by Cronbach and Gleser (1965), referring to the use of personality tests in making decisions serving an *individual* and decisions serving an *institution*. Dahlstrom, however, saw no ethical dilemma in either type of decision under normal circumstances. As an example of an institutional use of tests, let us consider the case where a candidate is being screened for an executive position in a particular company. Since the psychologist's loyalties to the company are clear to the candidate, there should be no ethical problem. Further, the applicant can choose to invalidate the procedure if he so desires by subtle noncooperation. Conflicts of interest, however, might arise for the psychologist in the event that information of real concern to society in general, such as murder or pyromania, were revealed in the course of the examination. Dahlstrom offered another plausible reason why many persons are conflicted about the use of personality tests in personnel selection. The reason is simply that the outcome of the testing session is often unfavorable to the respondent. In a sense, the information is used in a fashion that is at cross purposes with the respondent's own interests. As far as actual breaches of confidentiality with undesirable *general* consequences to the respondent are concerned, that is, the use of test results outside of the situation for which they were obtained, the 1965 Congressional hearings uncovered little or no evidence of such practices (Brayfield, 1965).

Two more points should be made regarding confidentiality. One is that a psychologist cannot legally assure his client that the test records will in fact be confidential. As noted by Brim (1965), "psychologists are misinformed in thinking that test responses have the character of privileged communication. Test results are subject to subpoena by any group with proper legal authority and easily can become a matter of public record" (p. 126).

The other point relates to confidentiality in a somewhat different context—the question of an individual's rights to know his own test results. Psychologists have traditionally been very reluctant to share this kind of information, for the reason that it might be misleading or harmful to the subject. Much of the reluctance stems from the fact that persons often tend to have distorted views of how much new personal information can be revealed by personality tests, and they regard test scores and interpretations as much more absolute and valid than they actually are. With regard to the belief that a person might be damaged in some manner by being informed about his test results, Brim (1965) has reported research evidence to demonstrate that high school students who were given information regarding ability tests appeared to have methods for defending themselves against any serious blows to their self-esteem. In other words, persons may not be as vulnerable to test interpretation as we think. Although the specific findings were with regard to aptitude measures, it is likely that the same applies to personality assessment. In reporting the work of the American Psychological Association's *ad hoc* committee on the social impact of psychological assessment, Berdie (1965) noted the recommendation that greater emphasis should "be given to research on the effects of communicating psychological information to parents, teachers, and students" (p. 146). His report also recommended research into different methods of communicating this information for maximum understanding.

In concluding our discussion of the confidentiality issue, it must not be overlooked that some people *do* have things to hide which may or may not be related to the assessment task at hand, but which would be potentially damaging to them if inadvertently revealed. Thus, in the context of a personality research program involving school children, Eron and Walder (1961) reported that one of the local citizens who had made efforts to harass the research team was later indicted for sodomy, though this was not in any way related to the research. How to permit such people to retain their rights to privacy in situations where the cooperation of a whole group is sought is indeed a difficult dilemma. Even if it is made known that persons who would rather not cooperate need not do so, such persons may become a focus of attention merely by their action in not participating. The same problem is present whenever questionnaires or inventories are administered with the instructions that respondents may omit any items which they would rather not answer. A glance at the answer sheet for omitted items reveals the areas of greatest personal sensitivity!

Inviolacy

Inviolacy is concerned with situations where there is no threat that the information that a person gives as part of an assessment procedure will be used against him; rather, we are concerned with the individual's right of personal privacy—his right not to have his privacy intruded upon. The question of inviolacy is relevant when people are questioned about aspects of their daily living that traditionally are not openly discussed in western culture. Thus, items on the MMPI regarding eliminative functions are hardly likely to provide material that might be self-incriminatory; however, in our society, toilet functions are very private matters, and many people are embarrassed to discuss them. In fact, one reason for negative reactions to such self-report items is that merely reading these items arouses anxiety about "taboo" topics. Another type of material which people object to discussing involves their cherished beliefs about human nature. Thus, Bennett (1967) stated that "A great many people seem to take comfort in believing that all children love and respect their parents, accept without question the teachings of their religion and live without sexual curiosity or urge until they attain the married state" (p. 9). In discussing behavioral research, Brim (1967) made the related point that much of the general concern about such research appears to come "not so much from the concern about methods and privacy, but about the inroads that behavioral science is making on ideas" (p. 30). There is the implication that security is found in the familiar, and that to be asked even to consider that there might be alternatives raises anxieties which are turned into aggression toward the test.

Some personality psychologists have placed considerable importance on the "need for inviolacy" as a personality characteristic. Brim (1965) has suggested that such people are also "authoritarian in interpersonal relations, intolerant of diversity in ideology or beliefs, and strongly opposed to most forms of social change" (p. 128). Jourard (1964) has written extensively on the topic of self-disclosure, by which he means one's readiness to be open and share one's self with others. Murray (1938) listed and discussed the need for inviolacy as one of his basic needs in his personality theory. And it has been found that for normal persons, the K (defensiveness) scale of the MMPI appears to be related to personality needs to remain cool, aloof, and wary, and to a general reluctance to reveal onself (Dahlstrom and Welsh, 1960).

To summarize, we have indicated that for a variety of reasons, some people resent being asked certain questions. These reasons do not necessarily concern the use to which the information will be put, but principally involve the negative feelings which result from being forced to confront the anxiety-arousing subject matter. Bennett (1967) has noted, in his excellent analysis of the problem, that every society has established rules or norms under which its members attain more benefits than would result from anarchy. These results periodically should be, and typically are, scrutinized and changed if found lacking. Those people who wish to initiate these changes have the responsibility for considering the consequences that even thinking about change would have on members of the society. Because such inquiry does cause considerable apprehension and anxiety, a reasonable degree of restraint must be exercised in asking members of a culture to give information about, or even to think about, certain of its important rules. If this restraint is not exercised, the effectiveness and professional image of the would-be changers of a society is bound to suffer. In the case of our contemporary American society, however desirable it may appear in the long run to gather certain information, psychologists and other social scientists will be ineffective and perhaps even seriously damage themselves if they do not recognize and respond to these very basic concerns and facts about social change.

Some positive responses to many of the criticisms previously discussed in this chapter suggest themselves when we consider the public image of psychology, especially of personality assessment. A clear statement of the poor state of this public image was offered by Nettler (1959) in an article entitled "Test Burning in Texas," which described the generalized unfavorable public reaction to a community-wide testing program. Eron and Walder (1961) reported, however, on another personality research program in which comprehensive and thoughtful procedures were instituted to prepare the community for the participation of both parents and children. Although some persons in the community produced publicity that was unfavorable and deliberately misleading, the foresight of the research team and their straightforwardness in dealing with community concerns and anxieties resulted in excellent cooperation from all but a handful of people. We suggest that psychologists might pay more careful attention to their public relations, particularly with regard to disseminating clear and accurate information about assessment procedures, and that this attention could do much to forestall unfavorable public reactions.

Before leaving the general area of invasion of privacy, we should note that there are certain situations in which there should be no question about the legitimacy of gathering personal information about a person for selection purposes; namely, those positions involving the public security. Bennett (1967) has identified three such situations: (1) where an individual may be susceptible to blackmail by unfriendly governments; (2) where a person may be assigned for important public duty overseas; and (3) where the position is that of policeman or guard. Bennett also pointed out that the amount of investigation to which an individual is subjected is proportional to the seriousness of making a poor selection decision. Thus, applicants for loans or credit are often subjected to a detailed investigation in the relevant areas, however private these areas may be. Perhaps the best example of a personality evaluation on an applicant is that given to a candidate for the presidency of the United States. First, his entire background is scrutinized by his rivals for any information which could possibly reflect negatively on him. Then, under guise of determining his position on substantive issues, the candidate is made the target of a blistering stress interview lasting many months, in which a single major error could cost him his goal. The degree of personal stability required to survive such a test is possessed by few, and the candidate who makes the best showing in this lengthy situational test is elected. The same applies, of course, to all political campaigns to some degree. In these circumstances, confidentiality or personal privacy traditionally has no meaning, and American society demands that the lives of important political figures be open to continual public scrutiny.

RESTRICTION OF FREEDOM

One further criticism of personality assessment which merits discussion involves those procedures which are claimed to restrict a person's individual freedom. For example, with regard to ability assessment, the use of intelligence tests in schools has often been criticized on the grounds that a child's opportunities tend to be restricted by the category into which the test score explicitly or implicitly places him (for example, Ebel, 1964a). This restriction has been documented in a series of research projects by Rosenthal (1966), who concluded that children tend to perform according to others' expectations of them, and that these expectations tend to get communicated regardless of efforts to control them. Since personality assessment interpretations lead us to develop expectations about others, we may subtly influence these others to fulfill our expectations. For example, if an assessment report suggests that a person is "untrustworthy," our constant suspiciousness may either produce ambiguous behavior, which we then interpret as justifying the label, or we may actually induce such behavior in the other person by our responses. One trend toward counteracting these effects can be seen in the current efforts to deemphasize the use of psychiatric diagnostic labels for patients in clinics and mental hospitals because they create strong expectations of patient behavior, a point of view which is supported, in rather different ways, by the writings of Kanfer and Saslow (1965) and of Szasz (1961).

Regarding the restriction of freedom, there is a somewhat different criticism which is made of personality assessment in the context of selection, namely the problem of "prevention of progress by encouraging the mundane and prosaic" (Guion, 1965, p. 372). Suppose a large industrial organization wishes to select the best executive applicants. The organization might follow the time-honored empirical procedure of exhaustively studying the best persons it has recruited for some years and using the results of this study to set the standards for selection. Thus, in the case of a company, a selection battery might be developed to choose applicants similar to the company's best executives over the past 15 years. Once the selection battery is in operation, the company has inadvertently assured itself of hiring executive trainees whose personality is currently adaptive and has been so in the recent past. Unfortunately, however, what is needed is persons who will best fit the company's needs in the future. There may be a serious error in assuming that the kind of executives most suited for running the company yesterday and today will be optimal in the future. At best, the talent pool becomes markedly narrowed by this procedure, and all executives in the company begin to look alike. At worst, if the management happens to be mediocre at the present time, this state of affairs is perpetuated. People with new and different ideas are never given a chance.

Selection programs need not involve this narrowing of talent and perpetuation of the present state of affairs. Once the nature of the present management staff is determined, the selection team in collaboration with management can then decide whether or not to continue this pattern. One reasonable approach might be to determine what trends are occurring in the industry, and to orient the selection criteria toward persons with characteristics most suitable for dealing with these trends. Also, diversity can deliberately be built in. Once the present managers are described, a deliberate plan can be developed to detect persons who differ from them in specified ways. These plans capitalize on the advantages of a selection program—knowing what kinds of people are being selected—without falling into the trap of making the organization's managers increasingly narrow in their outlook.

Summary

Personality assessment practices were subjected to a lengthy and careful scrutiny in 1965, when two sets of Congressional hearings were held. Although the avowed purpose of the hearings was to investigate invasion of privacy through the use of personality tests in federal government personnel selection practices, many more issues were explored. Complaints about personality assessment can be grouped under two headings: problems of *usage* and problems involving *moral issues*.

Usage problems are of two kinds: (1) test misuse, involving invalid use of an assessment procedure that has legitimate and validated uses; and (2) generalized test invalidity, involving the use of assessment procedures whose validity has not been established for any purpose. Test misuse is probably the most serious problem of all in the field of personality assessment, and much of the criticism is due to personnel selection practices in industry, particularly the use in this context of psychiatrically oriented instruments. Another potential misuse of personality tests is with cultural minority groups for whom the tests may not be valid, as has often been the case with the assessment of abilities. There is also a controversy over whether extensive training and experience are necessary for the valid use of projective instruments. A further misuse of personality assessment procedures is the tendency of clinical psychologists to try to derive from certain tests information which the tests were not designed to discover.

Concerning generalized test invalidity, one troublesome problem is that some assessment instruments were not designed with reference to any criteria, so that there is no reasonably straightforward use to which one can point as the "purpose" of such an instrument. Another serious problem is that of illusory correlation, which applies to tests that have traditionally been interpreted by reference to an accumulated fund of "clinical lore" or common-sense principles, and refers to the finding that many of these common-sense principles, although reliable, simply have no basis in fact.

There are two kinds of moral issues. One is that of confidentiality, referring to instances where test respondents are afraid that the information which they give might be used in some way against their interests. Once again, the most serious criticism probably arises in the context of personnel selection practices. Another problem arises when a respondent has something to hide that has nothing to do with the assessment at hand, but which may be damaging for other reasons if revealed. A different kind of confidentiality problem is related to an individual's right to know his own test results.

The second moral issue is connected with an individual's right to personal inviolacy, or privacy of his thoughts and behaviors. Many persons do not wish even to be required to think about certain topics, and being asked for responses to controversial statements is seen as a definite and unwarranted intrusion into their thoughts. However, in personnel selection situations where the public security is involved, a candidate's privacy often must be invaded. This situation might apply in assessing a person's suitability to be a policeman or an armed guard; and for candidates for political office, invasion of privacy has traditionally been the rule.

A final criticism of personality assessment procedures is that they tend to restrict an individual's freedom. This could happen through the "Rosenthal effect," in which a person's expectation of how another will behave sometimes influences the other's actual behavior. Another way in which assessment procedures can cause restriction is in the context of selection, if the criterion on which the selection procedure has been based is narrow and outmoded.

10 NEW DIRECTIONS IN PERSONALITY ASSESSMENT

We have discussed the most well-established approaches to personality assessment, and we have made occasional references to newer approaches, formulations, and techniques that appear to offer some promise for advancing assessment theory and technology. We shall now discuss some of these newer developments in more detail. It is probably fair to say that much of the research and exploration in new directions has been directly motivated by dissatisfaction because available assessment instruments and techniques are simply not as adequate as we would desire. We stated in Chapter 1 that most personality assessment techniques are atheoretical, and tend to be directed toward practical considerations; most of the newer developments in the field also tend to be of a practical nature. The fact that theoretical issues are still regarded as less important than practical ones supports the notion that personality assessment is still a fledging field, in which theoretical conceptualizations take a back seat to practical development.

Possible exceptions to this trend are two recent approaches to assessment which could be considered in part to be contributions of a theoretical nature, although both appear to have been developed as a result of dissatisfaction with existing frameworks and with the hope of ultimately producing greater accuracy in assessment. We are referring (1) to the approach to personality assessment within a behavioral learning theory framework, whose implications for assessment have been explored mainly by Kanfer and Saslow (1965), and (2) to the conceptualization of personality as a set of abilities (for example, Wallace, 1966, 1967).

Theoretical Approaches

Let us first consider the work of Kanfer and Saslow, who have addressed themselves to the problem of personality description within psychiatric settings. These authors regard personality as a set of complex behaviors which are learned and maintained through the actions of certain reinforcing consequences. In their view, the assessor or diagnostician should conduct a *functional analysis* of the behavior of the person; that is, he should attempt to formulate behavioral answers to the following questions:

(a) Which specific behavior patterns require changes in their frequency of occurrence, their intensity, their duration, or the conditions under which they occur;

(b) What are the best practical means which can produce the desired changes in this individual (manipulation of the environment, of the behavior, or the self-attitudes of the patient); and

(c) What factors are currently maintaining it and what are the conditions under which this behavior was acquired (1965, pp. 529–530).

In the behaviorally oriented approach to personality assessment, use would be made of a variety of sources of information, such as traditional interviewing and testing procedures, and also observation of the patient's daily behavior and his interaction with significant others. The functional analysis thus achieved is one oriented toward action, in that it serves both as a guide for collecting and organizing information and as a plan for initiating a program of behavior change. Kanfer and Saslow have limited their consideration to personality description or assessment of patients in psychiatric settings as a prerequisite for bringing about behavioral change, though their position would appear to have much greater generality.

Goldfried and Pomeranz (1968) have presented a similar viewpoint on the role of personality assessment with respect to psychological treatment. These authors argue that the most significant practical uses of assessments are in identifying areas where behavior changes are desirable, and in helping to determine how these changes might be brought about. They emphasize that it is important to consider covert behaviors (thoughts and feelings), as well as overt behaviors, as potential areas for modification. They have also noted that it is appropriate to inquire, as part of the assessment process, whether it might be desirable to try to bring about changes in environmental conditions which are causally related to the behavior in question. Wernimont and Campbell (1968) have raised the same issues in the context of industrial personnel practice.

Let us now consider how personality has been conceptualized as a set of abilities. A number of authors (for example Anastasi, 1967; Goldberg and Slovic, 1967; Wallace, 1966, 1967) have expressed dissatisfaction with the traditional viewpoint of personality as enduring response predispositions, which refer to what a person *really is*, and which are conceptualized as needs, traits, or drives—variables frequently considered as descriptive of the "essence" of the person. Wallace, who has written most fully on the topic, has suggested conceptualizing personality in terms of abilities or skills rather than in terms of predispositions or essence. He has suggested that personality concepts such as "aggressiveness," "dependency," and "leadership" be regarded as abilities or skills rather than as predispositions, much as we regard reading, operating a motor vehicle, or speaking a foreign language as skills rather than as predispositions. Thus, a person who has performed a sequence of behaviors that could be reliably labelled as "aggressive" would be regarded as having the skill or capacity of assuming an aggressive role or of emitting aggressive responses, without making any inferences about the centrality of this concept in the underlying personality structure or expressing any concern about the "level" at which it would be expected to operate.

With respect to his view of personality as abilities, Wallace (1967) has suggested two central questions: (1) that of response capability, which would inquire whether the individual has the appropriate response in his repertoire, and (2) that of response performance, which would inquire about the presence of the conditions which are necessary for the performance of this response. These interrelated questions are the focal concepts for Wallace's view of personality and have some direct implications for personality assessment. For example, assessment should be conducted under optimal conditions of measurement, much in the same way as skills are assessed, so that the respondent's performance on a personality test will fully reflect his response capacity. Thus, the assessment situation should be highly structured, ambiguity should be at a minimum, and it should be made known that there are "correct" response alternatives, as is the case with the measurement of abilities. To illustrate his approach to personality assessment, Wallace (1966) had undergraduates respond to TAT cards by writing "the most hostile story" of which they were capable, and "the most sexy story." The obtained results were considered to reflect individual differences in these two response capabilities or "personality abilities."

Wallace (1967) has proposed at least three sets of factors which can affect response performance in addition to response capability: reinforcement conditions or the individual learning history of the respondent, situation-specific hypotheses or the inferences the respondent must make about himself in responding to personality assessment devices (for example, in answering the self-report item "I am assertive"), and the formal properties or demand characteristics of the situation in which a prediction is to be made. The implications of this framework for personality assessment are rather similar to those generated by Kanfer and Saslow (1965), and by other proponents of behavior learning approaches for bringing about personality change (for example, Ullmann and Krasner, 1965), in that the focus is clearly upon the development of response repertoires in conjunction with the creation of conditions for the sustaining of those behaviors that are regarded as enhancing the effectiveness of the individual.

Regarding the prediction of behavior, Mischel (1968, pp. 288–290) has pointed to some promising results obtained by using measures of an individual's environment, rather than intrapsychic measures, as predictors of his socially significant behaviors. Thus, in one example Fairweather (1964) showed that the post-hospital adjustment of the psychiatric patients that he studied was highly related to the degree of supportiveness present in their new environments. Another way to use environmental measures would be to increase the accuracy of the existing intrapsychic predictors; for example, in the intellective field, Wolf (1966) was able to report a correlation of 0.87 between children's IQ scores and a predictor based on achievement test battery scores plus an "achievement-enhancing" rating of the environment, compared with a correlation of 0.76 between IQ and achievement scores alone.

The recent increasing interest in employing biographical and other factual information within a traditional personality assessment framework can also be viewed as consistent with the behavioral orientation which we have just described. It will be remembered that formalized personality assessment originated with Woodworth (see Chapter 2), whose Personal Data Sheet was simply a list of questions that psychiatrists might ask. After Woodworth, development of structured assessment devices proceeded in two directions. One, typified by the Strong Vocational Interest Blank and the MMPI, was to make no assumptions about the truth of the respondent's answers, but to treat these responses simply as data from which predictions might be possible. The other approach, employed initially by Woodworth, was to regard the answers as truthful information. Personality questionnaires based upon this latter approach soon came under fire as being highly vulnerable to simulation, and it is not surprising that psychologists became less willing to rely upon instruments which assumed that responses represented truthful reports. A third possible approach was recognized early by workers in the personnel field but was largely ignored by clinical psychologists. In this third approach, only *verifiable* information is collected—that is, objective information about actual events and actual behaviors. The use of such verifiable information as age, marital status, and sibling order in making specific predictions for socially significant behaviors has been previously discussed in Chapter 8. The use of life history data in identifying persons with creative talent and with managerial ability has also been widely explored (for example, Brodie, Owens, and Britt, 1968; Tucker, Cline, and Schmitt, 1967). However, in spite of a number of exhortations (for example, Fulkerson and Barry, 1961; Meehl, 1959b) to develop life history or biographical indices of clinically important personality characteristics, which are now usually assessed by traditional methods, relatively few such instruments are available for clinical use. Supporting the development of self-report instruments for gathering biographical information is some recent research by Walsh (1967, 1968), who showed that the data collected by the self-report method were acceptably accurate even when respondents were given a financial incentive to distort their answers.

Use of Computers

We next will consider a relatively recent innovation which has had considerable effect on personality assessment—the availability of electronic computers for high-speed calculation and data processing. The major impact of computer technology on personality assessment has been indirect, by permitting developments that could have taken place only as such labor-saving devices became available. This development is consistent with the impact of computer technology on other fields. In general, the main effect of the invention of high-speed computing and data-processing machinery has been not simply the performance of greater volumes of work, but developments and innovations in the kinds of work that can be performed. Thus, our computerized society is different from its former state in qualitative ways, and many of these differences were not anticipated, nor are they fully understood or fully developed as yet. Since the application of computer technology to personality assessment is so recent, thus far we have seen primarily quantitative changes in this field—that is, increases in the volume of work that can be performed. Thus it is possible, using optical scanners which "read" the specially prepared answer sheets for such self-report inventories as the MMPI and the California Psychological Inventory (CPI), to score a protocol and plot a profile almost instantaneously.

As another example of the potential labor saving function of computers, it is now feasible to attempt some of the more complex scoring procedures which have been proposed for inventories from time to time. One such procedure is Meehl's (1950) suggestion about configural scoring. Rather than depending upon the predictive usefulness of responses to single inventory items, Meehl suggested that we could examine responses to pairs of items, or triads, or even larger combinations. Such an approach would involve the pattern, organization, or configuration of item responses, which has traditionally been regarded as an important element in sophisticated clinical personality assessment.

The simplest type of configural scoring involves the simultaneous use of responses to pairs of items. Respondents would either have answered both items "true," both items "false," the first item "true" and the second item "false," or vice versa. Such configural patterns would then serve as the basis for developing empirical scoring keys, exactly as we have previously done in the case of responses to single items. The pairs or other combinations of items could be rationally selected as tapping some important domain or personality functioning, or could be empirically developed by the computer on a trial-and-error basis. The development of configural approaches to inventory scoring would involve sizeable amounts of computer time, but simply would not have been possible at all prior to the computer.

Meehl demonstrated that it would be possible for a configural scoring procedure to uncover pairs of items which singly have zero validity, but which are highly predictive when scored configurally. Configural scoring holds some promise for increasing the validity of personality inventories, in part through increasing the subtlety of the items, so that dissimulation is more difficult. These potential applications are also relevant, of course, for the modification of other psychometric devices beside inventories. A start in developing the necessary computational technology for configural scoring has been made by Williams and Kleinmuntz (1969).

Hints of other far-reaching changes in personality assessment procedures stemming from the use of computers are evident in the commercial availability of mail-order computer-produced *interpretations* of MMPI and CPI protocols. These mail-order services provide, at nominal cost, a profile of the inventory scale scores and a narrative description of the personality of the repondent based upon the profile. The potential range of mail-order services and the problem of ethical controls over them constitute important social issues. That the profession of psychology has not been prepared for these developments is indicated by the fact that the American Psychological Association did not formulate any policies and standards for them until they had become readily available commercially.

There is a very important confusion in the use of computer aids for interpretation in personality assessment. Mechanical or actuarial methods have been applied to personality assessment for some time. However, many of the advantages which have been attributed to computers are in fact due to the application of actuarial methods to profile interpretation. Thus, Eber (1965) and Piotrowski (1964) both stated that the validity of computer-reported personality assessments could be determined easily because such an assessment is objective and invariant, and not subject to human unreliability. In addition, developing a computer program for personality interpretation is said to force the psychologist to be specific, logical, and precise in his thinking. It should be clear that both of these advantages are only incidentally attributable to the computer. Objective information and precise thinking are prerequisites for the development of actuarial rules, which existed prior to the development of the computer, although the computer has facilitated the acceptance of an actuarial approach to personality assessment. The specific contribution of the computer to personality assessment has been *time-saving*, and the advantages derived from time-saving. Some of these advantages have been listed by Rome (Rome et al., 1962): the time of highly trained professional persons is freed for less routine activities, procedures may be simplified for the patient, and a variety of highly complex interpretive procedures can be tried (such as investigating the applicability of many different rules and indices) which were previously impracticable because of the time and labor involved.

The main difference to be noted between the manually applied actuarial rules of the 1950s and the computer applied rules of the 1960s is that the rules for computer use are many times more complex than rules for manual application, and they often take the form of representing as much as possible of what is known about a test. In principle, the clinician of the 1950's also could have tried to write down all his knowledge about a personality test in the form of actuarial rules, and then have his secretary interpret the tests for him. The fact that nobody did this suggests that clinicians felt there would simply be too many rules, making the task of checking them manually an extremely laborious one. Now that computers are available to store and check the rules, a number of psychologists have proceeded with the development of lengthy and complex test interpretation programs.

The Meehl-Dahlstrom rules (Meehl and Dahlstrom, 1960) for the discrimination of neurotic and psychotic patients by means of their MMPI profiles constitute one well-known example of the development of complex actuarial rules which are suitable for computer use. Kleinmuntz (1963), with the specific use of the computer in mind, developed a similiar set of MMPI rules for the identification of adjusted and maladjusted college students. The procedure employed by Kleinmuntz was to have several MMPI experts make a 14-category Q-sort of 126 MMPI profile sheets, with "least adjusted" at one extreme and "most adjusted" at the other. The expert who achieved the highest success rate was asked to repeat the sorting task, elaborating aloud on his reasons for placing each MMPI profile in the particular category to which he assigned it. Approximately 60 hours of recording tape was collected in this manner, and these verbalizations were carefully analyzed and used as the basis for developing a set of actuarial rules for sorting MMPI profiles into "adjusted" and "maladjusted" categories. The rules were then programmed for use by a computer, whose capacity for storage and high-speed retrieval permitted many further refinements to be made in the rules. The original rules derived from the expert's tape-recorded statements are given in flow chart form in Figure 10-1. Two additional MMPI scales are utilized in the rules: Barron's (1953) ego strength (*Es*) scale, and Kleinmuntz's (1960) college maladjustment (*Mt*) scale. (These scales are reported in raw score form in the figure.) The final set of rules is more complex and may be seen in Kleinmuntz's (1963) original monograph.

The first reported computer program for complete personality test interpretation was developed for the MMPI by Swenson at the Mayo Clinic (Rome et al., 1962). Taking each of the 13 common MMPl scales in turn, Swenson wrote interpretative statements to describe the personality implications of four different levels of scores on each scale. Eleven more statements were written to take into account important patterns of scores among the different scales. The computer prints out a personality description consisting of about 12 statements, most of which refer to the scores on single scales. The Mayo computer program is the basis for a program which has been in routine use at the Hartford Institute for Living, and it is also available as a commercial service (Pearson and Swenson, 1967). Another MMPI interpretation program has been described by Fowler (1965, 1969). Fowler's program, also commercially available, was originally developed to meet the author's practical need to make rapid interpretations of MMPI profiles in connection with diagnostic consultation. Because most clinicians who interpret the MMPI make use of configurations of scores rather than concentrating on the elevation of single scales, Fowler chose to base his program on the interpretation of the two highest scales of an MMPI profile. After developing a "two-point code library" of interpretive statements, additional statements were written to take

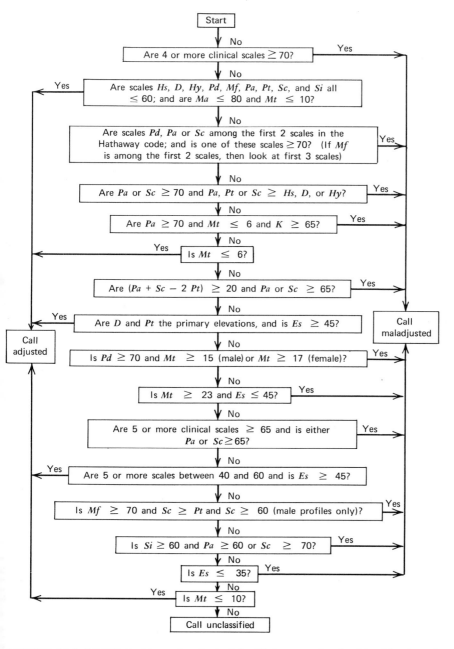

FIGURE 10-1. MMPI decision rules devised by Kleinmuntz for the identification of maladjustment in college students.

into account other scale elevations and configurations, as well as factors such as sex, age, and marital status.

The most complex MMPI interpretive program to date is that reported by Finney (1965). Finney's program, using the MMPI either alone or in combination with the CPI, utilizes up to 123 separate scales, as well as indices based on two or more scales, and "composes a lengthy, detailed, and highly organized psychological report" (1965, p. 1). In developing the program, Finney made rather elaborate efforts to meet certain methodological problems. For example, rules were written that would include appropriate conjunctions between descriptive phrases so that the reports would read sensibly. Special rules were written to deal with test profiles in which almost all scores are very high, in order to avoid producing a report in which the patient would be ascribed a wide and confusing array of pathology. Special efforts were also devoted to writing statements which would reconcile obviously conflicting findings in such a way as to make the report more meaningful.

Computer interpretation has also been applied to Rorschach responses. It is not surprising that this work should have been pioneered by Piotrowski (1964, 1969), who, of psychologists prominently identified with the Rorschach test, has been the most strongly interested in actuarial approaches (for example, Piotrowski, 1937, 1943). There are certain special problems which must be dealt with in attempting to employ interpretation with projective response materials. One problem is that the responses are unstandardized or idiosyncratic, and therefore must be reduced to units which can be handled in an actuarial manner. Piotrowski's latest program identifies more than 800 such response components and utilizes 937 interpretive rules, which are based to a greater extent on the formal aspects of the Rorschach test than upon content. Although computer processing of a Rorschach protocol is rapid, coding the protocol in preparation for processing is a slow and laborious task, and is reported to be a major difficulty in the use of the system at the present time.

Gorham (1967) described a computerized scoring system for 17 variables of the Holtzman Inkblot Technique (HIT), developed on protocols collected through group administration of the test. In order to reduce the response material to manageable proportions, Gorham originally limited each response to six words and eliminated the inquiry phase. In scoring a response, the computer makes use of a "dictionary" of 6100 words most commonly found in HIT responses, and assigns weights to each word according to its known contribution to each of the 17 variables. Gorham showed that this scoring procedure was as reliable as traditional scoring. His current scoring system allows more than six words per response and also incorporates a modified "location" score. Gorham's HIT program does not offer personality interpretation, but simply a rapid scoring system which is designed to facilitate use of the HIT.

A special advantage to the computer handling of responses to projective stimulus materials is that large masses of data can be processed. Thus it will become more feasible to use projective tests on a large scale, and hopefully it will be possible to examine validity issues more carefully. A special problem lies in the treatment of the response data, where a choice must be made as to whether responses should be highly restricted or whether extremely complex coding systems should be developed.

Comment. As stated above, we are predicting that the most important changes to be brought about by the use of computers in personality assessment and diagnosis will be qualitative. Increments in objectivity are primarily due to actuarial techniques, not to computers, although the labor-saving advantage of the computer enables much more complex actuarial procedures to be employed. There is a practical limit to how many rules a clerk can utilize in examining test data; there is also a practical limit to how many rules a computer can utilize, but it is many times greater. As Piotrowski (1964) has pointed out, there is no reason to limit a computer interpretation program to response material from just one test. Data from several different tests and also biographical and current status data could be employed to extend the information base from which descriptions and predictions are made. The professional clinician, relieved of some of his more routine duties in this manner, can spend his time doing work that cannot be performed automatically, at least at the present time. It will be when significant amounts of professional time can be saved by computers that the *qualitative* changes due to computer assistance will become more clearly evident.

Decision Making

Computer technology has been applied in a variety of complex ways to both diagnosis and treatment in psychiatry and in medicine generally. For example, Howell and Loy (1968) have discussed the identification of medical diseases by computer, and Spitzer and Endicott (1968) have reported on a computer program for psychiatric diagnosis. A classic theoretical paper by Ledley and Lusted (1959) in this area on medical diagnosis should also be noted. Reports of computer-assisted diagnosis have also been published for carcinoma of the lung or bronchus (Hollingsworth, 1959), thyrotoxicosis (Crooks, Murray, and Wayne, 1959), and nontoxic goiter (Boyle et al., 1966). An excellent introduction to this work is contained in the recent text by Lusted (1968).

There is a difference between medical diagnosis, as traditionally performed, and psychological diagnosis or personality assessment—a difference which makes for considerable difficulty when attempting to apply some of the complex medically oriented computer methods to the personality area. Medical diagnosis is presumed to mean the identification of a disease entity. That is, positive identification of some pathological process is presumed to be possible. A patient either has cancer or he does not. It is not possible, however, to treat personality assessment in this manner, because personality traits (and most psychiatric categories) are not *real* in the sense that cancer is real. Psychologists interested in computer-based actuarial techniques have tended, therefore, to direct their efforts in a somewhat different direction. Some have dispensed with the assessment or diagnosis step altogether, and have applied actuarial methods to help determine what should be done with the patient, or what action should be taken. In other words, they concentrate directly on the *decision* to be made.

The development of a decision-making orientation in the field of personality assessment came about in two ways. The first incursion was an outcome of a paper published in 1955 by Meehl and Rosen, who drew initial attention to the base rate problem which we previously discussed, namely, that accuracy of classifying patients into a diagnostic category depends on the overall size of that particular category in the population under study. The paper also implied, perhaps without intent, that percentage accuracy was the all-important criterion in diagnosis or classification. This paper elicited a number of rejoinders (for example Buchwald, 1965; Karson and Sells, 1956; Rimm, 1963) which insisted that it was the *utility* of a classification, not its accuracy, that should be used as the ultimate criterion for judging it. Taking account of utility involves a quantitative determination of the different consequences of the various possible classifications in terms of their costs to all concerned. For example, what would the overall costs be to the individual, to his family, to those professionals concerned with his treatment, and to society generally, of institutionalizing a patient at a given time; and, conversely, what would these costs be if the patient were to be maintained in the home?

The second important influence leading toward a decision-making orientation in personality assessment was the appearance of the first edition of *Psychological Tests and Personnel Decisions* by Cronbach and Gleser (1957), who offered a clear decision-making framework for the use of psychological tests, as an alternative to more traditional orientations. Among the issues raised was that of the expected utility or "payoff" of a particular kind of information in terms of the cost of obtaining this information relative to its yield in predictive accuracy. In other words, the cost of the testing program must be weighed against the increased efficiency of the selection process. Further discussion of this and other practical applications of the decision-making approach have been provided by Arthur (1966, 1969), Cole and Magnussen (1966), and Cronbach and Gleser (1965). Breger (1968) also has emphasized a decision-making orientation in his discussion of psychological testing.

Specifically, the decision-making approach focuses upon the consequences of various courses of action. Instead of describing a person according to such traditional personality dimensions as dominant, tolerant, and anxious, or classifying him according to traditional psychiatric categories, such as depressed, schizophrenic, and brain-damaged, the decision-making approach deals with the various courses of action open to those persons who are performing the assessment. For example, if a psychiatrist requests a "personality evaluation" of a patient so that he can decide whether to discharge the patient, keep him under intensive care, or send him to the back ward, these three options become the possible alternatives to be studied. There is no criterion for the accuracy of assessment, in the sense that a description of being high in dominance can be verified against peer ratings or the holding of leadership positions, or a diagnosis of schizophrenia can be checked for accuracy against a panel of expert judges, or a diagnosis of brain damage can be checked against physiological exploration. Rather, the criterion is one of cost and utility—the value of the decision. The aim is to make the decision-assessment that results in the most useful outcome, all things considered. How one decides upon and evaluates these "all things" will be discussed below, following an introduction to the way in which a decision-making orientation is employed in other fields.

Operations Research. During the second World War, the British government was faced with the problem of allocating its limited war resources to a wide variety of possible activities. The criterion for allocation was simple in principle—to maximize the effectiveness of these resources. Mathematical techniques were developed to assist in the kind of decisions that were necessary under these circumstances. After the war, it was realized that the decisions that had been faced were essentially the same as those facing business and industry in countless ways. For example, how many salesmen should a company hire, and where should they be sent, to sell a maximal amount of the company's products at the least cost? Or, how many check-out counters should a supermarket have in order to preserve an optimal balance between saving on clerks' time and losing customers because of their waiting too long? Again, how many plants should a company have, and where should they be located, in order to strike an optimal balance between the cost of transporting raw materials on the one hand, and the cost of transporting finished goods to their markets, on the other? The field of expertise in the complex engineering, mathematical, and business skills needed to approach such problems has come to be known as *operations research*. For an account of some of the techniques of this field, the reader is referred to Ackoff and Rivett (1963) for a brief introduction, and to Hillier and Lieberman (1967) for a more detailed treatment.

In business and industry, the criterion of utility traditionally employed is simple: monetary profit. Relationships can be quantified in terms of the money involved, and a system can then be devised which presumably will result in the greatest profit. A similar approach is possible in the context of psychological assessment; the assessment situation, however, is not quite so straightforward. A major problem is the determination of the values to be placed on the alternate available decisions. The values will at times be monetary, but a more important component is the social or cultural values involved. For example, how much is it worth, socially, to a person to avoid confining him in a psychiatric hospital? Or, how much is it worth to a community to have a particular person confined in a psychiatric hospital where his bizarre actions will not threaten others? Ways of determining such values and incorporating them into decision-making processes remain still to be developed in order to make full use of the potential of operations research technology. An interesting collection of papers relating to this problem has been published (Shelly and Byran, 1964).

It can be argued that social and cultural values are too complex to be quantified, and that it is foolish to hope for any success along these lines. However, as Arthur (1966) has pointed out, these values are estimated whenever an actual decision is made about a psychiatric patient, whether or not the decision maker is explicit about them. In other words, we cannot and do not avoid making judgments about these values in our actual behavior. The situation might be seen as analogous to a skilled clinician who integrates personality assessment information in his head and makes a diagnosis or a prediction about the respondent. He has combined certain specific pieces of information according to certain specific rules, whether or not he was aware of doing so. A task for the future is to understand and make explicit these implicit processes and values.

Mention should also be made of another term often used to describe the orientation discussed above: *systems analysis*. This is a much more general term than operations research, and is loosely used to refer to the employment of complex quantitative procedures and computers to problems involving a very large number of variables. It is used more specifically to refer to the analyses of complex situations where an attempt is made to identify *all* the variables which interact and influence the outcomes of interest. The situation, defined by those variables which need to be taken into account, is then called a system, and any part of any operation involved in quantifying processes within the system may become labelled as "systems analysis." Thus, in the context of assessment, Nathan (1967) has developed extensive sets of diagnostic rules for classifying psychiatric patients into traditional psychiatric categories, and he has referred to his work as a systems-analytic approach to the diagnosis of psychopathology. Nathan's work should not be confused with decision-making as discussed above, since the decisions to which he is referring concern placement into traditional diagnostic categories, and not alternate treatments or other courses of action.

Mention should be made of the application to personality assessment of one further concept from a decision-making context. It is possible to conceptualize a continuum which has at one extreme those assessment devices which yield a careful and thorough evaluation of a single, homogeneous psychological variable, such as clerical speed or cognitive slippage, and at the other extreme those which yield a more cursory examination of broad and complex variables, such as personal adjustment. Cronbach and Gleser (1957, 1965), using the language of information theory, have suggested using the term "band width" to describe the scope or variety of information obtainable from an assessment procedure and "fidelity" for the thoroughness or intensity with which the information is provided. Since increases in fidelity invariably lead to decreases in band width and vice versa, a dilemma is always posed in practical situations. Using some of the mathematical procedures of decision theory, Cronbach and Gleser (1957) have presented a technique for solving this dilemma, through the development of an "ideal" compromise. Included in their procedure are techniques for deciding when single tests fare better than many tests, and the optimal time to allocate to different tests.

Comment. We are neither predicting nor recommending that decision-making replace personality assessment as a discipline. But in certain practical circumstances (and contemporary society is currently much more interested in the practical than the theoretical) where personality assessment is traditionally utilized as one step in a process which ultimately results in a decision, a decision-making approach affords the possibility of bypassing the assessment step altogether. Psychologists have commonly used personality assessment instruments for making decisions, such as the use of the MMPI to decide whether or not a patient should be given electroshock therapy (Feldman, 1952). They now have the opportunity for being systematic about identifying the assessment situations in which the goal is to make a concrete decision, and treating these situations within a decision-making framework.

Moderator Variables

From time to time statisticians have discovered what appear to be tricks for making silk purses out of sows' ears. One of these tricks was seemingly embodied in the Taylor-Russell tables for determining the likelihood of selecting an acceptable candidate from a number of applicants, given the base rate of acceptable candidates, their scores on a predictive test, and the predictive validity of the test (Taylor and Russell, 1939). The tables are used to best advantage when there is an extreme selection ratio; that is, when there are many, many candidates from which to choose and only a few openings to fill. In such a case, even if the predictive validity of the test is very low, the few top scorers on the test are reasonably likely to be successful and the few bottom scorers likely to be unsuccessful on the job. Thus, the use of a mediocre test can result in reasonably good selection, when (and only when) certain rather specific conditions are present.

The use of *moderator variables* for improving prediction has come to be regarded with the same suspicion that is implied in the above paragraph, though the logic of their use is perfectly clear. What is necessary is a set of specific circumstances; given this, predictive accuracy can sometimes be enhanced.

The concept of moderator variables was originally identified by Ghiselli (1956, 1963) and by Saunders (1956). A moderator is a piece of information that can be used to predict, for a given respondent or set of respondents, the accuracy of another predictor. For example, if it is known that college grades for compulsive students can be effectively predicted from their aptitude test scores but grades for noncompulsive students cannot, then a measure of compulsivity could be used to moderate the prediction of grades from aptitude test scores—that is, to identify those students for whom the prediction will be relatively accurate and those for whom it will not. If we were to confine our interest to only the highly compulsive students, the predictive validity of college board scores would be higher than if we considered everybody. In other words, we have improved prediction at the expense of working only with those persons for whom we know prediction to be the most valid.

At first glance, the potentialities for improving prediction by the use of moderators in personality assessment seem enormous. They are probably already used informally in a wide number of instances; for example, if Dr. Jones is known to be expert at teasing out the differential personality dynamics of schizoid individuals who come to the clinic where he works, the intake interviewer may be more likely to send the schizoid clients to Dr. Jones for their personality workup. To extend the principle, there is the possibility for devising a moderator to indicate how much attention should be paid to a patient's Rorschach protocol or his MMPI profile in arriving at a psychiatric diagnosis. On a more complex level, it might be possible to determine whether, for a particular patient or group of patients, most attention should be paid to the Rorschach protocol, the Draw-A-Person, the MMPI, biographical information, or any other particular source of data.

Most of the research to date in developing moderator variables has been concerned with the prediction of success in academic or personnel areas. In attempting to enhance the prediction of earnings among cab drivers, Ghiselli (1960a) found that a moderator based on age and education could be used to indicate which of two ability measures (spatial and motor ability tests) was the better predictor. In this study, the spatial test was a better predictor for the older and less educated drivers. Ghiselli (1960b) also showed that it was possible to develop a moderator variable empirically by using a criterion groups approach. The characteristic to be predicted was sociability, as assessed by a questionnaire. The predictor, which showed a low correlation with sociability, was intelligence, defined by a rather arbitrary scale on a self-description inventory. To develop the moderator, two criterion groups were identified. The "predictable" group was composed of those persons whose scores fell at about the same point in the sociability and the intelligence distributions. The remainder constituted the "unpredictable" group. Responses to the self-description inventory were then examined to identify items which discriminated the two groups, and these items formed the moderator scale. Cross-validation on a new sample showed that the scale continued to identify the most predictable individuals.

Although the greatest success of moderator variables thus far has been in enhancing prediction of academic or job success, Fulkerson (1959) has demonstrated that the validity of a personality test for predicting general adjustment was related to the extroversion-introversion, or hysteric-psychasthenic, personality dimension, presumably because the introverted respondents were more careful in their responses. Further, in a study of clinical judgment, Tomlinson (1967) showed, among other things, that the judges with high achievement needs made more accurate client predictions than other judges after interviewing a client directly, but *less* accurate predictions than other judges when observing the client through a one-way mirror.

What is the basis for the utility of moderator variables? In the first two examples, the prediction of grades for college students and success among cab drivers, common-sense or rational explanations can be offered as to why certain subgroups should be more predictable than others. Thus, one would expect that compulsive students might be more likely to work to the limit of their abilities, while the less compulsive students would tend to devote time selectively to the courses which interested them. What is more difficult to explain is the fact that empirical moderator scales, with no obviously relevant content, can be developed in some instances. A discussion of possible psychometric explanations, though beyond our present scope, has been offered by Hobert and Dunnette (1967).

There are several limitations to the use of moderators in enhancing prediction. First, it may not be possible to develop moderator variables for all predictions. Smith and Lanyon (1968) used biographical data to post-dict juvenile offenders who violated their probation, and then attempted to build an empirical moderator scale, based on MMPI items, to improve the post-diction. Absolutely no improvement resulted, perhaps because the factors determining whether probation would be violated might have been circumstantial, and not present or ascertainable until the probation period had begun. Another potential limitation, not yet explored, is the possibility that moderators might work because some persons tend to be predictable as a general personality characteristic, while others are unpredictable. If this were the case, the clinical potential of moderators would be severely limited, because the same person who scored high on a moderator for the MMPI would score high on moderators for all other sources of personality information.

It is still too early to know what the long-term contribution of moderator variables to the field of personality assessment will be. A number of experts in the personality assessment and related fields, however, have predicted their increasing importance, among them Anastasi (1967) and Goldberg (1968b). It is fair to say that the exploration of moderator variables represents an advance in the technology of personality assessment, since it goes beyond a global search for validity, and explores the question of different degrees of validity for different kinds of persons under different circumstances.

Summary

Most of the recent developments in personality assessment have been of a technological rather than a theoretical nature. However, two new theoretical frameworks for personality assessment are worth noting. The first is in the context of behavioral learning theory, and proposes that psychological diagnosticians should conduct a functional analysis of the patient's behavior. This analysis would serve both as a guide for organizing information and as a plan for psychological treatments. In the second, personality characteristics are approached as abilities rather than dispositions, and the task of personality assessment becomes somewhat similar to the assessment of capabilities. This approach, like the former, tends to be consistent with behavioral learning approaches to personality. It should also be noted that there is a gradually increasing use of biographical and behavioral information for making assessments and predictions within the more traditional frameworks of personality assessment.

An important recent technological development in personality assessment has been the use of computers. Whereas the introduction of actuarial rules and techniques had afforded increases in the reliability and objectivity of interpretations, the use of computers has contributed immense savings of time. It is now feasible to develop highly sophisticated programs for both configural scoring and test interpretation, of a complexity that could never have been utilized with only manual clerical assistance. The most far-reaching changes to be brought about by computers will be qualitative; that is, changes in the nature of personality assessment and its applications. Since computers are a recent innovation in the field, these qualitative changes are not yet apparent. Several computer programs of varying degrees of complexity have been developed for interpretation of the MMPI, and attempts have been made to deal with methodological problems encountered in writing programs for composing automated psychological reports. An extensive computer program has also been prepared for Rorschach interpretation, although coding of the original responses remains a problem. A reliable computer scoring procedure, however, is available for the Holtzman Inkblot Technique.

Another important technological advance is signalled in recent attempts to conceptualize some aspects of personality assessment within a decision-making framework. In psychological assessment, contrary to medical assessment, a diagnosis or description cannot usually be checked against any real or verifiable criterion. Therefore, interest has developed in making choices among the options or outcomes available; that is, concentrating on the decision to be made. The adoption of a decision-making orientation makes available to psychologists the developments in decision-making technology from other fields and, in particular, the procedures utilized in business and industry known as operations research. A major problem with their application to personality assessment is that, associated with each possible outcome, there must be a quantifiable criterion of utility. In business and industry, these criteria may be specified in terms of monetary value; however, when decisions are to be made about people *qua* people, social and personal values become involved, and these are difficult to quantify.

The last development discussed is that of moderator variables. A moderator is any piece of information that can be used to predict, for a given person, how accurate another prediction is going to be. Thus, increased accuracy in prediction is potentially possible at the cost of making the prediction only for some proportion of the respondents. The majority of the research and interest in moderator variables to date has been in the contexts of academic and personnel predictions, but there is no reason why their use should not be explored for clinical and personality assessment. The way in which moderators function is not entirely clear, although a common-sense explanation appears adequate for some of their uses.

REFERENCES

Ackoff, R. L., and Rivett, P. *A manager's guide to operations research.* New York: Wiley, 1963.

Adorno, T. W., Frenkel-Brunswik, E., Levinson, D. J., and Sanford, R. N. *The authoritarian personality.* New York: Harper, 1950.

Ainsworth, M. D. Problems of validation. Chapter 14 in B. Klopfer, M. D. Ainsworth, W. G. Klopfer, and R. R. Holt, *Developments in the Rorschach technique: I. Technique and theory.* New York: Harcourt, Brace, and World, 1954.

Alex, C. *Personality tests: How to beat them and make top scores.* New York: Arco, 1965.

Allison, J., Blatt, S. J., and Zimet, C. N. *The interpretation of psychological tests.* New York: Harper and Row, 1968.

Allport, G. W. *Personality.* New York: Holt, 1937.

———, *Pattern and growth in personality.* New York: Holt, Rinehart, and Winston, 1961.

Allport, G. W., and Odbert, H. S. Trait names: a psycho-lexical study. *Psychological Monographs,* 1936, 47 (Whole No. 211).

Allport, G. W., Vernon, P. E., and Lindzey, G. *Study of Values* (third edition). Boston: Houghton-Mifflin, 1960.

American Psychological Association. Technical recommendations for psychological tests and diagnostic techniques. *Psychological Bulletin,* 1954, **51** (2, part 2).

———, Ethical standards of psychologists. *American Psychologist,* 1963, **18**, 56–60.

———, *Standards for educational and psychological tests and manuals.* Washington D.C.: APA, 1966.

———, *Casebook on ethical standards of psychologists.* Washington D.C.: APA, 1967.

Amrine, M. The 1965 congressional inquiry into testing: a commentary. *American Psychologist,* 1965, **20**, 859–870.

Anastasi, A. *Psychological testing* (second edition). New York: Macmillan, 1961.

————, Psychology, psychologists, and psychological testing. *American Psychologist*, 1967, **22**, 297–306.

Angyal, A. *Foundations for a science of personality.* New York and London: Commonwealth Fund and Oxford University Press, 1941.

Ansbacher, H. L. The history of the leaderless group discussion technique. *Psychological Bulletin*, 1951, **48**, 383–391.

Aronson, M. L. A study of the Freudian theory of paranoia by means of the Blacky pictures. *Journal of Projective Techniques*, 1953, **17**, 3–19.

Arthur, A. Z. A decision-making approach to psychological assessment in the clinic. *Journal of Consulting Psychology*, 1966, **30**, 435–438.

————, Diagnostic testing and the new alternatives. *Psychological Bulletin*, 1969, **72**, 183–192.

Auld, F., Jr., and Murray, E. J. Content-analysis studies of psychotherapy. *Psychological Bulletin*, 1955, **52**, 377–395.

Bales, R. F. *Interaction process analysis.* Cambridge: Addison-Wesley, 1950.

Bandura, A., Lipsher, D. H., and Miller, P. E. Psychotherapists' approach-avoidance reactions to patients' expressions of hostility. *Journal of Consulting Psychology*, 1960, **24**, 1–8.

Barker, R., Kounin, J., and Wright, H. F. (Eds.) *Child behavior and development.* New York: McGraw-Hill, 1943.

Barker, R., and Wright, H. F. *One boy's day.* New York: Harper, 1951.

————, *Midwest and its children. The psychological ecology of an American town.* New York: Harper and Row, 1955.

Barron, F. An ego-strength scale which predicts response to psychotherapy. *Journal of Consulting Psychology*, 1953, **17**, 327–333.

Barthell, C. N., and Holmes, D. S. High school yearbooks: a nonreactive measure of social isolation in graduates who later became schizophrenics. *Journal of Abnormal Psychology*, 1968, **73**, 313–316.

Bass, B. M. The leaderless group discussion. *Psychological Bulletin*, 1954, **51**, 465–492.

————, *Leadership, psychology and organizational behavior.* New York: Harper and Row, 1960.

Bass, B. M., and Coates, C. H. Forecasting officer potential using the leaderless group discussion. *Journal of Abnormal and Social Psychology*, 1952, **47**, 321–325.

Bechtoldt, H. P. Construct validity: a critique. *American Psychologist*, 1959, **14**, 619–629.

Beck, S. J., Beck, A. G., Levitt, E. E., and Molish, H. B. *Rorschach's test: I. Basic processes* (third edition). New York: Grune and Stratton, 1961.

Bell, H. M. *The Adjustment Inventory.* Palo Alto, California: Consulting Psychologists Press, 1939.

Bellak, L. *The Thematic Apperception Test and the Children's Apperception Test in clinical use.* New York: Grune and Stratton, 1954.

Bellows, R. M., and Estop, M. F. *Employment psychology: the interview.* New York: Rinehart, 1954.

Bender, L. A Visual motor test and its clinical use. *American Journal of Orthopsychiatry*, Research Monograph No. 3, 1938.

―――, *Instructions for the use of the Visual Motor Gestalt Test*. New York: American Orthopsychiatric Association, 1946.

Bennett, G. K. Testing and privacy. In W. W. Willingham (Ed.), Invasion of privacy in research and testing. *Journal of Educational Measurement*, 1967, **4**, 7–10 (supplement).

Berdie, R. F. The ad hoc committee on social impact of psychological assessment. *American Psychologist*, 1965, **20**, 143–146.

Berg, I. A. Response bias and personality: The deviation hypothesis. *Journal of Psychology*, 1955, **40**, 60–71.

―――, Deviant responses and deviant people: the formulation of the Deviation Hypothesis. *Journal of Counseling Psychology*, 1957, **4**, 154–161.

―――, The unimportance of test item content. Chapter 5 in B. M. Bass and I. A. Berg (Eds.), *Objective approaches to personality assessment*. Princeton: Van Nostrand, 1959.

Berg, I. A., Hunt, W. A., and Barnes, E. H. *The perceptual reaction test*. Evanston, Illinois: Authors, 1949.

Bernreuter, R. N. *The Personality Inventory*. Palo Alto, California: Consulting Psychologists Press, 1939.

Bieri, J., Atkins, A. L., Briar, S., Leaman, R. L., Miller, H., and Tripodi, T. *Clinical and social judgment*. New York: Wiley, 1966.

Billingslea, F. Y. The Bender-Gestalt: a review and a perspective. *Psychological Bulletin*, 1963, **60**, 233–251.

Bingham, W. V. D., and Moore, B. V. *How to interview* (fourth edition). New York: Harper and Row, 1959.

Blakemore, C. B. Review of the Bender-Gestalt. In O. K. Buros (Ed.), *The sixth mental measurements yearbook*. Highland Park, N.J.: Gryphon, 1965.

Block, J. *The Q-sort method in personality assessment and psychiatric research*. Springfield, Illinois: Thomas, 1961.

―――, *The challenge of response sets*. New York: Appleton-Century-Crofts, 1965.

Blum, G. S. A study of the psychoanalytic theory of psychosexual development. *Genetic Psychology Monographs*, 1949, **39**, 3–99.

―――, *The Blacky Pictures*. New York: Psychological Corporation, 1950.

―――, *Revised scoring system for the research use of the Blacky Pictures*. Unpublished mimeographed report, 1951.

―――, A guide for research use of the Blacky Pictures. *Journal of Projective Techniques*, 1962, **26**, 3–29.

Blum, G. S., and Kaufman, J. B. Two patterns of personality dynamics in male peptic ulcer patients as suggested by responses to the Blacky Pictures. *Journal of Clinical Psychology*, 1952, **8**, 273–278.

Boring, E. G. *A history of experimental psychology*. New York: Appleton-Century-Crofts, 1929.

Boyle, J. A., Greig, W. R., Franklin, D. A., Harden, R. Mc.G, Buchanan, W. W., and McGirr, E. M. Construction of a model for computer-assisted diagnosis: application to the problem of non-toxic goitre. *Quarterly Journal of Medicine*, 1966, New Series, **35**, 565–588.

Bray, D. W., and Grant, D. L. The assessment center in the measurement of potential for business management. *Psychological Monographs*, 1966, **80**, 1–17 (Whole No. 625).

Brayfield, A. H. (Ed). Testing and public policy. *American Psychologist*, 1965, **20**, 857–1005.

Breger, L. Psychological testing: treatment and research implications. *Journal of Consulting and Clinical Psychology*, 1968, **32**, 176–181.

Briggs, P. F. Eight item clusters for use with the M-B History Record. *Journal of Clinical Psychology*, 1959, **15**, 22–28.

Brim, O. G. American attitudes toward intelligence tests. *American Psychologist*. 1965, **20**, 123–124.

Brim, O. G. Reaction to the papers. In W. W. Willingham (Ed.), Invasion of privacy in research and testing. *Journal of Educational Measurement*, 1967, **4**, 29–31 (supplement).

Brock, T. C., and Giudice, C. D. Stealing and temporal orientation. *Journal of Abnormal and Social Psychology*, 1963, **66**, 91–94.

Brodie, W. M., Owens, W. A., and Britt, M. F. *Annotated bibliography on biographical* data. Greensboro, N.C.: Creativity Research Institute of the Richardson Foundation, 1968.

Buchwald, A. Values and the uses of tests. *Journal of Consulting Psychology*, 1965, **29**, 49–54.

Buck, J. N. The H-T-P test. *Journal of Clinical Psychology*, 1948, **4**, 151–159. (a)

———, The H-T-P technique: a qualitative and scoring manual. Part one. *Journal of Clinical Psychology*, 1948, **4**, 319–396. (b)

———, The H-T-P technique: a qualitative and scoring manual. Part two. *Journal of Clinical Psychology*, 1949, **5**, 37–76.

Burdock, E. I., and Hardesty, A. S. Psychological test for psychopathology. *Journal of Abnormal Psychology*, 1968, **73**, 62–69.

Burgess, E. W. Factors determining success or failure on parole. In A. A. Bruce (Ed.), *The workings of the indeterminate sentence law and the parole system in Illinois.* Springfield, Illinois: Illinois Board of Parole, 1928, 205–249.

Buros, O. K. *The sixth mental measurements yearbook.* Highland Park, N.J.: Gryphon, 1965.

Buss, A. H. The effect of item style on social desirability and frequency of endorsement. *Journal of Consulting Psychology*, 1959, **23**, 510–513.

———, *Psychopathology.* New York: Wiley, 1966.

Buss, A. H., and Durkee, A. An inventory for assessing different kinds of hostility. *Journal of Consulting Psychology*, 1957, **21**, 343–349.

Campbell, D. T. Factors relevant to the validity of experiments in social settings. *Psychological Bulletin*, 1957, **54**, 297–312.

Campbell, D. T., Siegman, C. R., and Rees, M. B. Direction-of-wording effects in the relationships between scales. *Psychological Bulletin*, 1967, **68**, 293–303.

Canter, F. M. Simulation on the California Psychological Inventory and the adjustment of the simulator. *Journal of Consulting Psychology*, 1963, **27**, 252–256.

Carp, A. L., and Shavzin, A. R. The susceptibility to falsification of the Rorschach psychodiagnostic technique. *Journal of Consulting Psychology*, 1950, **14**, 230–233.

Cattell, R. B. *Personality and motivation: structure and measurement.* Yonkers-on-Hudson: World Book, 1957.

———, Validity and reliability: a proposed more basic set of concepts. *Journal of Educational Psychology*, 1964, **55**, 1–22.

———, *The scientific analysis of personality.* Baltimore: Penguin, 1965.

Cattell, R. B., and Stice, G. F. *Handbook for the Sixteen Personality Factor Questionnaire.* Champaign, Illinois: Institute for Personality and Ability Testing, 1957.

Chapman, L. J. Illusory correlation in observational report. *Journal of Verbal Learning and Verbal Behavior*, 1967, 6, 151–155.

Chapman, L. J., and Chapman, J. P. Genesis of popular but erroneous psychodiagnostic observations. *Journal of Abnormal Psychology*, 1967, **72**, 193–204.

———, Illusory correlation as an obstacle to the use of valid psychodiagnostic signs. *Journal of Abnormal Psychology*, 1969, **74**, 271–280.

———, Associatively based illusory correlation as a source of psychodiagnostic folklore. In L. D. Goodstein and R. I. Lanyon (Eds.), *Readings in personality assessment.* New York: Wiley, 1971.

Cofer, C. N., Chance, J. E., and Judson, A. J. A study of malingering on the MMPI. *Journal of Psychology*, 1949, **27**, 491–499.

Cole, J. D., and Magnussen, M. G. Where the action is. *Journal of Consulting Psychology*, 1966, **30**, 539–543.

Couch, A., and Keniston, K. Yeasayers and naysayers: agreeing response set as a personality variable. *Journal of Abnormal and Social Psychology*, 1960, **60**, 151–174.

Craddick, R. A. WISC and WAIS IQs as a function of season of birth. *Psychological Reports*, 1966, **18**, 259–264.

Crites, J. O. The California Psychological Inventory: I. As a measure of normal personality. *Journal of Counseling Psychology*, 1964, **11**, 197–202.

Crites, J. O., Bechtoldt, H. P., Goodstein, L. D., and Heilbrun, A. B. A factor analysis of the California Psychology Inventory. *Journal of Applied Psychology*, 1961, **45**, 408–414.

Cronbach, L. J. An experimental comparison of the multiple true-false and multiple multiple-choice tests. *Journal of Educational Psychology*, 1941, **32**, 533–543.

———, Studies of acquiescence as a factor in the true-false test. *Journal of Educational Psychology*, 1942, **33**, 401–415.

————, Response sets and test validity. *Educational and Psychological Measurement*, 1946, **6**, 475–494.

————, Further evidence on response sets and test design. *Educational and Psychological Measurement*, 1950, **10**, 3–31.

————, *Essentials of psychological testing* (second edition). New York: Harper and Row, 1960.

Cronbach, L. J., and Gleser, G. C. *Psychological tests and personnel decisions.* Urbana, Ill.: University of Illinois Press, 1957. (Second edition, 1965).

Cronbach, L. J., and Meehl, P. E. Construct validity in psychological tests. *Psychological Bulletin*, 1955, **52**, 281–302.

Crooks, J., Murray, I. P. C., and Wayne, E. J. Statistical methods applied to the clinical diagnosis of thyrotoxicosis. *Quarterly Journal of Medicine*, 1959, New Series, **28**, 211–234.

Cureton, E. E. Reliability, validity, and baloney. *Educational and Psychological Measurement*, 1950, **10**, 94–96.

————, Recipe for cookbook. *Psychological Bulletin*, 1957, **54**, 494–497.

Dahlstrom, W. G. Invasion of privacy: how legitimate is the current concern over this issue? In J. N. Butcher (Ed.), *MMPI: Research developments and clinical applications.* New York: McGraw-Hill, 1969.

Dahlstrom, W. G., and Welsh, G. S. *An MMPI handbook.* Minneapolis: University of Minnesota Press, 1960.

D'Andrade, R. G. Trait psychology and componential analysis. *American Anthropologist*, 1965, **67**, 215–228.

Daston, P., and Sakheim, G. Prediction of successful suicide from the Rorschach test, using a sign approach. *Journal of Projective Techniques*, 1960, **24**, 355–365.

Davies, A. D. M. Season of birth, intelligence, and personality measures. *British Journal of Psychology*, 1964, **55**, 475–476.

Davies, J. D. *Phrenology: fad and science.* New Haven: Yale University Press, 1955.

Deutsch, M., Fishman, J. A., Kogan, L., North, R., and Whiteman, M. Guidelines for testing minority group children. *Journal of Social Issues*, 1964, **20** (2, Part 2), 127–145.

Dicken, C. F. Simulated patterns on the Edwards Personal Preference Schedule. *Journal of Applied Psychology*, 1959, **43**, 372–378.

Diggory, J. C. Calculation of some costs of suicide prevention using certain predictors of suicidal behavior. *Psychological Bulletin*, 1969, **71**, 373–386.

Doll, E. A. *The measurement of social competence.* Minneapolis: Educational Test Bureau, 1953.

————, *Vineland Social Maturity Scale: Condensed manual of directions.* Minneapolis: American Guidance Service Inc., 1965.

Dombrose, L. A., and Slobin, M. A. The IES Test. *Perceptual and Motor Skills*, 1958, **8**, 347–389.

Drake, L. E., and Oetting, E. R. *An MMPI Codebook for counselors*, Minneapolis: University of Minnesota Press, 1959.

Duff, F. L. Item subtlety in personality inventory scales. *Journal of Consulting Psychology*, 1965, **29**, 565–570.

Ebel, R. L. The social consequences of educational testing. *School and Society*, 1964, **92**, 331–334. (a)

———, Must all tests be valid? *American Psychologist*, 1964, **19**, 640–647. (b)

Eber, H. W. Computer reporting of 16 PF data. Paper read at the annual meeting of the South Eastern Psychological Association, Atlanta, April, 1965.

Edwards, A. L. The relationship between the judged desirability of a trait and the probability that the trait will be endorsed. *Journal of Applied Psychology*, 1953, **37**, 90–93.

———, *The social desirability variable in personality assessment and research*. New York: Dryden, 1957.

———, *Edwards Personal Preference Schedule*. New York: Psychological Corporation, 1959.

———, Social desirability and expected means on MMPI scales. *Educational and Psychological Measurement*, 1962, **22**, 71–76.

———, Prediction of mean scores on MMPI scales. *Journal of Consulting Psychology*, 1964, **28**, 183–185. (a)

———, Social desirability and performance on the MMPI. *Psychometrika*, 1964, **29**, 295–308. (b)

Edwards, A. L., and Diers, C. J. Social desirability and the factorial interpretation of the MMPI. *Educational and Psychological Measurement*, 1962, **22**, 501–509.

Edwards, A. L., and Heathers, L. B. The first factor of the MMPI: social desirability or ego strength? *Journal of Consulting Psychology*, 1962, **26**, 99–100.

Elizur, A. Content analysis of the Rorschach with regard to anxiety and hostility. *Rorschach Research Exchange*, 1949, **13**, 247–284.

England, G. W. *Development and use of weighted application blanks*. Dubuque, Iowa: Brown, 1961.

Eron, L. D. Frequencies of themes and identifications in the stories of schizophrenic patients and non-hospitalized college students. *Journal of Consulting Psychology*, 1948, **12**, 387–395.

Eron, L. D., and Walder, L. Test burning: II. *American Psychologist*, 1961, 237–244.

Ervin, S. J. Why Senate hearings on psychological tests in government? *American Psychologist*, 1965, **20**, 879–880.

Eysenck, H. J. The logical basis of factor analysis. *American Psychologist*, 1953, **8**, 105–114.

———, *The structure of human personality* (second edition). London: Methuen, 1960.

———, Review of the Holtzman Inkblot Technique. In O. K. Buros (Ed.), *The sixth mental measurements yearbook*. Highland Park, N.J.: Gryphon, 1965.

Fairweather, G. W. (Ed.) *Social psychology in treating mental illness: An experimental approach.* New York: Wiley, 1964.

Farberow, N. L., Shneidman, E. S., and Neuringer, C. Case history and hospitalization factors in suicides of neuropsychiatric hospital patients. *Journal of Nervous and Mental Disease,* 1966, **142**, 32–44.

Fear, R. A. *The evaluation interview.* New York: McGraw-Hill, 1958.

Feld, S., and Smith, C. P. An evaluation of the method of content analysis. In J. W. Atkinson (Ed.), *Motives in fantasy, action, and society.* Princeton: Van Nostrand.

Feldman, M. J. The use of the MMPI profile for prognosis and evaluation of shock therapy. *Journal of Consulting Psychology,* 1952, **16**, 376–382.

Feldman, M. J., and Graley, J. The effects of an experimental set to simulate abnormality on group Rorschach performance. *Journal of Projective Techniques,* 1954, **18**, 326–334.

Festinger, L., Riecken, H. W., and Schachter, S. *When prophecy fails.* Minneapolis: University of Minnesota Press, 1956.

Finney, J. C. Methodological problems in a programmed composition of psychological test reports. Paper read at the annual meeting of the American Psychological Association, New York, May, 1965.

Flanagan, J. C. The critical incident technique. *Psychological Bulletin,* 1954, **51**, 327–358.

Forehand, G. A. Comments on comments on testing. *Educational and Psychological Measurement,* 1964, **24**, 853–859.

Forer, B. R. The fallacy of personal validation: a classroom demonstration of gullibility. *Journal of Abnormal and Social Psychology,* 1949, **44**, 118–123.

———, A structured sentence completion test. *Journal of Projective Techniques,* 1950, **14**, 15–29.

———, Review of the Holtzman Inkblot Technique. In O. K. Buros (Ed.), *The sixth mental measurements yearbook.* Highland Park, N.J.: Gryphon, 1965.

Fosberg, I. A. Rorschach reactions under varied instructions. *Rorschach Research Exchange,* 1938, **3**, 12–30.

———, An experimental study of the reliability of the Rorschach psycho-diagnostic technique. *Rorschach Research Exchange,* 1941, **5**, 72–84.

Fowler, R. D. Three approaches to the automatic interpretation of the MMPI: Purposes and usefulness of the Alabama program. Paper read at the annual meeting of the American Psychological Association, Chicago, September 1965.

———, Automated interpretation of personality test data. Chapter 6 in J. G. Butcher (Ed.), *MMPI: Research developments and clinical applications.* New York: McGraw-Hill, 1969.

Frank, L. K. Projective methods for the study of personality. *Journal of Psychology,* 1939, **8**, 389–413.

Freeberg, N. E. The biographical information blank as a predictor of student achievement: A review. *Psychological Reports,* 1967, **20**, 911–925.

Freedman, N., Rosen, B., Engelhardt, D. M., and Margolis, R. Prediction of psychiatric hospitalization: I. The measurement of hospital proneness. *Journal of Abnormal Psychology*, 1967, **72**, 468–477.

Fulkerson, S. C. Individual differences in response validity. *Journal of Clinical Psychology*, 1959, 15, 169–173.

Fulkerson, S. C., and Barry, J. R. Methodology and research on the prognostic use of psychological tests. *Psychological Bulletin*, 1961, 58, 178–204.

Gallagher, C. E. Opening remarks. In "Testimony before house special subcommittee on invasion of privacy of the committee on government operations." *American Psychologist*, 1965, **20**, 955–988.

Galton, F. Measurement of character. *Fortnightly Review*, 1884, **42**, 179–185.

Garfield, S. L., and Sundland, D. M. Prognostic scales in schizophrenia. *Journal of Consulting Psychology*, 1966, **30**, 18–24.

Ghiselli, E. E. Differentiation of individuals in terms of their predictability. *Journal of Applied Psychology*, 1956, **40**, 374–377.

———, Differentiation of tests in terms of the accuracy with which they predict for a given individual. *Educational and Psychological Measurement*, 1960, **20**, 675–684. (a)

———, The prediction of predictability. *Educational and Psychological Measurement*, 1960, **20**, 3–8. (b)

———, Moderating effects and differential reliability and validity. *Journal of Applied Psychology*, 1963, **47**, 81–86.

———, *Theory of psychological measurement.* New York: McGraw-Hill, 1964.

Gilberstadt, H., and Duker, J. *A handbook for clinical and actuarial MMPI interpretation.* Philadelphia: Saunders, 1965.

Glueck, S., and Glueck, E. T. *500 criminal careers.* New York: Knopf, 1930.

Goheen, H. W., and Mosel, J. N. Validity of the Employment Recommendation Questionnaire. II. Comparison with field investigations. *Personnel Psychology*, 1959, **12**, 297–302.

Goldberg, L. R. The effectiveness of clinicians' judgments: the diagnosis of organic brain damage from the Bender-Gestalt test. *Journal of Consulting Psychology*, 1959, **23**, 25–33.

———, Diagnosticians vs. diagnostic signs: The diagnosis of psychosis vs. neurosis from the MMPI. *Psychological Monographs*, 1965, **79**, 9 (Whole No. 602).

———, Seer over sign: the first good example? *Journal of Experimental Research in Personality*, 1968, **3**, 168–171. (a)

———, Simple models or simple processes? Some research on clinical judgments. *American Psychologist*, 1968, **23**, 483–496. (b)

———, Man vs. model of man: a rationale, plus some evidence, for a method of improving on clinical inferences. *Psychological Bulletin*, 1970, **73**, 422–432. (a)

———, Why measure *that* trait: An historical analysis of personality scales and inventories. Tutorial address presented at the meetings of the Western Psychological Association, Los Angeles, April, 1970. (b)

Goldberg, L. R., and Slovic, P. Importance of test item content: an analysis of a corollary of the deviation hypothesis. *Journal of Counseling Psychology*, 1967, **14**, 462–472.

Goldberg, L. R., and Werts, C. E. The reliability of clinicians' judgments: a multitrait-multimethod approach. *Journal of Consulting Psychology*, 1966, **30**, 199–206.

Goldberg, P. A. A review of sentence completion methods in personality assessment. *Journal of Projective Techniques and Personality Assessment*, 1965, **29**, 12–45.

Golden, M. Some effects of combining psychological tests on clinical inferences. *Journal of Consulting Psychology*, 1964, **28**, 440–446.

Goldfried, M. R., and Pomeranz, D. M. The role of assessment in behavior modification. *Psychological Reports*, 1968, **23**, 75–87.

Goldsmith, D. B. The use of the personal history blank as a salesmanship test. *Journal of Applied Psychology*, 1922, **6**, 149–155.

Goodenough, F. L. *Measurement of intelligence by drawings.* Yonkers-on-Hudson, New York: World Book Co., 1926.

Goodstein, L. D., Crites, J. O., Heilbrun, A. B., Jr., and Rempel, P. P. The use of the California Psychological Inventory in a university counseling service. *Journal of Counseling Psychology*, 1961, **8**, 147–153.

Gordon, L. V. *Gordon Personal Profile manual (Revised).* New York: Harcourt, Brace, and World, 1963.

————, Clinical, psychometric and work-sample approaches in the prediction of success in Peace Corps training. *Journal of Applied Psychology*, 1967, **51**, 111–119.

Gorham, D. R. Validity and reliability studies of a computer-based scoring system for inkblot responses. *Journal of Consulting Psychology*, 1967, **31**, 65–70.

Gottschalk, L. A., and Gleser, G. C. *The measurement of psychological states through the content analysis of verbal behavior.* Berkeley: University of California Press, 1969.

Gough, H. G. Simulated patterns on the MMPI. *Journal of Abnormal and Social Psychology*, 1947, **42**, 215–225.

————, The construction of a personality scale to predict scholastic achievement. *Journal of Applied Psychology*, 1953, **37**, 361–366.

————, *California Psychological Inventory: manual.* Palo Alto: Consulting Psychologists Press, 1957 (revised 1964).

————, Clinical versus statistical prediction in psychology. Chapter 9 in L. Postman (Ed.), *Psychology in the making.* New York: Knopf, 1962.

Gough, H. G., and Heilbrun, A. B., Jr. *Manual for the Adjective Check List.* Palo Alto: Consulting Psychologists Press, 1964.

Gough, H. G., McClosky, H., and Meehl, P. E. A personality scale for dominance. *Journal of Abnormal and Social Psychology*, 1951, **46**, 360–366.

Gough, H. G., and Peterson, D. R. The identification and measurement of predispositional factors in crime and delinquency. *Journal of Consulting Psychology*, 1952, **16**, 207–212.

Grayson, H. M., and Olinger, L. B. Simulation of "normalcy" by psychiatric patients on the MMPI. *Journal of Consulting Psychology*, 1957, **21**, 73–77.

Gross, L. R. Effects of verbal and non-verbal reinforcement in the Rorschach. *Journal of Consulting Psychology*, 1959, **23**, 66–68.

Gross, M. L. *The brain watchers*. New York: Random House, 1962.

———, Testimony before House special subcommitte on invasion of privacy of the committee on government operations. *American Psychologist*, 1965, **20**, 958–960.

Guilford, J. P. *An inventory of factors STDCR*. Beverly Hills, California: Sheridan Supply Co., 1940.

Guilford, J. P. (Ed.) *Printed classification tests*. Washington: Government Printing Office, 1947.

Guilford, J. P. *Personality*. New York: McGraw-Hill, 1959.

Guilford, J. P., and Martin, H. G. *Personnel Inventory: Manual of directions and norms*. Beverly Hills, California: Sheridan Supply Co., 1943 (a).

Guilford, J. P., and Martin, H. G. *The Guilford-Martin inventory of factors GAMIN: Manual of directions and norms*. Beverly Hills, California: Sheridan Supply Co., 1943 (b).

Guilford, J. P., and Zimmerman, W. S. *The Guilford-Zimmerman Temperament Survey: Manual of instructions and interpretations*. Beverly Hills, California: Sheridan Supply Co., 1949.

Guion, R. M. *Personnel testing*. New York: McGraw-Hill, 1965.

Haggerty, M. E., Olson, W. C., and Wichman, E. K. Haggerty-Olson-Wichman Behavior Rating Schedules. Yonkers-on-Hudson, New York: World Book Co., 1930.

Halbower, C. C. A comparison of actuarial versus clinical prediction to classes discriminated by MMPI. Unpublished doctoral dissertation, University of Minnesota, 1955.

Hall, C. S., and Lindzey, G. *Theories of personality*. New York: Wiley, 1957.

Hall, L. P., and LaDriere, L. Patterns of performance on WISC similarities in emotionally disturbed and brain damaged children. *Journal of Consulting and Clinical Psychology*, 1969, **33**, 357–364.

Hammer, E. F. (Ed.) *The clinical application of projective drawings*. Springfield, Ill.: Thomas, 1958.

Hammer, E. F. Projective drawings. Chapter 12 in A. I. Rabin (Ed.), *Projective techniques in personality assessment*. New York: Springer, 1968.

Hammond, K. R., and Summers, D. A. Cognitive dependence on linear and nonlinear cues. *Psychological Review*, 1965, **72**, 215–224.

Hart, H. Predicting parole success. *Journal of Criminal Law and Criminology*, 1923, **14**, 405–413.

Hartshorne, H., and May, M. A. *Studies in deceit.* New York: Macmillan, 1928.

————, *Studies in the nature of character: II. Studies in service and self-control.* New York: Macmillan, 1929.

Hartshorne, H., May, M. A., and Shuttleworth, F. K. *Studies in the nature of character: III. Studies in the organization of character.* New York: Macmillan, 1930.

Hartwell, S. W., Hutt, M. L., Andrew, G., and Walton, R. E. The Michigan Picture Test: diagnostic and therapeutic possibilities of a new projective test for children. *American Journal of Orthopsychiatry,* 1951, **21,** 124–137.

Hase, H. D., and Goldberg, L. R. Comparative validities of different strategies of constructing personality inventory scales. *Psychological Bulletin,* 1967, **67,** 231–248.

Hathaway, S. R. Clinical intuition and inferential accuracy. *Journal of Personality,* 1956, **24,** 223–250. (a)

————, Scales 5 (Masculinity-Femininity), 6 (Paranoia), and 8 (Schizophrenia). Article 10 in G. S. Welsh and W. G. Dahlstrom (Eds.), *Basic readings on the MMPI in psychology and medicine.* Minneapolis: University of Minnesota Press, 1956. (b)

————, Increasing clinical efficiency. In B. M. Bass and I. A. Berg (Eds.)., *Objective approaches to personality assessment.* Princeton: Van Nostrand, 1959.

————, MMPI: Professional use by professional people. *American Psychologist,* 1964, **19,** 204–210.

Hathaway, S. R., and McKinley, J. C. A multiphasic personality schedule (Minnesota): I. Construction of the schedule. *Journal of Psychology,* 1940, **10,** 249–254.

————, *Minnesota Multiphasic Personality Inventory: manual.* New York: Psychological Corporation, 1951.

Hathaway, S. R., and Monachesi, E. D. *Adolescent personality and behavior.* Minneapolis: University of Minnesota Press, 1963.

Heilbrun, A. B. The psychological significance of the MMPI *K* scale in a normal population. *Journal of Consulting Psychology,* 1961, **25,** 486–491.

————, Revision of the MMPI *K* correction procedure for improved detection of maladjustment in a normal college population. *Journal of Consulting Psychology,* 1963, **25,** 161–165.

————, Social-learning theory, social desirability, and the MMPI. *Psychological Bulletin,* 1964, **61,** 377–387.

Heilbrun, A. B., and Goodstein, L. D. Social desirability response set: error or predictor variable. *Journal of Psychology,* 1961, **51,** 321–329. (a)

————, The relationships between individually defined and group defined social desirability and performance on the Edwards Personal Preference Schedule. *Journal of Consulting Psychology,* 1961, **25,** 200–204. (b)

Henry, E. M., and Rotter, J. B. Situational influences on Rorschach responses. *Journal of Consulting Psychology*, 1956, **20**, 457–462.

Henry, W. E. *The analysis of fantasy.* New York: Wiley, 1956.

Hertz, M. R. *Frequency tables for scoring responses to the Rorschach inkblot test* (third edition). Cleveland: Western Reserve University Press, 1951.

Heymans, G., and Wiersma, E. Beitrage zur Speziellen Psychologie auf Grund einer Massenunterschung. *Zeitschrift fur Psychologie*, 1906, **43**, 81–127, 258–301.

Hiler, E. W., and Nesvig, D. An evaluation of criteria used by clinicians to infer pathology from figure drawings. *Journal of Consulting Psychology*, 1965, **29**, 520–529.

Hillier, F. S., and Lieberman, G. J. *Introduction to operations research.* San Francisco: Holden-Day, 1967.

Hobert, R., and Dunnette, M. D. Development of moderator variables to enhance the prediction of managerial effectiveness. *Journal of Applied Psychology*, 1967, **51**, 50–64.

Hoch, A., and Amsden, G. S. A guide to the descriptive study of personality. *Review of Neurology and Psychiatry*, 1913, **11**, 577–587.

Hoffman, P. J., Slovic, P., and Rorer, L. G. An analysis-of-variance model for the assessment of configural cue utilization in clinical judgment. *Psychological Bulletin*, 1968, 69, 338–349.

Hollingsworth, T. L. Using an electronic computer in a problem of medical diagnosis. *Journal of the Royal Statistical Society of Britain*, 1959, **122**, 221–231.

Holmen, M. G., Katter, R. V., Jones, A. M., and Richardson, I. F. An assessment program for OCS candidates. *HumRRO Technical Reports*, 1956, 26.

Holt, R. R. Clinical and statistical prediction: a reformulation and some new data. *Journal of Abnormal and Social Psychology*, 1958, **56**, 1–12.

Holt, R. R., and Luborsky, L. *Personality patterns of psychiatrists.* New York: Basic Books, 1958.

Holtzman, W. H., Thorpe, J. S., Swartz, J. D., and Herron, E. W. *Inkblot perception and personality: Holtzman inkblot technique.* Austin: University of Texas Press, 1961.

Holzberg, J. D. Reliability re-examined. Chapter 13 in M. A. Rickers-Ovsiankina (Ed.), *Rorschach psychology.* New York: Wiley, 1960.

Horst, P. *Psychological measurement and prediction.* Belmont, California: Wadsworth, 1966.

Hovey, H. B., and Stauffacher, J. C. Intuitive versus objective prediction from a test. *Journal of Clinical Psychology*, 1953, **9**, 349–351.

Howell, R. W., and Loy, R. M. Disease coding by computer: the fruit machine method. *British Journal of Preventive and Social Medicine*, 1968, **22**, 178–181.

Huff, F. W. Use of actuarial description of abnormal personality in a mental hospital. *Psychological Reports*, 1965, **17**, 224.

Hughes, J. F., Dunn, J. F., and Baxter, B. The validity of selection instruments under operating conditions (The Prudential Insurance Company of America). *Personnel Psychology*, 1956, **9**, 321–324.

Humm, D. G., and Wadsworth, G. W. The Humm-Wadsworth Temperament Scale. *American Journal of Psychiatry*, 1935, **92**, 163–200.

Hundleby, J. D. Review of the Study of Values. In O. K. Buros (Ed.), *The sixth mental measurements yearbook*. Highland Park, N.J.: Gryphon, 1965.

Hursch, C. J., Hammond, K. R., and Hursch, J. L. Some methodological considerations in multiple-cue probability studies. *Psychological Review*, 1964, **71**, 42–60.

Husek, T. R. Acquiescence as a response set and as a personality characteristic. *Educational and Psychological Measurement*, 1961, **21**, 295–307.

Jackson, D. N., and Messick, S. Content and style in personality assessment. *Psychological Bulletin*, 1958, **55**, 243–252.

————, Response styles on the MMPI: comparison of clinical and normal samples. *Journal of Abnormal and Social Psychology*, 1962, **65**, 285–299.

Jacobs, A., and Schlaff, A. *Falsification scales for the Guilford-Zimmerman Temperament Survey*. Beverly Hills, California: Sheridan Supply Co., 1955.

Johnston, R., and McNeal, B. F. Statistical versus clinical prediction: length of neuropsychiatric hospital stay. *Journal of Abnormal Psychology*, 1967, **72**, 335–340.

Jourard, S. *The transparent self*. Princeton: Van Nostrand, 1964.

Jung, C. G. The association method. *American Journal of Psychology*, 1910, **21**, 219–269.

Kahn, R. L., and Cannell, C. F. *The dynamics of interviewing*. New York: Wiley, 1957.

Kanfer, F. H., and Saslow, G. Behavioral analysis: an alternative to diagnostic classification. *Archives of General Psychiatry*, 1965, **12**, 529–538.

Kantor, R. E., Wallner, J. M., and Winder, C. L. Process and reactive schizophrenia. *Journal of Consulting Psychology*, 1953, **17**, 157–162.

Kaplan, M. F., and Eron, L. D. Test sophistication and faking in the TAT situation. *Journal of Projective Techniques*, 1965, **29**, 498–503.

Karson, S., and Sells, S. B. Comments on Meehl and Rosen's paper. *Psychological Bulletin*, 1956, **53**, 335–337.

Kelly, G. A. *The psychology of personal constructs*. New York: Norton, 1955.

Kelly, E. L. Review of the California Psychological Inventory. In O. K. Buros (Ed.), *The sixth mental measurements yearbook*. Highland Park. N.J.: Gryphon, 1965.

Kelly, E. L., and Fiske, D. W. *The prediction of performance in clinical psychology*. Ann Arbor: University of Michigan Press, 1951.

Kelly, E. L., and Goldberg, L. R. Correlates of later performance and specialization in psychology. *Psychological Monographs*, 1959, 73 (No. 12, Whole No. 482).

Kent, G. H., and Rosanoff, A. J. A study of association in insanity. *American Journal of Insanity*, 1910, **67**, 37–96 and 317–390.

Kleinmuntz, B. Identification of maladjusted college students. *Journal of Counseling Psychology*, 1960, **7**, 209–211.

————, MMPI decision rules for the identification of college maladjustment: a digital computer approach. *Psychological Monographs*, 1963, **77** (14, Whole No. 577).

Klett, W. G., and Vestre, N. D. Demographic and prognostic characteristics of psychiatric patients classified by gross MMPI measures. *American Psychologist*, 1967, **22**, 562. (abstract)

Klopfer, B., Ainsworth, M. D., Klopfer, W. G., and Holt, R. R. *Developments in the Rorschach technique: I. Technique and theory*. New York: Harcourt, Brace and World, 1954.

Klopfer, B., and Davidson, H. H. *The Rorschach technique: an introductory manual*. New York: Harcourt, Brace, and World, 1962.

Klopfer, B., Kirkner, F., Wisham, W., and Baker, G. Rorschach prognostic rating scale. *Journal of Projective Techniques*, 1951, **15**, 425–428.

Kostlan, A. A method of the empirical study of psychodiagnosis. *Journal of Consulting Psychology*, 1954, **18**, 83–88.

Kuder, G. F. *Examiner manual for the Kuder Preference Record*. Chicago: Science Research Associates, 1951.

Kuder, G. F., and Richardson, M. W. The theory of the estimation of test reliability. *Psychometrika*, 1937, **2**, 151–160.

Lang, P. J., and Lazovik, A. D. Experimental desensitization of a phobia. *Journal of Abnormal and Social Psychology*, 1963, **66**, 519–525.

Lanyon, R. I. Measurement of social competence in college males. *Journal of Consulting Psychology*, 1967, **31**, 495–498. (a)

————, Simulation of normal and psychopathic MMPI personality patterns. *Journal of Consulting Psychology*, 1967, **31**, 94–97. (b)

————, *A handbook of MMPI group profiles*. Minneapolis: University of Minnesota Press, 1968.

————, Development and validation of a psychological screening inventory. *Journal of Consulting and Clinical Psychology*, 1970, **35** (No. 1, Part 2), 1–24.

Laurent, H. The early identification of management potential. Paper presented to the American Psychological Association, St. Louis, September 1962.

Ledley, R. S., and Lusted, L. B. Reasoning foundations of medical diagnosis. *Science*, 1959, **130**, 9–21.

Levy, L. H. *Psychological interpretation*. New York: Holt, Rinehart, and Winston, 1963.

Lewinsohn, P. M. Psychological correlates of overall quality of figure drawings. *Journal of Consulting Psychology*, 1965, **29**, 504–512.

————, *Projective techniques and cross-cultural research*. New York: Appleton-Century-Crofts, 1961.

Lindzey, G. Seer versus sign. *Journal of Experimental Research in Personality*, 1965, **1**, 17–26.

Lindzey, G., and Kalnins, D. Thematic Apperception Test: some evidence bearing on the "hero assumption." *Journal of Abnormal and Social Psychology*, 1958, **57**, 76–83.

Little, K. B., and Shneidman, E. S. Congruencies among interpretations of psychological test and anamnestic data. *Psychological Monographs*, 1959, **73**, (6, Whole No. 476).

Loevinger, J. Objective tests as instruments of psychological theory. *Psychological Reports*, 1957, **3**, 635–694.

Lorr, M. Review of the Sixteen Personality Factors questionnaire. In O. K. Buros (Ed.), *Sixth mental measurements yearbook*. Highland Park, N.J.: Gryphon, 1965.

Lovell, V. R. The human use of personality tests: a dissenting view. *American Psychologist*, 1967, **22**, 383–393.

Lusted, L. B. *Introduction to medical decision making*. Springfield, Illinois: Thomas, 1968.

Machover, K. *Personality projection in the drawing of the human figure*. Springfield, Illinois: Thomas, 1949.

Mahl, G. F. Disturbances and silences in the patient's speech in psychotherapy. *Journal of Abnormal and Social Psychology*, 1956, **53**, 1–15.

MacKinnon, D. W. The personality correlates of creativity: A study of American architects. In G. S. Nielsen (Ed.), *Proceedings of XIV International Congress of Applied Psychology, Copenhagen*, 1961. Volume 2. Copenhagen: Munksgaard, 1962.

Marks, P. A., and Seeman, W. *The actuarial description of abnormal personality*. Baltimore: Williams and Wilkins, 1963.

Marx, M. H. *Theories in contemporary psychology*. New York: Macmillan, 1963.

Matarazzo, J. D. The interview. In B. B. Wolman (Ed.), *Handbook of clinical psychology*. New York: McGraw-Hill, 1965.

McClelland, D. C., Atkinson, J. W., Clark, R. A., and Lowell, E. L. *The achievement motive*. New York: Appleton-Century-Crofts, 1953.

Meehl, P. E. Configural scoring. *Journal of Consulting Psychology*, 1950, **14**, 165–171.

———, *Clinical versus statistical prediction*. Minneapolis: University of Minnesota Press, 1954.

———, Wanted—a good cookbook. *American Psychologist*, 1956, **11**, 263–272.

———, A comparison of clinicians with five statistical methods of identifying psychotic MMPI profiles. *Journal of Counseling Psychology*, 1959, **6**, 102–109. (a)

———, Some ruminations on the validation of clinical procedures. *Canadian Journal of Psychology*, 1959, **13**, 102–128. (b)

———, The cognitive activity of the clinician. *American Psychologist*, 1960, **15**, 19–27.

———, Seer over sign: the first good example, *Journal of Experimental Research in Personality*, 1965, **1**, 27–32.

Meehl, P. E., and Dahlstrom, W. G. Objective configural rules for discriminating psychotic from neurotic MMPI profiles. *Journal of Consulting Psychology*, 1960, **24**, 375–387.

Meehl, P. E., and Hathaway, S. R. The *K* factor as a suppressor variable in the MMPI. *Journal of Applied Psychology*, 1946, **30**, 525–564.

Meehl, P. E., and Rosen, A. Antecedent probability and the efficiency of psychometric signs, patterns, or cutting scores. *Psychological Bulletin*, 1955, **52**, 194–216.

Meltzoff, J. The effect of mental set and item structure upon responses to a projective test. *Journal of Abnormal and Social Psychology*, 1951, **46**, 177–189.

Messick, S. Personality assessment and the ethics of assessment. *American Psychologist*, 1965, **20**, 136–142.

Mills, R. B., McDevitt, R. J., and Tonkin, S. Situational tests in metropolitan police recruit selection. *Journal of Criminal Law, Criminology, and Police Science*, 1966, **57**, 99–106.

Mischel, W. *Personality and assessment*. New York: Wiley, 1968.

————, Continuity and change in personality. *American Psychologist*, 1969, **24**, 1012–1018.

Mitchell, J. V., and Pierce-Jones, J. A factor analysis of Gough's California Psychological Inventory. *Journal of Consulting Psychology*, 1960, **24**, 453–456.

Mogar, R. E. Three versions of the F scale and performance on the semantic differential. *Journal of Abnormal and Social Psychology*, 1960, **60**, 262–265.

Moos, R. H. Behavioral effects of being observed: reactions to a wireless transmitter. *Journal of Consulting and Clinical Psychology*, 1968, **32**, 383–388.

Moreno, J. L. *Who shall survive?* Washington: Nervous and Mental Disease Publishing Co., 1934.

Morgan, C. D., and Murray, H. A. A method for investigating fantasies: the Thematic Apperception Test. *Archives of Neurology and Psychiatry*, 1935, **34**, 289–306.

Mosel, J. N., and Wade, R. R. A weighted application blank for reduction of turnover in department store sales clerks. *Personnel Psychology*, 1951, **4**, 177–184.

Murray, H. A. *Explorations in personality*. New York: Oxford, 1938.

————, *Thematic Apperception Test manual*. Cambridge, Massachusetts: Harvard University Press, 1943.

Murstein, B. I. *Theory and research in projective techniques (emphasizing the TAT)*. New York: Wiley, 1963.

————, Introduction to Study 49. In B. I. Murstein (Ed.), *Handbook of projective techniques*. New York: Basic Books, 1965.

Nathan, P. E. *Cues, decisions, and diagnosis: A systems-analytic approach to the diagnosis of psychopathology*. New York: Academic Press, 1967.

Nettler, G. Test burning in Texas. *American Psychologist*, 1959, **14**, 682–683.

Norman, W. T. Personality assessment, faking and detection: An assessment method for use in personnel selection. *Journal of Applied Psychology,* 1963, **47**, 225–241. (a)

——, Relative importance of test item content. *Journal of Consulting Psychology,* 1963, **27**, 166–174. (b)

——, Toward an adequate taxonomy of personality attributes: replicated factor structure in peer nomination personality ratings. *Journal of Abnormal and Social Psychology,* 1963, **66**, 574–583. (c)

——, On estimating psychological relationships: social desirability and self-report. *Psychological Bulletin,* 1967, **67**, 273–293.

Nunnally, J. C. *Popular conceptions of mental health,* New York: Holt, Rinehart, and Winston, 1961.

——, *Psychometric theory.* New York: McGraw-Hill, 1967.

Orme, J. E. Ability and season of birth. *British Journal of Psychology,* 1965, **56**, 471–475.

Osgood, C. E. The nature and measurement of meaning. *Psychological Bulletin,* 1952, **49**, 197–237.

Osgood, C. E., Suci, G. J., and Tannenbaum, P. H. *The measurement of meaning.* Urbana: University of Illinois Press, 1957.

Oskamp, S. The relationship of clinical experience and training methods to several criteria of clinical prediction. *Psychological Monographs,* 1962, **76** (28, Whole No. 547).

——, Overconfidence in case-study judgments. *Journal of Consulting Psychology,* 1965, **29**, 261–265.

OSS Assessment Staff. *Assessment of men.* New York: Rinehart, 1948.

Owens, W. A., and Henry, E. R. *Biographical data in industrial psychology: a review and evaluation.* Greensboro, N.C.: Richardson Foundation, 1966.

Pascal, G. R., and Suttell, B. J. *The Bender-Gestalt Test.* New York: Grune and Stratton, 1951.

Passini, F. T., and Norman, W. T. A universal conception of personality structure? *Journal of Personality and Social Psychology,* 1966, **4**, 44–49.

Payne, F. D., and Wiggins, J. S. Effects of rule relaxation and system combination on classification rates in two MMPI "cookbook" systems. *Journal of Consulting and Clinical Psychology,* 1968, **32**, 734–736.

Peak, H. Problems of objective observation. In L. Festinger and D. Katz (Eds.), *Research methods in the behavioral sciences.* New York: Dryden, 1953.

Pearson, J. S., and Swenson, W. M. *A user's guide to the Mayo Clinic automated MMPI program.* New York: Psychological Corporation, 1967.

Peterson, D. R. Scope and generality of verbally defined personality factors. *Psychological Review,* 1965, **72**, 48–59.

——, *The clinical study of social behavior.* New York: Appleton-Century-Crofts, 1968.

Phillips, L. Case history data and prognosis in schizophrenia. *Journal of Nervous and Mental Disease,* 1953, **117**, 515–525.

Phillips, L., and Smith, J. G. *Rorschach interpretation: advanced technique.* New York: Grune and Stratton, 1953.

Pintner, R., and Forlano, G. Season of birth and mental differences. *Psychological Bulletin*, 1943, **40**, 25–35.

Piotrowski, Z. A. The Rorschach inkblot method in organic disturbances of the central nervous system. *Journal of Nervous and Mental Disease*, 1937, **86**, 525–537.

————, Tentative Rorschach formulae for educational and vocational guidance in adolescence. *Rorschach Research Exchange*, 1943, **7**, 16–27.

————, Digital-computer interpretation of inkblot test data. *Psychiatric Quarterly*, 1964, **38**, 1–26.

————, Personal communication, 1969.

Piotrowski, Z. A., and Briklin, B. A second validation of a long-term Rorschach prognostic index for schizophrenic patients. *Journal of Consulting Psychology*, 1961, **25**, 123–128.

Pressey, S. L., and Pressey, L. W. "Cross-out" tests, with suggestions as to a group scale of the emotions. *Journal of Applied Psychology*, 1919, **3**, 138–150.

Radcliffe, J. A. Review of the EPPS. In O. K. Buros (Ed.), *The sixth mental measurements yearbook.* Highland Park, N.J.: Gryphon, 1965.

Reznikoff, M. Social Desirability in TAT themes. *Journal of Projective Techniques*, 1961, **25**, 87–89.

Richardson, M. W. An empirical study of the forced-choice performance report. *American Psychologist*, 1949, **4**, 278–279. (Abstract).

Rimm, D. Cost efficiency and test prediction. *Journal of Consulting Psychology*, 1963, **27**, 89–91.

Roback, H. B. Human figure drawings: their utility in the clinical psychologist's armentarium for personality assessment. *Psychological Bulletin*, 1968, **70**, 1–19.

Robins, A. J. Prognostic studies in mental disorder. *American Journal of Psychiatry*, 1954, **111**, 434–444.

Rodnick, E. H., and Garmezy, N. An experimental approach to the study of motivation in schizophrenia. In M. R. Jones (Ed.) *Nebraska symposium on motivation: 1957.* Lincoln: University of Nebraska Press, 1957.

Rogers, C. R., and Dymond, R. F. *Psychotherapy and personality change.* Chicago: University of Chicago Press, 1954.

Rohde, A. R. *The sentence completion method: its diagnostic and clinical application to mental disorders.* New York: Ronald, 1957.

Rome, H. P., et al. Symposium on automation technics in personality assessment. *Proceedings of the Staff Meetings of the Mayo Clinic*, 1962, **37**, 61–82.

Rorer, L. G. The great response-style myth. *Psychological Bulletin*, 1965, **63**, 129–156.

Rorer, L. G., Hoffman, P. J., Dickman, H. R., and Slovic, P. Configural judgments revealed. *Proceedings of the 75th Annual Convention of the American Psychological Association,* 1967, **2,** 195–196.

Rorschach, H. *Psychodiagnostics.* Bern, Switzerland: Huber, 1942. (New York: Grune and Stratton, 1951).

Rosen, A. Detection of suicidal patients: an example of some limitations in the prediction of infrequent events. *Journal of Consulting Psychology,* 1954, **18,** 397–403.

Rosenthal, R. *Experimenter effects in behavioral research.* New York: Appleton-Century-Crofts, 1966.

Rosenzweig, S. The picture-association method and its application in a study of reactions to frustration. *Journal of Personality,* 1945, **21,** 3–23.

Rotter, J. B., and Rafferty, J. E. *Manual: The Rotter Incomplete Sentences Blank.* New York: Psychological Corporation, 1950.

Rundquist, E. A. Item and response characteristics in attitude and personality measurements: a reaction to L. G. Rorer's "The great response-style myth." *Psychological Bulletin,* 1966, **66,** 166–177.

Sanford, N. Personality: its place in psychology. In S. Koch (Ed.), *Psychology: A study of a science.* Volume 5. New York: McGraw-Hill, 1963.

Sappenfield, B. R. Review of the Blacky Pictures. In O. K. Buros (Ed.), *The sixth mental measurement yearbook.* Highland Park, N.J.: Gryphon, 1965.

Sarason, S. B. *The clinical interaction with special reference to the Rorschach.* New York: Harper, 1954.

Sarbin, T. R. Ontology recapitulates philology: the mythic nature of anxiety. *American Psychologist,* 1968, **23,** 411–418.

Sarbin, T. R., Taft, R., and Bailey, D. E. *Clinical inference and cognitive theory.* New York: Holt, Rinehart, and Winston, 1960.

Satz, P., Fennell, E., and Reilly, C. The predictive validity of six neurodiagnostic tests: A decision theory analysis. *Journal of Consulting and Clinical Psychology,* 1970, **34,** 375–381.

Saunders, D. S. Moderator variables in prediction. *Educational and Psychological Measurement,* 1956, **16,** 209–222.

Sawyer, J. Measurement *and* prediction, clinical *and* statistical. *Psychological Bulletin,* 1966, **66,** 178–200.

Schwartz, L. A. Social-situation pictures in the psychiatric interview. *American Journal of Orthopsychiatry,* 1932, **2,** 124–133.

Schwartz, M. M., Cohen, B. D., and Pavlik, W. B. The effects of subject- and experimenter-induced defensive response sets on Picture-Frustration Test reactions. *Journal of Projective Techniques,* 1964, **28,** 341–345.

Schwarz, J. C. Comment on "High school yearbooks: a nonreactive measure of social isolation in graduates who later became schizophrenic." *Journal of Abnormal Psychology,* 1970, **75,** 317–318.

Scollay, R. W. Personal history data as a predictor of success. *Personnel Psychology,* 1957, **10,** 23–26.

Scott, R. D., and Johnson, R. W. Use of weighted application blank in selecting unskilled employees. *Journal of Applied Psychology*, 1967, **51**, 393–395.

Scott, W. A. Comparative validities of forced-choice and single-stimulus tests. *Psychological Bulletin*, 1968, **70**, 231–244.

Sechrest, L. Incremental validity: a recommendation. *Educational and Psychological Measurement*, 1963, **23**, 153–157.

Sechrest, L., Gallimore, R., and Hersch, P. D. Feedback and accuracy of clinical predictions. *Journal of Consulting Psychology*, 1967, **31**, 1–11.

Sechrest, L., and Jackson, D. N. The generality of deviant response tendencies. *Journal of Consulting Psychology*, 1962, **26**, 395–401.

———, Deviant response tendencies: Their measurement and interpretation. *Educational and Psychological Measurement*, 1963, **23**, 33–53.

Seeman, W. "Subtlety" in structured personality tests. *Journal of Consulting Psychology*, 1952, **16**, 278–283.

———, Concept of "subtlety" in structured psychiatric and personality tests: an experimental approach. *Journal of Abnormal and Social Psychology*, 1953, **48**, 239–247.

———, The compleat clinician: Constituting some reflections on diagnostic decision-making and on theorizing. Unpublished manuscript, 1969.

Selltiz, C., Jahoda, M., Deutsch, M., and Cook, S. W. *Research methods in social problems*. New York: Holt, Rinehart, and Winston, 1959.

Sheldon, W. H., Stevens, S. S., and Tucker, W. B. *The varieties of human physique*. New York: Harper and Row, 1940.

Shelly, M. W., and Bryan, G. L. *Human judgments and optimality*. New York: Wiley, 1964.

Shneidman, E. S. *Thematic test analysis*. New York: Grune and Stratton, 1951.

Sines, L. K. The relative contribution of four kinds of data to accuracy in personality assessment. *Journal of Consulting Psychology*, 1959, **23**, 483–492.

Sines, J. O. Actuarial methods in personality assessment. In B. A. Maher (Ed.), *Progress in experimental personality research*, Volume 3. New York: Academic Press, 1966.

Smith, E. E. Defensiveness, insight, and the *K* scale. *Journal of Consulting Psychology*, 1959, **23**, 275–277.

Smith, J., and Lanyon, R. I. Prediction of juvenile probation violators. *Journal of Consulting and Clinical Psychology*, 1968, **32**, 54–58.

Soskin, W. F., and John, V. P. The study of spontaneous talk. In R. G. Barker (Ed.), *The stream of behavior*. New York: Appleton-Century-Crofts, 1963, 228–281.

Spencer, G. J., and Worthington, R. Validity of a projective technique in predicting sales effectiveness. *Personnel Psychology*, 1952, **5**, 125–144.

Spitzer, R. L., and Endicott, J. DIAGNO: A computer program for psychiatric diagnosis. *Archives of General Psychiatry*, 1968, **18**, 746–756.

Spranger, E. *Types of men*. Translated from the 5th German edition of *Lebensformen* by P. J. W. Pigors. Halle: Max Niemeyer Verlag, 1928.

Stein, M. I. *Volunteers for peace: the first group of Peace Corps volunteers in a rural community development in Colombia.* New York: Wiley, 1966.

————, The use of a sentence completion test for the diagnosis of personality. *Journal of Clinical Psychology*, 1947, **3**, 47–56.

Stephenson, W. *The study of behavior.* Chicago: University of Chicago Press, 1953.

Stern, G. G., Stein, M. I., and Bloom, B. S. *Methods in personality assessment.* Glencoe, Illinois: Free Press, 1956.

Stricker, L. J. Review of the EPPS. In O. K. Buros (Ed.), *The sixth mental measurements yearbook.* Highland Park, N.J.: Gryphon, 1965.

Strong, E. K. A vocational interest test. *Educational Record*, 1927, **8**, 107–121.

Sullivan, H. S. *The psychiatric interview.* New York: Norton, 1954.

Sundberg, N. D. The practice of psychological testing in clinical services in the United States. *American Psychologist*, 1961, **16**, 79–83.

Swensen, C. H. Empirical evaluations of human figure drawings. *Psychological Bulletin*, 1957, **54**, 431–466.

————, Empirical evaluations of human figure drawings, 1957–1966. *Psychological Bulletin*, 1968, **70**, 20–44.

Symonds, P. M. *Diagnosing personality and conduct.* New York: Appleton-Century, 1931.

Szasz, T. *The myth of mental illness.* New York: Hoeber, 1961.

Taft, R. The ability to judge people. *Psychological Bulletin*, 1955, **52**, 1–23.

————, Multiple methods of personality assessment. *Psychological Bulletin*, 1959, **56**, 333–352.

Tallent, N. On individualizing the psychologist's clinical evaluation. *Journal of Clinical Psychology*, 1958, **14**, 243–244.

Taylor, C. W., and Ellison, R. L. Biographical predictors of specific performance. *Science*, 1967, **155**, 1075–1080.

Taylor, H. C., and Russell, J. T. The relationship of validity coefficients to the practical effectiveness of tests in selection: Discussion and tables. *Journal of Applied Psychology*, 1939, **23**, 565–578.

Taylor, J. B. Social desirability and MMPI performance: the individual case. *Journal of Consulting Psychology*, 1959, **23**, 514–517.

Thetford, W. N. Review of the Holtzman Inkblot test. In O. K. Buros (Ed.), *The sixth mental measurements yearbook.* Highland Park, N.J.: Gryphon, 1965.

Thurstone, L. L. *Thurstone Temperament Schedule.* Chicago: Science Research Associates, 1949.

————, The dimensions of temperament. *Psychometrika*, 1951, **16**, 11–20.

Tomlinson, J. R. Situational and personality correlates of predictive accuracy. *Journal of Consulting Psychology*, 1967, **31**, 19–22.

Toomey, L. C., and Rickers-Ovsiankina, M. A. Tabular comparison of scoring systems. In M. A. Rickers-Ovsiankina (Ed.), *Rorschach Psychology.* New York: Wiley, 1960.

Toops, H. A. The criterion. *Educational and Psychological Measurement,* 1944, **4,** 271–297.

Tucker, M. F., Cline, V. B., and Schmitt, J. R. Prediction of creativity and other performance measures from biographical information among pharmaceutical scientists. *Journal of Applied Psychology,* 1967, **51,** 131–138.

Turner, D. R. Predictive efficiency as a function of amount of information and level of professional experience. *Journal of Projective Techniques and Personality Assessment,* 1966, **30,** 4–11.

Ullmann, L. P., and Krasner, L. *Case studies in behavior modification.* New York: Holt, Rinehart, and Winston, 1965.

Ulrich, L., and Trumbo, D. The selection interview since 1949. *Psychological Bulletin,* 1965, **63,** 100–116.

Van Lennep, D. J. The Four-Picture Test. In H. H. Anderson and G. L. Anderson (Eds.) *An introduction to projective techniques.* Englewood Cliffs, N.J.: Prentice-Hall, 1951.

Vernon, P. E. The validation of civil service selection board procedures. *Occupational Psychology,* 1950, **24,** 75–95.

——, *Personality assessment: a critical survey.* London: Methuen, 1964.

Vernon, P. E., and Allport, G. W. A test for personal value. *Journal of Abnormal and Social Psychology,* 1931, **26,** 231–248.

Wallace, J. An abilities conception of personality: some implications for personality measurement. *American Psychologist,* 1966, **21,** 132–138.

——, What units shall we employ? Allport's question revisited. *Journal of Consulting Psychology,* 1967, **31,** 56–64.

Walsh, W. B. Validity of self-report. *Journal of Counseling Psychology,* 1967, **14,** 18–23.

——, Validity of self-report: another look. *Journal of Consulting Psychology,* 1968, **15,** 180–186.

Webb, E. Character and intelligence. *British Journal of Psychology Monograph Supplement,* 1915, **III.**

Webb, E. J., Campbell, D. T., Schwartz, R. D., and Sechrest, L. *Unobtrusive measures: nonreactive research in the social sciences.* Chicago: Rand McNally, 1966.

Webster, E. C. *Decision making in the employment interview.* Montreal: Industrial Relations Centre, McGill University, 1967.

Weisskopf, E. A., and Dieppa, J. J. Experimentally induced faking of TAT responses. *Journal of Consulting Psychology,* 1951, **15,** 469–474.

Wells, F. L. The systematic observation of the personality—in its relation to the hygiene of the mind. *Psychological Review,* 1914, **21,** 295–333.

Welsh, G. S. Factor dimensions A and R. In G. S. Welsh and W. G. Dahlstrom (Eds.), *Basic readings on the MMPI in psychology and medicine.* Minneapolis: University of Minnesota Press, 1956.

Welsh, G. S., and Dahlstrom, W. G. *Basic readings on the MMPI in psychology and medicine.* Minneapolis: University of Minnesota Press, 1956.

Wernimont, P. F., and Campbell, J. P. Signs, samples, and criteria. *Journal of Applied Psychology*, 1968, **52**, 372–376.

Whyte, W. H., Jr. *The organization man.* New York: Simon and Schuster, 1956, 201–222.

Wiggins, J. S. Strategic, method, and stylistic variance in the MMPI. *Psychological Bulletin*, 1962, **59**, 224–242.

———, Personality structure. *Annual Review of Psychology*, 1968, **19**, 293–350.

Wiggins, N. L., and Hoffman, P. J. Three models of clinical judgment. *Journal of Abnormal Psychology*, 1968, **73**, 70–77.

Willingham, W. W. Foreword. In W. W. Willingham (Ed.), Invasion of privacy in research and testing. *Journal of Educational Measurement*, 1967, **4**, 1–31 (supplement).

Williams, J. G., and Kleinmuntz, B. A process for detecting correlations between dichotomous variables. In B. Kleinmuntz (Ed.), *Clinical information processing by computer.* New York: Holt, Rinehart, and Winston, 1969.

Williams, T. R. *Field methods in the study of culture.* New York: Holt, Rinehart and Winston, 1967.

Wittenborn, J. R. *Wittenborn psychiatric rating scales.* New York: Psychological Corporation, 1955 (Revised, 1964).

Wittman, P. A scale for measuring prognosis in schizophrenic patients. *Elgin State Hospital Papers*, 1941, **4**, 20–33.

Wolf, R. The measurement of environments. In A. Anastasi (Ed.), *Testing problems in perspective.* Washington D.C.: American Council on Education, 1966, 491–503.

Zigler, E., and Phillips, L. Social effectiveness and symptomatic behaviors. *Journal of Abnormal and Social Psychology*, 1960, **61**, 231–238.

———, Social competence and the process-reactive distinction in schizophrenia. *Journal of Abnormal and Social Psychology*, 1962, **65**, 215–222.

Zubin, J. Failures of the Rorschach technique. *Journal of Projective Techniques*, 1954, **18**, 303–315.

Zubin, J., Eron, L. D., and Schumer, F. *An experimental approach to projective techniques.* New York: Wiley, 1965.

AUTHOR INDEX

SUBJECT INDEX

Astrology, 1-2, 5-6
  horoscope, 1-2
  moment of birth, 1-2
  season of birth, 2
Aunt Fanny error, 3

Bales Interaction Check List, 100
Band width of assessment device, 219
Barnum effect, 3
Base expectancy tables, 15
Base rates, 3, 80, 133-137, 169-171, 187,
    216
  actuarial prediction, 161
  chance prediction, 134
  cutting scores, 134-137
  decision-making, 170-171
  hit-and-miss validity, 133-137, 169-171
  importance of, 169-171
  improper usage of tests, 187
  improvement over, 170
  outcome values, 170-171
  parole violation, 171
  prediction, of brain disease, 170-171, 187
    of suicide, 136-137
  predictive accuracy, 133-137
  relative costs, 134
  test usefulness, 169-170
Basic concepts in personality assessment,
    19-36
Batteries of tests, limited utility of, 178-179
Behavior samples, 15-16, 32, 94-102
  anecdotal records, 102
  content validity of, 129
  controlled, 97-102
  critical incident technique, 102
  hidden observation, 96
  historical records, 96
  natural, 95-97
  participant observation, 95-96
  unsystematic, 102-103
  use of references, 103
Behavior theory approaches to assessment,
    22, 28, 205-209
  assessment of abilities, 206-208
  biographical data, 208
  in personnel practice, 206
  rules for, 207
Behavior therapy, 16
Bell Adjustment Inventory, 13
Bender Gestalt test, 64-66, 179, 189

  confidence in interpretation, 179
  instructions for administration, 64
  intelligence and, 65
  interpretation, 64
  quantitative scoring, 64
  training and accuracy, 189
  validity, 65-66
Bernreuter Personality Inventory, 13
  defensiveness, 151
Bile, *see* Humoural theory
Binet, Alfred, 7, 8
  intelligence tests, 7
Biographical data, 8, 15-16, 32, 103-110,
    172-173, 208-209
  compared with other information, 172-
    173
  faking, 107
  M-B history record, 106
  personal documents, 107
  psychopathology, 104
  scholastic achievement, 104
  social competence, 105-106
  weighted biographical data sheet, 103-104
  Worthington Personal History Blank, 106
  written methods in, 103-107
Biographic method, 8
Birth, moment of, 1
  season of, 2
Blacky Pictures test, 12, 31, 40, 62-64
  instructions for administration, 63
  reliability, 63
  scoring and interpretation, 63
  validity, 64
Body types, 5, 7
British Civil Service, situational tests, 99
British War Office Selection Board, 17
Brain disease, assessment of, 170-171, 187

CAT, 12, 53
California F scale, and acquiescence, 143
California Psychological Inventory (CPI),
    80-84, 91
  computer interpretation of, 210, 214
  construction of, 80-81
  defensiveness, 152
  factor analysis of, 81
  interpretation, 82-84
  profile, 83
  scales, 80-81
  validity, 82